At Home on the Range with a Texas Hunter

Henry Chappell

Republic of Texas Press
Plano, Texas

Library of Congress Cataloging-in-Publication Data

Chappell, Henry.
 At home on the range with a Texas hunter / Henry Chappell.
   p. cm.
 ISBN 1-55622-836-8
 1. Fowling—Texas. I. Title.

 SK313 .C44 2001
 799.2'4'09764—dc21   00-051813
                                              CIP

Republic of Texas Press is an imprint of Wordware Publishing, Inc.
No part of this book may be reproduced in any form or by
any means without permission in writing from
Wordware Publishing, Inc.

Printed in the United States of America

ISBN 1-55622-836-8
10 9 8 7 6 5 4 3 2 1
2011

All inquiries for volume purchases of this book should be addressed to
Wordware Publishing, Inc., at 2320 Los Rios Boulevard, Plano, Texas 75074.
Telephone inquiries may be made by calling:
(972) 423-0090

For Dad who showed me the wild places then gave me the freedom to know them.

Table of Contents

Some of the essays in this collection first appeared in the following magazines whose editorial staffs I wish to thank and acknowledge:

"Big Country Bobwhites" in a slightly different form in *Gun Dog* (June/July 1994)

"Rosie" under a different title in *Gray's Sporting Journal* (November 1994)

"Chihuahuan Desert Duo" in a shorter form in *Wing & Shot* (August/September 1997)

Parts of "Oklahoma" in *Wing & Shot* (February/March 1998 and April/May 1998)

"Prairie Grouse, More or Less" in a much shorter form in *Gun Dog* (February/March 1999)

"Rebuilding" in *Concho River Review* (Fall 1995)

Special thanks go to *Southern Outdoors* for permission to reprint "On-the-Job Training" (June 1997)

Acknowledgments

Many of the people who helped with this book are named in the pages ahead. My debts to them are obvious and heavy.

I also want to express my appreciation to Bob Rogers of the Texas Parks and Wildlife Department for introducing me to legendary wildlife biologist Dick DeArment, and I am indebted to Roger Applegate of the Kansas Department of Wildlife and Parks who arose in the wee hours one freezing April morning to guide me to a Flint Hills prairie chicken blind.

I am eternally grateful to my editor, Ginnie Siena Bivona, for believing in this project and to the members of the DFW Writers' Workshop for their support, guidance, gentle criticism, and friendship.

Author's Introduction

This morning I finished two days of High Plains waterfowl hunting in the Texas Panhandle east of Amarillo. Around nine o'clock my friend and host Kevin Mote and I gathered his decoys from the few square yards of open water we had stomped out in the ice just before dawn, and I headed east toward the edge of the caprock. A good trip, hunting with good people. As I came off the Staked Plains west of Quitaque and drove down through the rough, gray, juniper-studded breaks of the Caprock Escarpment, I felt that tired dreaminess that comes after a hard hunt in unfamiliar country.

I drove out of the breaks and eastward through Turkey, Texas, home of swing legend Bob Wells and two dozen or so cut-out plywood cowboys and cowgirls leaning against the store-front columns along Main Street. Then south to Matador and over Quitaque Creek and the North Pease, then east to the breaks of the Middle Pease for a day and half of bobwhite quail hunting. Around noon, I stopped the truck at a favorite spot overlooking the river bottom—miles of midgrass, ragweed, sand sage, cholla, plum, and chittam and the copper-colored cliffs above the northern bank. I let Molly, my German shorthaired pointer, out of her box to stretch and snuffle about while I set up the camp stove on the tailgate and brewed a hellishly strong pot of coffee. Molly was more than ready to hunt after being cooped up in her box for most of two days while three Labs did all the work. I wasn't. The time would be right soon enough when the birds moved out of the brush and onto the sandy ragweed flats to stuff their crops before going to roost. I tethered Molly to a handy mesquite, put on my down jacket, and sat on the dog food bucket in the sun with my back to the passenger side door. I sipped coffee, dozed, and with binoculars tried occasionally and mostly in vain to identify the half dozen or so species of sparrows, warblers, and buntings that flitted about in the mesquite. Rufous-crowned sparrow, lark bunting, and eastern bluebird for sure; dark-eyed junco and song sparrow maybe. Mostly though, I dozed. It felt good to be back in my country.

Mid-afternoon I awoke refreshed, plunked Molly on the tailgate, and forced myself to take my sweet time taping her boots on against the grass burrs that waited in the river bottom. As always, I wondered how coyotes deal with grass burrs. Molly whined and shivered more with anticipation than the cold. It was early still; I forced myself again to slow down on the little chores: shell sorting, water bottle filling, twenty-gauge assembly. Molly pranced on the tailgate, then on top of her dog box, then again on the tailgate. To hell with it; we were going, early or not.

I felt light and springy, happy to be out of the heavy duck-hunting garb. My twenty-gauge Beretta felt like a wand after toting the heavy twelve-gauge magnum for two days. I walked down the two-track toward the river and, by the tinkling of the little brass bell on her collar, kept track of Molly as she bustled about in the mesquite and broom weed. In the bottom, we swung westward right into the sun—a brilliant tactical move —but I was more interested in visiting a favorite stretch of river than in tactics. Molly worked ahead of me in perfect feeding cover, a mixture of thick ragweed, clumps of little bluestem, and sand sage.

Her busy tail got suddenly busier. She snuffled loudly and started to point then thought better of it and looped back into the breeze for another try. Then again. Nothing. Who knows? We moved on, plowing through several islands of thick woolly grass and mature mesquite where no self-respecting bobwhite would be. Then through tall reeds rank with the smell of wild hogs, and at last to the river, a broken string of clear, salty pools. Molly waded in belly deep, drank greedily, then paddled about for a few minutes to cool off. Obviously feeling better and grinning piggishly, she slogged through a miasmic black ooze at the tail of the pool and headed westward, resembling some Pleistocene beast that had just narrowly escaped the La Brea tar pits.

Just ahead, a copse of cottonwoods promised well-drained sandy soil and good quail cover. We plowed through the last of the rank stuff and emerged into a nice weedy flat. Two hundred yards ahead four whitetail does stood frozen, watching me. When I first hunted this place eight years ago, mule deer far outnumbered whitetails. But the brush is getting thicker and so are whitetail deer, and there's a solid feeling in knowing you've stayed with a piece of country, hunting it through years of drought and years of fecundity to see the subtle changes. I took another step and long, elegant white flags bobbed away to the west.

Molly got birdy then pointed. I knew the birds would run in the sparse ground cover, and sure enough, her sidelong glance told me the birds had moved. I sent her on and she bustled off the flat and into the grass and sage and quickly pulled up high and hard. No question about it this time. I walked by her, flushed a nice covey, picked out a bird, and shot behind it twice knowing full well each time I slapped the trigger that I was going to miss.

No matter. The birds flew south out of the river bottom, and I felt sure they'd be spread nicely about in the mesquite just over the top of the nearest hill. I called Molly in for a drink and a breather to give the singles time to settle in and put out a little scent. Molly didn't care to drink or rest; she wanted those birds and whined piteously while I made her sit. Then she added a nice outer crust to her coat with a good roll in the sand. I let go all hope of a *Gun Dog* cover shot.

After five minutes of her chafing, I sent her on. Then, picking my way through a plum thicket, I walked up a second covey, which flew over the same hill. Excellent. I find singles much easier to deal with than discombobulating covey rises. But the hillside was covered in aromatic snakeweed. We hunted into the wind, with the wind, across the wind. Molly's tail told me that she smelled birds the entire time, but she never pointed and we flushed nothing. I stopped to wipe the sweat from my glasses and just as I was shoving the handkerchief back into a hip pocket, a single flushed from a clump of mesquite behind me. I missed badly. Hearing the shots, Molly came bounding down the hill toward me—bird dogs are born optimists—and ran up another bird at a spot I'd have sworn we'd already stepped on at least twice.

We worked our way down the hill toward a weedy draw, flushing and missing birds all the way. I was getting mad, and Molly, frustrated now, was pushing too hard. (If you don't believe dogs sense and feel frustration, you might as well stop reading right now. We won't agree on anything.) Molly needed a bird. *I* needed a bird. Down in the draw and out of the snakeweed, Molly began to trail. Several times she pointed then softened as the birds ran. We came to the head of the draw and she locked up hard on a clump of sage. No sidelong glance this time. Her nostrils were flared and her stiff tail quivered like a tuning fork. God, it was good to be back home in my country!

***

Home. Home just north of Dallas where I live happily with my wife, daughters, and bird dogs. Home as in my home hunting grounds on the western edge of the Rolling Plains, the rough sandhill, midgrass, and river breaks country in the eastern half of the Texas Panhandle. Or home water—a half dozen prairie tanks and a stretch of the Brazos River that snakes through the oak, cedar, and mesquite country of the western Cross Timbers.

I'm not sure when my old friend and hunting partner Brad Carter and I started referring to *our country.* For the first quarter century of my life, I couldn't imagine hunting and fishing anywhere other than the green, rolling hardwood farm country in central Kentucky where I was born and raised. My first few years in Texas, I hopped from one lease to the next, hunting deer all over the state. I enjoyed the deer hunting immensely but never really got to know a piece of country in any meaningful way. A dozen or so years ago I got back into bird hunting. I hunted quail for a while on my own before Brad and I stumbled across each other at work. We made a trip together to West Texas and have been more or less a permanent team ever since.

Brad and I have since hunted together all over creation, but given a choice we'll hunt bobwhite quail in a certain piece of river breaks country in the southeastern corner of the Texas Panhandle. Somewhere along the line it became our home country even though we live near Dallas, 250 miles and four and a half hours to the east. We'll be in Kansas hunting prairie chickens or in the Piney Woods after woodcock, and one of us will say something like, "You know, I believe *our country* is a little harder on dogs." Or, "Back *home*, we'd be worrying about rattlesnakes."

I can be seduced by postcard country as well as anyone. Brad and I often talk dreamily of green mountains, grouse hunting, cold trout streams, and plenty of open land. Hunting in Texas comes with a unique set of aggravations that could eventually push me away to other places. For now, though, I might vacation in the Rockies, but I'll do my serious hunting at home in the country I know best and love the most: rough, dry, windy, brushy, rocky, thorny country with lots of quail, deer, ducks, turkey, and dried cow flops.

***

I wish I could tell you about a perfect shot and brisk retrieve. But the bird flushed to my right and flew up the hill, and I never caught up with it. As I write this I'm suffering through one of the worst shooting slumps of my life. We were about halfway back to the mouth of the draw when the unmistakable *koi-lee* wafted down the hill to the west. I sent Molly up the hill, but the bird flushed wild and I dropped him into a prickly pear cactus bed.

Molly gingerly plucked it from the nasty spines and brought it in. We picked up a second bird over a nice staunch point on the way back to the truck.

Two birds from two coveys in an hour and a half of hunting in West Texas. Nothing to brag about, certainly. But there's satisfaction in knowing that in this day and time you can still go out and shoot a few wild bobwhites over your own dogs in familiar country without a guide or a lease. To some degree I hunt the big, beat-up public areas out of financial necessity, but there are other reasons too, and I'll get to those a bit later.

Back at the truck I cleaned my two birds and listened to the scattered singles whistling in the draw, gathering to roost for the night. I won't harry them tomorrow morning. I know of other coveys in other draws, and I need to check some favorite spots to see which have grown too woolly over the wet summer and which pastures, heavily grazed last year, have since come back in ragweed and croton. I've been away far too long. It's high time for me to take care of things here at home.

H.C.
Paducah, Texas
November 1997

Big Country Bobwhites

 West Texas. Southeastern Panhandle to be more exact. (But not too exact.) Your dog's beeper collar is nearly out of range and tough to locate in the hot, dry, late morning wind. You're sure of at least one hill between the two of you so you hold your breath and listen, half hoping she's stopped to squat or listen for your whistle. But the beeping continues. You start down the hill, trying at first to keep your feet, but after a few yards you give up and ride the seat of your pants.

You slide into a dry creek bed and stop again, straining to hear. Why does the beeping always sound different—urgent —when she really has her birds? You cross the creek and start up the hill, slipping and clawing. The hillside, denuded a century ago by grazing, is covered with loose sand and gravel populated here and there with cedar, ragweed, and clumps of little bluestem. Pretty good bobwhite cover created by rapacious land use.

Your heavy, ragged breathing drowns the beeping. You hold your breath for three agonizing seconds. Got it.

You find her on point in the brush just over the top of the hill, head and tail high, just like the dogs in John Cowan's paintings, except that her tail is docked to one-third length. You're a German shorthair man in English pointer country and a little smug about it, although you'll admit to yourself (and only yourself) that you'd run pointers if you hunted for a living. But you don't, and you like your birds—woodcock and doves included—retrieved to hand with as little swearing on your part as possible.

She's pointing the base of a big, low hanging cedar—a near impossible situation for a lone hunter. You walk in wondering how she's able to just lock up and stop panting after running a half dozen miles. The birds blow out the opposite side of the cedar and fly over the hill. You don't bother with the gun.

You water the dog from your canteen, send her on, and check your compass. About the time you decide that you know *about* where you are, the beeper goes off again, barely audible, somewhere back across the creek and over the hill.

***

In South Texas and on the Rolling Plains around Albany, Throckmorton, Rotan, and Sweetwater, bobwhite hunters ride in specially equipped quail rigs following big-running pointers. Here, the gentle terrain and careful brush control ensure ideal conditions for hunters as well as quail. In good years, hunters often move thirty coveys per day, and I'm told that collecting a limit can be easy, but I can't be sure. This sort of hunting is way beyond my means.

A few seasons back, I destroyed a pair of kangaroo feather-weight hunting boots in fourteen days of hunting in West Texas. For me, quail hunting means serious walking. The places I hunt aren't managed for hunters if they are managed at all, and a dozen or more coveys moved doesn't necessarily mean a limit of birds.

I grew up following my father's pointers and setters along south central Kentucky's fence rows and field edges in the sixties and early seventies. We found birds in most of the likely places, and as often as not, the singles sat down in the open where an unscrupulous hunter with a good dog could wipe them out. A 200-acre farm could be covered in short order by hunting the obvious objectives. Sometimes, on really nasty days, Dad and I sat in the station wagon while the dogs ran the fence rows and checked the brush piles in the small fields. No big deal. Hunt a few hours and shoot a limit.

Modern farming practices have nearly finished the quail hunting in my part of Kentucky. But fate smiled, and I ended up in Texas with a pretty good German shorthair pup and an understanding wife. I fancied myself a real quail hunter until I got on a 2,000-acre lease in the Palo Pinto country between Fort Worth and Abilene. Dense mesquite flats and live oak mottes separated by ragweed, bunch grass, and cactus, and dry, brush choked creek bottoms formed a bobwhite Eden. Things looked a bit different from my perspective. The first day out, Heidi, my German shorthair, and I stumbled into thirteen coveys, and I slunk back to camp with three or four birds. I didn't shoot badly, but I heard twenty birds for every one I actually saw, and we couldn't find the singles. Worse yet, the wind blew my tent, with my daughter Jamie in it, into a mesquite tree.

Things improved though. I remembered to stake the tent down and picked up a few more birds, but I couldn't shake the feeling that there was easier hunting out there.

The following April I met a well-known quail guide who had some smaller leases on the Rolling Plains north of Abilene that either were or were not within my budget, depending on whether you talked to me or to Jane. After admitting that even he couldn't afford to hunt on any of his better leases, he showed my buddy Jay Chesley and I a beautiful Fisher County section that he had covered in his quail rig several times the previous season. He assured us that the place had never failed to produce a dozen or so coveys. It had all the essentials: gentle terrain, several brushy draws, a couple of stock tanks, and strips of mesquite separated by grama and weeds. I sent him a check a week later.

When I drove through the gate in September, I didn't recognize the place. Drought seared, it hadn't gotten a drop of rain since March. By early December we had identified only three coveys of bobwhites. I called the guide and complained. He apologized but said he had spent the previous month driving high-paying customers over his best leases, and they had done no better than we had. Jay and I declared our lease finished by mid-December. That season's birds cost me about $100 each. They made one good meal.

That spring, on a whim, Jay and I decided to look at a big state wildlife management area. The drought had finally broken, and the place was gorgeous—cactus and prickly poppy in full bloom; brimming stock tanks; lush stands of ragweed and croton; Indian blanket spread over the hills and savannahs; and more whistling bobwhites than we could count.

After six hours of backslapping and self-congratulation, we decided against another season lease. The guys at the local Quail Unlimited meetings were aghast that we would stoop to public land, and I'll admit that deep down I had a nagging feeling that my reputation as a real hard case was in jeopardy.

Next season Jay, Brad Carter, and I hunted our management area exclusively. We found birds—not a lot of them—but about as many as the guys with leases. Granted, it was a bad year for quail hunting statewide, despite ample spring rains, but we felt pretty smug nonetheless. We've had some big years, including some dozen-covey days, and occasionally we've come out on top when the coveys were tallied at the end of the day at the local diner. Still, I dread the inevitable question: "So where's your lease?"

***

Take a thousand acres of prime West Texas quail habitat—midgrass prairie interspersed with low brush—with a bobwhite density of a bird per acre, and protect it completely. Disallow all grazing and tilling. Suppress fire completely. Add

photo by Brad Carter

ample rainfall. Within a half-dozen years you'll have a rank stand of grass, more brush, no quail, and little other wildlife. Bobwhites and other seedeaters depend on soil disturbance to create openings and stimulate food producing forbs and legumes. Forget popular environmentalism; violent disturbance —fire and trampling and grazing by large ungulates—have been an integral part of the mixed prairie's ecology for tens of thousands of years. But traditional bobwhite management (brush control, disking and burning) costs big money. A Texas Parks and Wildlife biologist told me that bulldozer time costs $200 an hour. Prescribed burning on a large scale probably runs an order of magnitude higher. Enter the poor, maligned cow. Although it upsets preservationists, controlled *overgrazing*, also called "spot" or "shock" grazing, clears perennial vegetation, creates bare ground, and causes the soil disturbance needed to bring on the native forbs bobwhites require. Carefully controlled grazing is the most important technique used on most of the wildlife management areas in West and South Texas. Even the relatively heavy grazing done with no regard for wildlife on ranches all over the western two-thirds of the state typically produces excellent bobwhite habitat. This year's ugly razed draw might well hold next year's prime feeding cover if the cattle are removed before the spring rains come. Unfortunately, grazing does nothing to improve shooting conditions. People with money, connections, or both enjoy shooting in what the magazines call "The Grand Tradition." The rest of us spend a lot of time stumbling around in heavy mesquite worrying about rattlesnakes.

Hard hunted bobwhites are much like educated trout; you might know they're around in good numbers—you might even see them—but that doesn't mean you can get them. Every season we end up naming coveys that elude us time and again. The Ox covey; the Sand Creek covey; we nearly always find them, but they flush before we can get within shotgun range, or they run off into the brush and then flush or otherwise engage in unsporting tactics not generally recognized as part of the classic (I'm truly sick of that word) upland shooting experience.

I've remarked offhandedly to nonresidents that I usually restrict my shooting to covey rises. Once I achieve the desired effect, I admit that this is only because I can't find the singles. Hunting rough, unmanaged rangeland presents a different set of problems than the farmland situations in which the fence row covey always flies into the woods, or the covey behind the barn usually heads for the creek bottom.

Biologists tell me that bobwhites rarely fly further than eighty yards at a time. I believe this is true over most of their range. More times than I can remember, however, I've watched entire coveys fly at least a third of a mile across the Pease River bottom. Most often though, the birds are visible for only the first twenty yards. After that you have no idea where they've gone, and there's always a sea of escape cover in all directions.

We go after singles, get sidetracked by new coveys, change plans a dozen times, and end up miles from the original flush. Things could be far worse.

***

The English pointer: archetypal Texas bird dog. Lean, fast, and scarred by cactus and mesquite, he's independent to the point of being a near renegade. But he gets it done right day in and day out for little more than a pat and an occasional kind word. Texans like this image; it reflects the way we like to perceive ourselves. The huge, flat spreads call for big-running dogs. Hunters and dog handlers sit high in their rigs or on horseback where they can see over the brush, and the dogs can run flat out; when they begin to tire, replacements are put down.

But tradition for a few and reality for the masses are rarely the same. In the southeastern Panhandle where I do most of my hunting, steep hills and deep draws make hunting from a

photo by Henry Chappell

vehicle a chancy if not dangerous proposition, and a dog on point a quarter mile away in the cedar brakes might as well be lost. Pull into a motel parking lot just after dark in this country and the dogs you will see tied to truck bumpers and stake-outs are as likely to be setters, shorthairs, and Brittanys as pointers.

I spent my first six seasons in Texas hunting behind one dog. Heidi, my German shorthair, could hunt all day for three consecutive days, holding that smooth shorthair jog like a marathon runner. Incredulous weekend hunters with trailers full of untrained pointers regarded me with condescension.

"Why the hell would anyone drive all the way out here with only one dog?"

I usually tried to be pleasant. "We're doing okay. What's the shock collar for?"

"Son, I hunt over big-running dogs. You get a real bird dog out there, runnin' big and workin' good, and sometimes you need a little juice. I shocked the shit out of a hardheaded old bitch this morning. Straightened her little ass out right now."

"Huh. Well I'll be."

***

Heidi developed her own techniques for dealing with ungentlemanly, arid country bobwhites. Stylish and intense, with high head and eleven o'clock tail, she points and breaks of her own volition as many times as it takes to pin a running covey. Magazine editors don't seem to care for my dog training articles.

Field trial purists would be horrified, but I get a charge watching her stalk running coveys through the brush. It can be quite a suspense building production though, and by the time she finally pins her birds, I do well to remember to push the safety off.

I based all of my early sporting opinions on classic (that word again) upland shooting literature. Bird dogs should be steady to wing and shot, quarter in tight cover, and hunt edges and objectives when required. Proper respect for the quarry and all that. It took very few lost cripples to convince me that I could live with dogs that go with their birds. Clear objectives, I noticed, are scarce in a 1,000-acre mesquite flat, and as Brad once observed, West Texas is one big edge.

Nowadays we point the dogs in a promising direction and saunter along behind them watching for arrowheads, deer rubs, and wild hogs. Not very technical, I realize, but easy on the nerves. We do shoot a bird every now and then.

***

An overused axiom says, "In Texas, rain equals birds." Or, "When it rains in Texas, it rains quail." Why, then, do the drought prone regions provide the best hunting? Texas's quail population does fluctuate wildly depending on rainfall. But the rain must come at the right time, in the right amount, and without drought, we wouldn't experience the "boom" years.

I've gradually learned to see drought as part of a natural cycle that's tough to live with but impossible to live without. Rain brings on the annual forbs that feed the quail, but it also gives rise to grass and other perennial vegetation. After two or three consecutive wet years, the grass begins to dominate and the quail population starts to slide. Then drought hits and all but wipes the birds out. Only the most genetically superior bobwhites survive. If you doubt this, try to approach a covey late in a drought year. But things always improve. Spring and fall rains return, the food-producing forbs spring up in place of the drought-seared grass, and the quail comeback begins. You can see it in the annual August census data for my country in the southeastern Panhandle. In 1994 biologists counted eighty-two bobwhites along a 20-mile census route. In 1995 they counted none. Five in 1996. Twenty-three in 1997. Perfection—very elegant; very brutal.

Unlike the majority, Brad and Jay and I hunt hard during the bad years, running ourselves and the dogs into the ground for a half dozen drought-honed, unapproachable coveys. At the other extreme, the big years draw hunters from all over the country to crowd the public areas and book every affordable day lease months in advance. For me, the best years fall between boom and bust. There are fewer hunters, plenty of birds, and room to hunt.

Texans have a tendency to take their quail hunting for granted. It's been good since the old days and always will be, or so the reasoning goes. But we have a troublesome little irony to sort out. Prior to the "old days," grasslands covered the western two-thirds of the state—bison probably outnumbered bobwhites. Wildfire kept the brush back, and the nomadic bison laid waste to large areas then moved on. Then buffalo hunters came and slaughtered the bison, and later settlers suppressed the rejuvenating, brush-clearing prairie fires. Cattle, held in place by barbed wire, razed the plains as they had never been razed, and brush and bobwhites moved in. Destructive land use created the country's best bobwhite habitat. Bothersome? I need to go quail hunting and think about it.

***

You find your dog again after another arduous climb. This time the birds more or less behave and you manage to take a straggler. You hunt your way down out of the hills and out into a broad river bottom where you move another eight coveys. You don't get a limit, but you get enough. You clean the last bird in the dark while the dogs snore in their box.

Back in town, you see dog trailers worth more than your truck and quail rigs equipped with grain dispensers sitting on trailers in the diner parking lot. At the ratty little motel, three men corner you to complain about lousy hunting. They've spent the past three days driving around on 80,000 acres and haven't done well at all. You nod sympathetically then excuse yourself. You have blisters to attend to.

On-The-Job Training

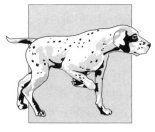

I run a pair of competent bird dogs. They're nothing to brag about really, just a couple of rawboned German shorthaired pointers out of solid bloodlines. But they hunt hard, point staunchly, back and search diligently for dead and crippled birds, which they retrieve reliably to hand. They also occasionally bump birds, chase jackrabbits, ignore my whistle, and leave too many tooth marks, but I wouldn't be embarrassed to put them down anywhere in front of anybody.

Outside of basic obedience and a few debacles involving planted pigeons that wouldn't fly and pen-reared quail that couldn't fly, the dogs learned their trade by practicing it in pretty good quail country. I tell people my dogs were trained on the job, but if I'm completely honest, I have to say that they've taught me a lot more than I've taught them.

When I was a boy hunting with my father, our approach was simple—hunt crop-field edges early and late, and fence rows, brush piles, and bois d'arc in the middle of the day. Toward the end of the season, we sometimes found birds in the woods. I didn't understand why we did things that way—I never really thought about it. Dad probably thought it was obvious. He handled the dogs and I shot a few birds and fancied myself an accomplished quail hunter.

In the early eighties, Jane and I graduated from college and moved to Texas—real bobwhite country, I was told. I bought a pretty good German shorthair pup, Heidi, from a kennel in Idaho. After a bit of arduous negotiations with Jane, I wrote a check worth two weeks' pay and began chasing quail all over a 2,000-acre lease in the Palo Pinto country west of Fort Worth. No cornfields, fence rows, or brush piles here. Just thousands of acres of mesquites, live oak, shin oak, cedar, bunch grass, sunflowers, ragweed, goatweed, prickly-pear cactus, cholla, and countless other species of barb producing vegetation with no respect for brush pants.

We found birds—or I should say, Heidi found birds—mostly in places I would never have thought to look. Fortunately for me, she was a patient (or indifferent) instructor, and gradually the patterns began to sink in: ragweed, croton, and sunflower early and late, always a short distance from heavy escape cover; and low brush—open at ground level for easy movement—during the middle of the day. Some places began to look and feel birdy. Other very similar places didn't. How high is too high? How thick is too thick? I followed and watched and learned. How could she have known these things in her first season? She taught me to never underestimate the benefits of hundreds of generations of selective breeding.

She got better and so did I. A covey flushed, and I fired twice at a bird that never missed a beat. Before I could break open my gun and drop in a pair of fresh rounds, Heidi was out of sight somewhere off in the direction the bird had flown. I thought I had marked most of the rest of the covey in another direction. My whistle quickly gave way to shouts, threats, and expletives. I cut a switch and went looking for her. She found me before I found her and brought me the dead cock. What could she have seen in that bird's flight that told her it had been hit? I haven't cut a switch since, and I've taken home lots of birds I thought I had missed.

Bobwhite quail are the gentleman's game bird. Everyone knows that. Havilah Babcock and Robert Ruark told us so. I believe they told the truth—at least it was true when they wrote it. The dogs point; you walk in and flush the birds (or, if you hunt in the right circles, an assistant gets them up with a flushing whip); the birds fly straight away; and the singles settle nicely in the open sedge about eighty yards away. Of course all this happens between 9 A.M. and 4 P.M. I was born forty years too late.

Jay and I had hunted hard one morning on some public land in northeastern Texas but had found nothing. Heidi got birdy on a grassy knoll, and sure enough, we found a roost in the little bluestem. After several minutes of animated searching, she pointed in a tangled mess of oak and greenbrier along the edge of the woods. As Jay and I eased into the thicket, we heard the soft, unmistakable clucking that anyone who has spent time around a game farm would recognize. The birds couldn't have been more than ten yards away. We gave each other the thumbs-up and moved in. Nothing. We walked quickly into the woods and made several looping casts. Still nothing. I sent Heidi on and she followed the scent trail thirty yards into the woods to a complete dead end. So you think you're getting a lot of false points? I'd probably blame the birds instead of the dog.

Brad and I watched a nice covey run across a West Texas ranch road. We don't road hunt, but we felt that his Brittany, Dee, who was then a year-old pup, needed the bird contact. We decided to put Heidi down too, just for insurance. She was trailing before we had our guns loaded. We walked into the pasture and saw her and Dee disappear into the mesquite at least a hundred yards away. I got on my whistle, sure that she was off looking for another covey. She came back in and immediately picked up the scent trail and followed it back into the mesquite. Then she pulled up to back Dee, who had found the covey while she was coming to my whistle. She has taught me to assume, despite conventional wisdom, that bobwhites are going to run. I'm a much better hunter because of that lesson, but looking back, I shudder to think of the times I've called her off birds.

My younger dog, Molly, comes from a line of big-running field trial dogs with names that German shorthair people would recognize. Where Heidi hunts with finesse and patience, Molly gets it done with speed and flash and physical ability. (Brad nicknamed her *Velocitus maximus maximus.*) She came into her prime in a year when the quail hunting was way off because of drought. She taught me that to get birds in "bust" years, you've got to cover ground from daylight to dark, and heaven knows she's good at that. After all the sensible hunters had quit for the year, Molly found scattered coveys out on the horizon with me a quarter mile behind her panting, sweating, trying to keep up.

Molly is maturing, developing finesse and bird sense to go along her strength and speed. With her style, so much different than Heidi's, she'll undoubtedly show me things in a new light. Most importantly though, when it's late in the day and rubber legs and blistered feet are making me think of supper, fire, and a sleeping bag, she's out on the horizon, running hard, doing what she was bred to do—reminding me that if you want to find quail, you have to hunt for them.

Heidi's muzzle is almost completely gray now, but she continues to instruct me. A few years ago, freezing rain had turned the West Texas river bottom we were hunting into a crystalline jungle of frozen mesquite and bluestem—breathtakingly beautiful but hell on dogs. A hard hour's walk from the truck, Heidi began losing control of her hindquarters. We took a break then started for the truck. She picked up a tendril of scent, followed it, and pointed a covey in a big ragweed flat. As I walked in, I noticed that she was unable to get her normally erect tail up. I shot a bird on the rise, and she staggered badly as she brought it in. We rested, then I called her to heel and we walked on.

A half-mile from the truck, she bolted into the weeds along the ranch road and pointed. Then her hind legs gave way, but she held her point. I walked in, flushed a single bird, and missed with both barrels. I carried her the rest of the way to the truck.

There's a lesson in that story too, or at least an example— one I hope I'm man enough to follow.[1]

photo by Henry Chappell

---

1   Printed by permission of *Southern Outdoors*, 5845 Carmichael Road, Montgomery, AL 36117.

Rosie: A Short Story

Fannie saw the beagle before I did, and not being much of a warrior, she immediately came over and sat down beside me. Then she started growling.

The beagle stopped and stared, its over-sized ears pricked up and out like sails.

Fannie let go a bark, and the little hound strode right into camp and up to Fannie, who made a hell of a show of ignoring him. I called him to me, and he rolled onto his back. I scratched his belly, and he worked his hind legs, first one then the other as I moved around his underside. He was young, maybe two, and handsome with a nice houndy head, and rich colors—black, tan, and white each cut cleanly one from the others. His collar had a name plate with a local phone number scratched on it.

It was mid-January, late in the East Texas woodcock season, but that morning I was focused more on the coffeepot than on woodcock. The hunting had been good the past three days; I was only two birds shy of the possession limit, but it had rained all night—a cold rain—and it had slackened just enough that I could get out of the tent and start a little fire.

I had been awakened by hounds running just after daylight. The young Forest Service clear-cuts are full of rabbits, and after deer season the only people I ever see in the woods are rabbit hunters. I've never met another woodcock hunter.

I played with the beagle for a few minutes and was wondering what to do with him, when I heard a truck coming. A red, three-quarter-ton Ford pulled off the road and up the hill into camp. A big man with a sandy beard climbed out grinning and said, "Tryin' to steal my dog are you?" He was wearing an orange cap, a heavy wool shirt, and tattered, muddy canvas overalls with a stitched rectangle on the chest where shell loops had been.

He held out a big, freckled hand and I shook it. "Anson Shipp," he said. He motioned toward the truck. "That's my boy Travis. Trav, come on out here."

The boy, I'd guess him to have been about eleven, got out, and Fannie jumped up and jogged over to meet him. He knelt and made a fuss over her, and she licked his face. "Travis don't care a thing about dogs," Anson said. I said I could see as much. Anson picked the beagle up, stroked his ears, and took him over to the truck and put him into a homemade dog box.

I offered coffee, and Anson allowed he had time for one cup. I offered the boy a soft drink and he declined saying, "Daddy lets me have coffee."

"Lord, don't tell his mama," Anson said. He and Travis grinned and exchanged conspiratorial glances.

Anson looked at Fannie. "Good lookin' pointer you got there. What are you after? Quail?"

"Woodcock," I said. "Seen any?"

"Bogsuckers huh? Yeah, we flushed a couple along Sandy Creek this mornin'. I can't hit the damn things. Travis killed one the other day though. We like to never got it away from old Ted." He motioned toward his truck. "Had to pick him up over my head to get him to turn loose."

I thought of my rabbit-hunting days as a kid in Kentucky and the nights spent driving along the back roads looking for lost hounds. I asked him if he had ever lost one for good.

He took a big gulp of the scalding coffee and didn't even blink. "Naw. There's a lot of hound people around here, and we keep an eye out for everybody's dogs. I've never lost one for good and don't know anybody who has." He pulled out a bandanna and blew his nose with one hand. "Oh I've had deer hounds gone for a couple of days but somebody always picked 'em up and called me," he said. "I had to go clear up to Burrantown one time to pick up a gyp that disappeared over by Apple Springs. I don't know how in the hell she got all the way up there."

"Sometimes we stayed out all night lookin'," Travis said.

Anson smiled and nodded at his son. "Never found one that way, but I just can't sleep with a dog missin'."

He emptied his cup and I motioned toward the pot. "Awful nice of you," he said. "Believe I will." He got his coffee and stood by the fire with one hand in his pocket. "Of course now I don't spend much time lookin' for dogs since they made us quit runnin' deer with 'em. I like these little rabbit dogs, but they just don't run like real hounds. Don't sound like 'em neither."

Travis cleared his throat and nodded like he knew what was coming.

Anson worked the fire with the toe of his boot. "I've killed eleven deer in my lifetime," he said. "Started after 'em with hounds before I was Travis's age. Learned it from my uncle. On the other hand, a man down the road from me goes over to the Hill Country, sits in a tree, and gets his two deer every year—over a feeder." He looked past his truck and across the road toward the third growth covered hills and Sandy Creek beyond. "Hell, I got up one day and it was against the law to do what I'd done most of my life. Nobody ever asked me about it. Nobody I know has any problem with hounds."

I just nodded. I was an outsider and felt it.

"Gave my pack to my wife's cousin over in Mississippi," Anson said. "What the hell was I gonna do with five deer hounds I couldn't run?"

"Mama cried," Travis said.

Anson rolled his eyes. "Lord. Thousand wonders she didn't leave me. I did keep old Rosie though. Her and Travis came up together. Born two days apart. I just couldn't do without her. Besides, she'll run a rabbit as soon as she'll run deer, and she's gotten so old and slow she won't run it aground."

I asked what kind of hound she was and regretted it in the same breath.

"A deer hound, by God," Anson said. He saw my discomfort and smiled. "Most of my dogs came out of fox hound lines. We don't get too hung up in papers around here."

I thought he might get Rosie out and show her off—he kept glancing at his truck while he talked about her. I think now he wanted me to ask to see her, but knowing that hound men don't parade their dogs around the way bird hunters do, I didn't, and I've regretted it ever since.

Anson offered me a chew of tobacco and I declined, remembering the time I bit off a hunk of Mammoth Cave Twist to demonstrate what a good ol' boy I was.

He stuffed his cheek. "Trav, I guess we better go shoot us a rabbit."

The dog box doors rattled and several sets of nostrils appeared through the quarter-sized air holes as we leaned over the bed of his truck. I wondered which nose, if any, belonged to Rosie. I could picture her curled up in the back of her box, watching the door through cataract clouds. Travis poked his fingers through the holes and grinned, more with his eyes than his mouth.

Fannie reared up on a tire for a better sniff and then trotted back to the fire and sat down, clearly disgusted that her camp had been invaded by a truckload of hounds. Anson laughed out loud and shook his head. "Don't take none of this for granted," he said.

I wished them luck. We shook hands, and they left heading east.

The drizzle picked up a bit but not enough to drown the fire. I put on my poncho, fed the flames, and refilled my cup. Fannie curled up beneath the truck. Off to the east, along the Neches, a hound opened up. The long, low, bawl wafted out of the river bottom and through the pines and seemed much closer than the frantic, higher pitched voices that joined it. The woodcock were out there, I knew, and conditions were right, but I felt I should sit and listen while I could.

At Home on the Range

We can be ethical only in relation to something we can see, feel, understand, love, or otherwise have faith in.

Aldo Leopold, "The Land Ethic"

I live amid some of the best hunting and fishing country in North America. I say *amid* instead of *in* because I have to drive about a hundred miles in any direction to get out of that dreary, sprawling, concrete and Bermuda grass prairie, the Dallas-Fort Worth metroplex, to find it. And then, since nearly all of it is on private property, I generally have no access to it. Other than dove shooting around the milo fields and ponds and waterfowl on the big impoundments, there is little hunting to speak of in the Dallas area, so I drive westward for quail, eastward for woodcock, and in either direction for waterfowl.

We do have good fishing on some of the area lakes—Lavon, Ray Hubbard, Lewisville—those huge impoundments that rate a weekly fishing report in the local newspapers. But I prefer a canoe and a fly rod over bass boat and bait casting gear, so despite the cheap gunwale pads, I have dents and bare spots on the roof of my pickup cab from hauling my canoe to the rivers and modest still waters.

Why do I stay? I probably won't. Presently, though, I'm anchored by children, inertia, the need for sustenance, and something else—some amorphous attachment I can't fully explain. And as far as urban areas go, I live in a good one.

Yet other places beckon. Of Texas's ten ecological regions, the Blackland Prairie, where I live, is by far the most tame. Of eleven million or so acres of once virgin prairie, only a few thousand remain, most of them under control of the Nature Conservancy. The "country," if you can call it that, is mostly Bermuda pasture, fence to fence milo, and the big reservoirs intermingled with a few old farms and mobile home parks and subdivisions that claim to offer country living because the lots are a little more than an acre in size. Even if the agricultural lands provided decent wildlife habitat—and discounting mourning doves, cattle egrets, starlings, meadow larks, and fire ants, they don't—some of the area farmers form cooperatives and mutually agree to disallow hunting.

In theory, I could hunt on the Corps of Engineers land around the big reservoirs—there are a few doves there in September—but the bait buckets, beer cans, discarded tampon applicators, low water stench, and thousands of fire ant hills do little for the aesthetics. Bank fishing for crappie and sand bass can be very good on the big lakes, and I'm occasionally tempted, but then I'll drive across one of the bridges over Lake Lavon and there'll be a dozen people sitting in their lawn chairs amid the industrial-looking detritus, fishing the water around a partially submerged piece of living room furniture. I hear that you can safely eat the fish.

***

Texas: 267,338 square miles; 80,000 miles of flowing water; hundreds of miles of coastline—the most ecologically diverse state in the country with ten distinct ecological regions encompassing beaches, coastal marshes, pine and hardwood forests, prairies, desert, and mountains. I have visited all ten regions, some very briefly. Carrying a shotgun and fly rod, I've come to know six of the regions in the small way you can know country that is almost completely privately owned. About 98 percent of Texas's land is privately held. Upon joining the Union, the state retained ownership of its unsettled lands then, depending on your point of view, either promptly gave them away or stole them from the Comanches, Kiowa, and Apaches, then gave them away. The bulk of the remaining public two percent is made up of state and national park lands. I love the "nonconsumptive" outdoor activities—hiking, birding, and so forth—but to really know a place in a personal way I must hunt or fish there. Call me boorish, but there it is. And since hunting is generally prohibited on park lands, I'm forced to choose between an expensive lease and the relatively paltry amount of land open to public hunting. You simply don't drive up to the rancher's house and ask for permission to hunt or fish. On the big spreads, you're likely to be stopped and interrogated before you find the house. Get caught trespassing and you'll go to jail or worse.

Leased hunting varies widely in price and quality. You can get a pretty good Rolling Plains quail lease for two or three dollars per acre, but a decent Hill Country deer lease may run you five dollars an acre. The better South Texas leases may cost even more. Good hunting lands close to metropolitan areas are off the charts. If five dollars per acre doesn't sound like much, consider that two people with good dogs will need a minimum of 2,000 acres for a decent season's quail hunting. Of course deer hunters can get by with considerably less land, but the price per acre goes up sharply with the quality of the bucks. We have nearly 3.5 million deer, but short of a miracle, a true trophy-quality buck will cost as much as a fairly nice used pickup truck. There are all sorts of day leasing arrangements, risky affairs that cost $100 per day and up. Guided quail hunts on the Rolling Plains or in South Texas, complete with specially equipped quail rigs and big-running dogs, go for around $500 per day per gun; expensive, yes, but you'll probably be into fifteen or twenty coveys before lunch.

Most native Texans, especially those who can afford it but also a good many who can't but who participate anyway, seem completely comfortable with leased hunting. Few, I suspect, have even thought about it. Boosters and most outdoor writers, particularly Texas writers, pooh-pooh the high prices and claim that there's a lease to fit everyone's budget. Most of the *serious* hunters I've talked with aren't aware that public hunting exists in Texas. Everyone knows you have to have a lease. We are, after all, talking about Texas.

Okay, I suppose I am primarily a weekend hunter and probably a cheapskate to boot, but it goes much deeper than that. I'm willing to do with fewer birds flushed and fish landed to become intimate with the places I hunt, fish, and love. I must be able to visit these places whenever the urge strikes. I need to feel that these places belong to me. I have leased hunting rights before, and I enjoyed more covey rises then than I do now. I had year-round access, but I never felt intimate with these places. Perhaps it was the limited guest privileges and the knowledge that my continued access depended on a thousand dollars I really couldn't afford. Mostly, though, I think it was the fact that I was a paying guest. I owned no part of the land, had no say as to its management outside of my ability to influence the landowner with extra money, which is to say I had no influence at all. On the other hand, I can always vote against a public land-grabbing politician.

When I decided I could no longer afford the lease, I mailed my gate key to the lease manager. Strangely, I have trouble picturing that lease although it was beautiful and the hunting was marvelous. I haven't moved twenty coveys of quail in a day since I returned my key, but I don't feel cheated. I know the places I now hunt like I know the contours of my dogs' faces, and I can see the draws and dry creeks and cedar hills, sloughs, and pine plantations in fine detail when I'm away from them. There's nothing surprising about this. We are, after all, talking about my land.

Texas's rivers provide passage into otherwise inaccessible country. Yet there are problems here as well. The beds of navigable rivers are publicly owned, thus the axiom, "If you can float it, you can fish it." But put in and take out points are few and far between. Private property begins above the permanent high water mark, but some landowners dispute even this, asserting that narrow or shallow stretches aren't navigable, or that private property begins above the high water line during normal flow. Some even claim ownership of the stream bed under authority of the Spanish land grants. So step onto the bank in response to nature's call or to line or portage a rapid and you're trespassing. Want to camp? Find an island.

We canoeists carry much of the blame. Low impact camping hasn't found its way into common use in Texas. Yet tolerance seems in desperately short supply. Landowners should be tolerant, and river runners should be respectful and considerate. No problem. Right?

***

Jim Fergus, in his excellent book *A Hunter's Road*, tells of a conversation on a motorized, guided quail hunt on a huge South Texas ranch. He asked a member of the hunting party, a conservative Republican, if he was concerned about so much of the prime hunting land in America being tied up in leases. "I think we've got a goddamn socialist among us!" the man answered. Whereupon their young guide explained, "Sport is not for the masses."

I find the entire exchange chilling, never mind the ability of "the masses" to vote hunting out of existence and the sickening pomposity of both the guide and the well-to-do hunter. Without access to country—the wild and semi-wild places that hold most of America's wildlife—the individuals who make up the masses simply aren't going to develop a land ethic. People rarely care about things that don't touch their lives. So instead of a utopia in which the almighty market decides who is worthy to hunt, fish, camp, backpack, and bird, we would have a very undemocratic situation, much like the one that exists in socialist countries: The proletariat is separated from the land which is then exploited in the best interest of the ruling power—an autocratic government in the case of socialism; the all powerful market in the case of complete private ownership and restricted access. It's difficult to love something you have little chance of experiencing. Bird life was virtually nonexistent in East Berlin when the wall came down; the rodents near Chernobyl are still mutating; subdivisions continue to spread across erstwhile Texas prairie. If the majority of us are locked off the land, will we care enough to set reasonable limits on development?

Business, after all, is business, and most ranchers have their price. *We need jobs, growth. We can't have all that land lying around and nobody making any money on it. Anyway, I've got my lake house and my lease in South Texas.*

***

"Landowners are the best stewards," the argument goes. They can and should be. In some cases they are. But how much of Texas's abundant wildlife in general and game in particular is the result of stewardship? Bobwhite quail and whitetail deer, our two most popular resident game species, thrive on heavily grazed rangeland. In fact, we wouldn't enjoy the quail and deer hunting we have today were it not for the forbs, legumes, and brush that quickly invade overgrazed prairie. I don't worry much for deer and quail.

Lesser prairie chickens, however, are not tolerant of heavy grazing. Early plains settlers encountered them in staggering numbers, but in recent years we've been able to afford only a two-day hunting season in a few Panhandle counties. Worse yet, as of this writing, the U.S. Fish and Wildlife Service is considering a petition to list the birds as threatened. A South Texas subspecies, the Attwater's prairie chicken, is officially endangered and is likely already in the extinction vortex. What are the odds that we will ever again see prairie chickens in significant numbers if neither Texas hunters nor the federal government is willing to pay landowners enough to make it lucrative to leave large areas untilled and lightly grazed? Just the market in action, I suppose.

A few years ago, after an extended drought and several poor bobwhite seasons, a number of West Texas ranchers, citing their concern for the birds' long-term well-being, pressured the Parks and Wildlife Department to shorten quail season by one half. Wildlife managers pointed out that landowners can limit hunting on their own land as they see fit. By the way, we all wanted to know would they be reducing season leasing fees accordingly? Both rain and quail came back, and as far as I can tell, leasing fees have since about doubled.

But ranchers have to make a living, and we suburbanites need beef and cotton. So the government, through the Conservation Reserve Program (CRP) and similar initiatives, pays landowners to take highly erodible lands out of cultivation and plant them in native grasses and wildlife food plots. We hunters then pay again to hunt these areas. Fair enough, except that much of the CRP land in Texas, particularly on the High Plains, ends up covered in monocultures of Old World bluestem or weeping lovegrass, imported species worthless to wildlife. The reason? Wildlife-friendly native grass mixtures are much more expensive to establish. Pheasants and prairie chickens are nice, but business is business.

Meanwhile, prairie dogs, much hated by generations of cattlemen because they dig troublesome holes and allegedly compete with cattle for grass, have been shot and poisoned by the millions. The U.S. Fish and Wildlife Service has considered giving the prairie dog threatened status, and the scientific community now recognizes them as a shortgrass prairie indicator species—a wildlife species whose general well-being reflects the overall health of its ecosystem. If you merely want to see prairie dogs in their natural habitat, they can still be found on the Rita Blanca National Grassland and at MacKenzie State Park. But if you're looking for some free target practice, you'll have little trouble finding ranchers willing to let you come out to their prairie dog towns and melt your barrel.

Yet I can't blame the ranchers and farmers. Very few are getting rich, and many are going broke despite their best efforts and family ranching traditions that reach back into the last century. They're forced to operate in a brutal agricultural economy seemingly designed to keep them in the red if not in ruin. We want our commodities cheap, and we'll have them right now, thank-you. And you hayseeds should stop abusing your land.

It's easy to be poetic about indicator species when you don't draw your livelihood from the soil. And let's face it, the most beat-up rangeland or toxic cotton field in Texas is infinitely preferable to another strip mall or subdivision. If farmers and ranchers have to be paid twice to set aside some habitat for wildlife, then I'm all for it. The last thing we need is for more third-generation ranchers to be bought out by huge concerns run by cretins who never set foot on the land.

But don't expect me to buy the landowner stewardship argument just yet. The real stewardship test will come when landowners have enough financial maneuvering room to cut stocking rates, reduce chemical use, and leave marginal areas out of production and still earn a reasonable measure of security. Then we'll see if farmers and ranchers value wildlife for its own sake or if it's just another cash crop. We'll see if a swift fox matters as much as a pheasant; if burrowing owls are worth a few rows of milo. We'll see, then, how much they really love their land and its wild residents. First, though, the rest of us will have to decide if prairie chickens and golden-cheeked warblers and native prairie are worth a 200 percent increase in the price of blue jeans, bread, and beef. Then we'll know if our hearts match our rhetoric. We'll know if we really love the land and the wild things that live on it.

***

We do have some land open to public hunting here in Texas. Even a tiny percentage of nearly 300,000 square miles is a fair amount of country. We have about 700,000 acres of national forest in the East Texas Piney Woods and 170,000 acres of national grassland scattered about the north central and northwestern parts of the state. Woodcock and waterfowl hunting can be very good in the national forests. But while many nonresident hunters would consider the deer hunting pretty good, it pales compared to that available on private land in the Hill Country, South Texas, and the Rolling Plains. You can hunt doves, quail,

squirrels, rabbits, waterfowl, and deer on the national grasslands and even pronghorn antelope on the Rita Blanca National
Grasslands in far northwestern Texas. I rate the national grasslands hunting as poor, but the price is right and I often take
advantage of it. Sometimes I even manage to bring home a few
birds. Game is scarce, but so are people. I consider our national
grasslands a treasure—cattle, gas wells, and all.

The best public hunting is found on the state wildlife management areas. Presently we have around fifty of these ranging
in size from a few hundred acres to a bit over 100,000 acres.
Hunting quality varies widely, but the Texas Parks and
Wildlife Department does wonders with an ever shrinking
budget; hunting on a few of the best management areas rivals
that on all but the best private lands. Needless to say, competition for space on these areas is fierce. All totaled, the state of
Texas provides around a million acres under its public hunting
and wildlife management program, and more acreage is added
each year. You get the feeling that at least a few people in
Austin understand the problem and actually care about the poor
and the cheap.

Federal wildlife refuges—we have fourteen of them—provide still more public hunting and fishing, but on most of them
you have to basically win the state lottery to get a hunting permit. The lottery winners generally do very well, however.

So counting state and federal land, we Texans have around
two million acres open to public hunting. Sounds like a lot. It
would be in Vermont or Rhode Island, but Texas has a population of 15 million people, and the Parks and Wildlife
Department sells nearly a million hunting licenses each year.
Maybe a third of that two million acres actually provides decent
hunting, and then there are the ever increasing numbers of hik-
ers, bird watchers, and mountain bikers who have just as much
right to wide open spaces as we hunters do—yes even during
hunting season. For the most part, things have remained civil,

but with our burgeoning population, user conflicts are inevitable.

So I look long and hard for good public hunting and fishing and space and solitude. I hunt bobwhite quail west of Fort Worth in the Cross Timbers and on the Rolling Plains and blue quail on the High Plains. In January I head southeast into the Piney Woods for woodcock. Although I often fish well-known local waters in the interest of time, I know of some small, hidden ponds on public land, and I love moving water so I try to fish remote sections of the Brazos whenever I can. And I know about a piece of a small Rolling Plains river—nothing more than a string of small crystal-clear pools in the summer—where two-pound bass will rise and take a well-presented grasshopper pattern.

It has taken me fifteen years to accumulate these places. They are all on public land, so you can visit them too, but you'll have to find them yourself. Some of my best spots are well hidden, but not well enough. I have to share them with more and more people every year, so I'm always on the lookout for new places. I need to hunt bobwhite and blue quail down in the South Texas brush country and blues and Gamble's in the Trans-Pecos desert. And there's waterfowl hunting on the Gulf prairies and marshes and fishing in the spring-fed Hill Country streams.

The secret places are out there, and there are more of them than I can possibly find in a lifetime, but they are scattered about a huge state. The route to one of my favorite places takes me past a sign on Interstate 20: El Paso—526 Miles. I can't pass that sign without looking and thinking beyond the 98th meridian, into New Mexico and the public land states to the west.

***

If I were to move tomorrow, where would I go? The Rocky Mountains come immediately to mind. Nearly unlimited

photo by Brad Carter

hunting, fishing, and, if you're willing to work at it, solitude. A few years back, in June, I spent a week with Jane and the girls in a remote cabin at 9,300 feet in western Colorado. Our cabin was Spartan and used by elk and bear hunters in the fall. No electricity, phone, or television. Coleman lanterns provided the only artificial light. The ranch covers around 60,000 acres. The northern boundary abuts another 4 million acres of national forest. From the front door, I could see snow-capped peaks in Utah, and sixty yards away, trout rose and rolled in a ten-acre lake. Mule deer visited the yard every evening at dusk. Hummingbirds hovered around hanging feeders and just as often, our heads.

Taciturn cowhands, on their way up the mountain after cattle, their blue heeler cow dogs constantly and tenuously among the horses' hooves, came by every other morning to check on us. One morning the foreman said, "So what does a Texan think about all this game, fish, and space?" I don't remember my reply, but I remember my thoughts: That, hunting quail in Texas, I often see thirty or forty deer in a day without looking for them, and that on a good night on my tanks, twenty bass will rise to smash my deer hair frog; and that after cleaning my birds, I can rinse my hands in the Pease River just upstream from where Texas Rangers recaptured Cynthia Ann Parker. Kneeling there on the sandy bank, I can watch a pale autumn moon—a Comanche moon—rise from behind the red cliffs to the northeast. I can listen to hysterical sounding coyotes protesting my presence and know that tonight, no artificial light will taint my view of the firmament.

There are other places too. I could live in northern Idaho, where I've caught cutthroat trout in the Coeur d'Alene River, and hunt grouse and waterfowl in September and October before snow keeps me out of the mountains. And Vermont, maybe the prettiest, cleanest place I've been; grouse, woodcock, trout, pike, smallmouth bass, and funky politics. The tiny communities, clusters of white homes, stores and churches and libraries. I could learn about cross-country skiing and snowshoes and drive into Maine every spring to run the rivers and fish for brook trout.

And Kentucky, my boyhood home, where English sounds right and access to country is as simple as knocking on a farmer's door. There are ruffed grouse and smallmouth bass and trout in the eastern mountains and muskie in the clear, deep lakes, squirrels in the hardwoods, and deer nearly everywhere. I could go on and on.

Why would anyone who doesn't own a good-sized piece of land, who cares about country and freedom to roam at will, stay in Texas? Yes, the hunting and fishing are both good here, and you can find space and solitude if you're diligent, although they might cost you much more than sweat. There's history, too, if you care about it, and most Texans care deeply. For me, it's part of that amorphous attachment. Of course every region has its human history, but here it seems uniquely tied to the landscape and to our sense of identity and place. Stand at any creek or river ford in the Cross Timbers or Rolling Plains or watch the moon rise over the Llano Estacado, and if you care to, you can feel some of what you feel on hallowed ground at Shiloh or Vicksburg. But the things you feel and the screams you imagine come from Ranger, Comanche and Kiowa, vaquero, white settler, and black soldier.

On a spring afternoon I made the long drive on farm to market roads to the Adobe Walls battle site on the Canadian River northeast of Amarillo near Stinnett. There on June 27, 1874, Quanah Parker, under the spell of a soon to be disgraced prophet named Isa-Tai, led 700 Comanche, Cheyenne, and Kiowa warriors against 28 white buffalo hunters encamped inside the adobe walled trading post. The white hunters cut the raiders to pieces with their 50-caliber Sharps rifles. The enraged warriors then split up, struck the hunters' camps wherever they found them, and left hacked bodies all over the northern Panhandle.

I stood between the two simple monuments—one honoring the Indians, the other memorializing the white hunters. Across the broad, green river bottom, the northern breaks rose to rough juniper-studded hills and buttes. Several blue quail ran one at a time across the gravel road. Behind me a middle-aged couple probed the knee-high grass for artifacts. Looking for something to take, I suppose.

Only a fool would see romance there. But the history of the place matters. I wanted to touch it. To cross the fence and walk up the hill where the raiders gathered before sunrise that morning. To walk out into the river bottom where incomprehensible numbers of bison surely grazed. Or just to walk into the pasture and flush a few quail in country that moves me. But no.

I drove back toward the highway past signs on either side of the road:

NO TRESPASSING
STAY ON THE ROAD!

I know. I know. That's just the way things have turned out.

It's Hell Being a Bird Dog

Heidi looked truly pathetic. Judging from the pitiful expression on her face, you'd have thought she was awaiting a flogging. Instead, she stood soaking wet and shivering on the tailgate while I taped a set of Cordura dog boots onto her feet for the afternoon hunting.

We had spent the morning chasing late season bobwhites in a slow, cold, steady drizzle in the shin oak hills near Paducah, Texas. My cousin Todd Smith, Heidi, and I had gotten into a few coveys, but we were showing some wear. My feet squished in wet boots, and the clammy facing on my brush pants clung to my skin despite an hour-long lunch break in the cab with heater going full blast.

Todd, a Georgian by way of Mississippi, stood patiently in the rain, watching me apply duct tape. "Poor Haadi," he said. "Hit's hay-ull bein' a bird dog, ain't it girl?"

***

I hate thinking about it, but I probably shortened Heidi's career if not her life. Early on, she was my only bird dog, and unfortunately for her, her prime years coincided with my late twenties. Back then we hunted all day from first shooting light until thirty minutes past sunset and the end of legal shooting hours. If things were slow, we might take an hour lunch break. And since we hunted on weekends, I expected her to put in two consecutive days unless I happened to have Friday or Monday

off in which case I expected three straight days of dawn to dusk work.

In those days she'd ride atop the gear in the back of my Jeep Cherokee—I didn't have a portable kennel. We'd get home well after dark, and she'd be unable to get out of the Jeep. I'd sheepishly carry her past Jane and the girls and into the kitchen where I could see to pull the cactus spines from her ears and underside. Her teats would be unrecognizable scabs; her eyes would be nearly gummed shut. Her hindquarters would tremble when she tried to stand. After pulling all the spines I could find, I would treat her cuts and abrasions with antiseptic, squirt ophthalmic ointment under her eyelids, and feed her double the normal amount. She sometimes ate and drank lying down. Then I'd carry her into the study and lay her on a foam pad where as best I could tell she would sleep through the night without moving.

Inevitably, Jane would suggest that I might be pushing her too hard, and just as inevitably, I would point to Heidi and launch my "This is a by god working dog" speech. Next morning, Heidi would be up sniffing about and weakly wagging her bobtail. By afternoon, she'd be jogging around the backyard and barking insanely at whomever or whatever happened to be in the alley. Now recovered, she was ready to sleep outside in the dog house until it was time for me to run her into the ground again.

I never worried; instead, I likened her post-hunt condition to my football days when I could barely stand, let alone walk after a game. (It has since occurred to me that my football years might yet shorten *my* career.) Heidi is a small German shorthair, just over forty pounds, lithe and tough. In her prime, she covered ground with a lovely, smooth, energy efficient gait; graceful yet businesslike—like a little dancer, Jane used to say.

At five years old she was unstoppable. She still had the tools and knew how to use them. She'd occasionally flag a bit late in the morning and again around mid-afternoon, but she maintained a reserve somewhere—in her heart I think—and always drew on it during the magical hour just before dark when the birds are most active, frantically filling their crops before nightfall. Brad would watch her working some distant hillside, shake his head, and wonder aloud what she could possibly be running on.

At six she began to fail. And I don't mean she slowed down a bit. I'd put her down first thing in the morning and within two hours she'd be obviously hurting. At first I blamed it on conditioning and assumed she'd toughen up as the season wore on. By mid-season it was clear that I wasn't conditioning her; I was simply hurting her.

So I cut her workload way back. I'd run her for an hour or so first thing in the morning then again the last two hours before dark. At times she seemed to be herself again, especially late in the day when she worked birds. But she was running on heart alone, I think. Nevertheless, she made good use of her time and we shot a lot of birds over her that year. I reminded myself that dogs *do* eventually slow, and by that time Molly was aboard, still a pup but already working wild birds. I felt good about the season, but there's no escaping reality. Heidi's slowing was too abrupt, and I know exactly where the blame rests.

***

Texas's quail country is murder on bird dogs. On the Rolling Plains, where I do most of my hunting, you'll find prickly pear cactus—scads in dry years—several species of cholla, mesquite thorns, cat claw, and shin oak which grows to a height perfect for destroying a dog's underside. Every woody plant comes equipped to tear holes in your brush pants. Imagine what it can do to a dog's hide.

Amazingly, most bird dogs quickly learn to avoid cactus—even prickly pear, which often grows in huge patches virtually hidden in the little bluestem. But occasionally even a mature dog will come ripping by with a cholla branch or prickly pear pad stuck to some part of her anatomy—usually her head—and I'll have to call her in for barb removal. A pup sometimes will become so badly festooned he'll actually stop and wait for help.

But there's one unavoidable hazard, nastier than all the others combined, that will stop the toughest most maniacal pointer ever whelped: the grass burr or sand burr, a wicked multi-spiked little grass seed with no redeeming qualities that I can see. In dry years, they carpet entire pastures, especially sandy riparian areas that just happen to be ideal bobwhite habitat. Pull one off your boot lace and you'll spend the next five minutes trying to let go of it. They're as hard as steel and needle sharp. They'll punch pinholes through your ground cloth, tent floor, and Thermarest pad. They'll cover the bottoms of your boots and your steel belted radials. They're too bad to be true.

Dogs can deal with grass burs on their pads. But let one find its way between the pads and the dog *will* stop and go to work on her feet. Dog boots are the only practical answer. Brad and I have tried every available style: molded rubber boots, boots made from bicycle inner tubes, leather Australian sheep dog boots, and Cordura boots. We've settled on the Cordura boots for most situations. They're not cheap, but they go on easily and wear well. And unlike the other styles, they don't hamper a dog's swimming ability. If anything, they serve as fins. Just wrap the dog's ankles with Vetrap, slip the boots on, and tighten the Velcro straps. Then affix the boots to the Vetrap—*not the dog's hair*—with duct tape. Carry a small roll of duct tape, a roll of Vetrap, and a spare boot in your game vest. If worse comes to worse and a dog loses more than one boot, you can just wrap his entire foot (not too tightly) with a layer of Vetrap followed by a layer of duct tape. Dogs hate it, but the alternative involves stopping every two minutes for burr removal. I'm still trying to figure out how coyotes deal with sand burrs.

Extremely rocky terrain calls for molded rubber boots. They're expensive, but in rocky country a hard going dog can shear a pad right off, and Cordura doesn't provide adequate protection. Molly destroyed four sets of Cordura boots in as many days in the rocky foothills of the Florida mountains in New Mexico. By the second day her pads were battered so badly she could barely walk. I kept her going by padding her feet with several layers of gauze and Vetrap beneath the boots.

One night in a motel parking lot, I watched a man pulling duct tape directly from his pointer's feet. The dog yelped and cried like he was being tortured with a cattle prod. The man's teary-eyed wife held and comforted the dog. The man would jerk a piece of tape loose; the dog would yelp and lurch; and the man would blurt, "Oh god, boy, I'm sorry. Bless your heart."

The couple had come to Texas from the Southeast and had quickly become acquainted with the sand burr problem. A local had suggested wrapping the dog's feet with duct tape. I gave him a couple rolls of Vetrap and probably saved his marriage.

You'll read and hear about other approaches involving waterproof first-aid tape and baby socks and tube socks and so forth. Go ahead and try them if you must; we did. Or you can go directly to our approach and save yourself a lot of hassle and expense. End of discussion.

Still, I hear about dogs that never need boots. "Old Missy, by god, she just plops down and bites them burrs right off." Some people should be required to spend two minutes rolling a handful of sand burs around in their mouths.

One more thing on boots: If your dog has never worn them be sure to try them at home before going into the field. You'll want to be ready with your video camera. You'll see what I mean.

***

We sometimes get cold, damp, drizzly, or even freezing weather in West Texas. Generally though, the weather is quite nice, even in January. I hate it. Rattlesnakes and golfers are out, and since I can't put fresh dogs down every thirty minutes, I have to carry a half gallon of water just to keep Molly and Heidi going for a couple of hours. Like most people, I enjoy standing around in sixty-five degree weather. But trudging around in the Panhandle sandhills all day in that kind of heat is another matter.

I've met few other Texans who carry water for their dogs. (Yes, I realize they're *just* dogs.) Old Thug is about to expire from heat exhaustion; his tongue, which he's about to step on, is covered with grass burrs and sand, and the boss says, "By god, a cold one sure would go good about now."

Brad carries a canteen on a strap; I carry one or two Nalgene water bottles in my game bag. The weight pulls at my shoulders and the back of my neck at first, but the water goes fast. On warm days, two dogs might need a quart per hour to stay at their best. And they'll need water even on cold days, so unless we're going to be out less than an hour or happen to be hunting near an abundance of surface water, I always carry at least a quart.

Get into birds and you might have trouble getting your dogs to drink, even if they're in bad shape for water. A good dog might flag a bit in the heat, but let her smell birds and she'll go until she falls over on her nose. I sometimes force my dogs into shade and make them sit until they're relaxed enough to drink, especially after they've had extended bird contact. Their mouths will be covered with sticky feathers; they'll be wild-eyed and wheezing with every breath, but for a few minutes, they might be too excited to drink. It takes discipline on everyone's part to call them in when a dozen singles are spread nicely about, but the dogs will do a better job if they're not on the verge of heat exhaustion. Besides, the short rest will give the air-washed singles time to settle in and put out scent.

On extended death marches, water conservation methods overshadow shotgunning technique. For years I let my dogs lap water from my cupped hand. As much water spilled to the ground as went down the dogs' throats. I've since used empty margarine tubs, Tupperware bowls, Dixie cups, aluminum pie plates, and squirt bottles among other things. Finally Brad went to the toy department at Wal-mart and bought a small, inflated rubber ball, cut it in two, gave one half to me and kept the other. The resulting flexible bowl fits nicely in my palm and provides a smooth surface for the dogs to drink from. And it's a conversation piece.

Occasionally the dogs will find a bit of shade, dig a hole, and lie down—a sure sign that a break is in order. Field trial purists would be horrified; a real bird dog, we're told, starts fast and finishes at the same speed. Sounds impressive, but our heats typically run longer than a half hour.

***

I've yet to see a rattlesnake in Texas during quail season. I know they're around though; I see scores during the warm months. Of course the risk is far greater in South Texas where snakes never really hibernate, but I have no firsthand experience down there. That country is locked up, and access is way beyond my means.

I did see a massasauga in New Mexico, and I was edgy the entire time I hunted in Arizona. My hosts all wore snake boots or chaps; several of their dogs have been bitten over the years. Still, I chose to more or less ignore the danger. I should hire a pro to run Molly through snake avoidance training, but thus far I've talked myself out of the trouble and expense.

I do take precautions however. I won't run my dogs immediately after several consecutive warm days and mild nights. This past season Brad and I decided to forgo opening weekend for that very reason. Sure enough, opening day on our favorite West Texas management area, a rattler struck a Mississippi hunter's pointer on the head. The dog pulled through and was back at work the following week. But not before his head swelled to about twice normal size.

Rattlesnakes do kill bird dogs. In Texas, prairie rattlers occasionally get a dog, but the western diamondback is the most common assassin. I've stopped killing rattlesnakes as a matter of course, but this snake sorely tests me. It's aggressive, with an exceptionally toxic venom and, among the rattlesnakes, grows to a size eclipsed only by the eastern diamondback. Years ago Jay and I killed a big western diamondback on my quail lease in the Cross Timbers. It was about an inch shorter than me and I'm six two. Jay stepped within six inches of it as it lay along a cattle trail. The unusually cool weather that April morning spared Jay a rough trip to the emergency room.

Of course rattlesnakes theoretically buzz to warn us of their presence. I've been within striking distance of several that never made a sound until they were assaulted with a stout stick or a rock. I suspect most dogs are hit as they come suddenly upon a downwind snake, which might rattle after it strikes if it rattles at all. I often wonder how many rattlers my dogs have encountered on warm days back in the brush—or how many I've missed by few feet. I try not to dwell on it.

I briefly considered carrying anti-venom. The stuff costs about $200 per dose, must be refrigerated, has a shelf life of about a year, and must be administered intravenously by a veterinarian. And if a dog gets a full load of venom in the right place, especially between the ear and shoulder, you probably can't get him to the vet in time to save him.

Fortunately, dogs usually get bitten on the head or forelegs, areas with relatively little tissue and few blood vessels. And snakes rarely unload a full dose of venom when they strike defensively. Discounting folk remedies and shock treatment, it's probably best to just pick the dog up and get him to the vet as soon as possible. With fluids and confinement, he'll probably pull through fine. I'm not so sure about doting owners suffering from cardiac arrest.

If porcupines were poisonous, Brad and I would be out of dogs. I keep a hemostat in my game vest just for pulling quills. Every encounter, and the resulting load of quills, makes Dee and Molly all the more determined to rid the world of porcupines. Last time she jumped a porky, Molly caught several dozen quills inside her mouth. Enraged, she went back for another round. By the time I got to her, blood was pouring from the roof of her mouth, and there was no way to fashion a muzzle. I stuck my fingers in her mouth and jerked the blood engorged quills out with the hemostat. She cried pathetically but never once snapped at my hand. After some furious head shaking and a quick drink, she galloped over the hill and nailed a covey. That night as I watched her happily chomping her dry dog food, it occurred to me that we humans are frail creatures.

Six years ago Brad and I began seeing a few feral hogs on our Panhandle hunting grounds. Lately they seem to be taking over the world. We see them most often at dusk, leggy black monsters that melt into the brush at the first whiff of a human. Sport hunting doesn't make a dent in their population. They're spookier than deer. They tear up riparian areas and eat everything, including the eggs of ground nesting birds. In East Texas, several eastern wild turkey restoration efforts failed miserably until wildlife managers got serious about removing hogs.

A couple of years ago on our favorite management area, a bird dog was neatly unzipped when he ran amongst a sow and her pigs. I never learned whether or not he pulled through. These days I'll often hear porcine squealing in the mesquite above the Pease River bottom, and Molly will come sprinting out of the brush with her ears laid back. Some people can shrug philosophically, but I don't consider feral swine a natural hazard like rattlesnakes and porcupines.

I nearly had a heart attack last year when Molly and Brad's young setter, Buck, caught a wild, squealing piglet on the Caddo National Grasslands. We pulled them away while the angry adults squealed and popped their teeth a few yards away in the brush. The dogs had no idea what to do with their hysterical captive and seemed quite relieved to be ordered out of combat. We probably should've given them both a good switching.

***

Early on, Brad and I hauled Heidi and Dee in the extended cab area of my truck. On rainy days, it was "Back you wretched beasts!" while we tried to eat our soggy pimento loaf sandwiches. By mid-season the inside of my truck resembled the interior of an earthen hut. Naturally I saw no reason to clean it up while quail season was on. Jane, on the other hand, would neither ride in the truck nor acknowledge co-ownership.

That summer I moved up a caste when I bought a two-hole fiberglass box to go behind the cab. It's light and well ventilated, yet dogs quickly warm the compartments in all but the coldest weather. I can load and unload it with ease. I threw in a foam pad and Heidi rode in comfort, and I noticed immediately that she seemed much less crippled after riding home in her box than she did after riding amid a pile of shifting equipment.

Naturally it wasn't good enough. Brad and I needed equipment to match our ardor. We went in together on a battered but solid three-hole dog trailer. Brad did the refurbishment; I came over occasionally to hand him tools. He lengthened the tongue and added a webbed steel platform for water jugs, installed Plexiglas door windows with adjustable vents, added cargo rails on top, and mounted a spare tire. I pick my hunting buddies carefully.

Now the dogs ride in insulated steel compartments. I'll open one of the doors in freezing weather, and doggy heat will billow out and fog my glasses. We've pulled our trailer, loaded with dogs and everything but a rocking chair lashed on top, all over creation. It serves as a cooking platform, a workbench, and a veterinary table. But more importantly, it marks us as *serious* bird hunters. Pulling our trailer westward, we exchange greetings with other serious hunters, secure in our position in the upper caste. Then we'll meet a West Texas guide pulling a dual axle, twenty-eight-hole, double decked trailer with an air conditioning unit on top.

***

Too many bird dogs really do live in hell. There was the pointer I saw tied to a flatbed trailer in ten-degree weather. For bedding, his thoughtful owner had thrown a few handfuls of straw down on the frozen gravel. I could go on and on. Dogs shoved three and four at a time into a single compartment and left to fight all night long. Dogs left in uninsulated metal boxes with no bedding. Yet they get up and put in a good day's work for masters who shouldn't be allowed to own a dog.

The mistreated dogs are nearly always English pointers; tough, stoic, the hands-down choice of serious hunters, professional guides, and callous assholes. I run into the latter every season—know-it-alls who like to blow about "culling" dogs. They want you to believe they shot the dogs when in reality they abandoned them—just left them in the field. Perhaps the dogs really are worthless as hunters, but I'm betting on worthless owners. And even a sorry dog deserves better than that. A bullet between the eyes would be more humane than abandonment, but the gutless owners won't dirty their hands with it. Far easier to keep it out of sight and out of mind. Just leave it to the coyotes.

The rest of us deal with emaciated dogs that show up in camp or along ranch roads, starved for human affection as much as food, their ribs and spine in sharp relief against their dull coats. They want to run to you, but they hold back, unsure. They wonder: Will you merely shoo them away, or, consistent with their past, kick the hell out of them?

Dogs do occasionally get lost. A youngster might chase a deer out of the country or get separated from her boss and head in the wrong direction. So you look for identification on the collar and make the call, knowing that nine chances in ten the owner will refuse to come after the dog. He'll tell you he doesn't care what you do with the worthless son-of-a-bitch. But you call anyway, hoping for the one out of ten that will thank you, offer to pay you for your trouble, praise the Lord, then jump in his pickup and drive 300 miles to get his dog. More than likely, though, you'll be left wondering what you're going to do with this poor dog.

Brutal jerks heap extended suffering on trusting animals and get away with it. But hook one of these creeps in the side of the head like he deserves and you'll go to jail. Still, at times you have to wonder how long you'd be locked up.

***

Heidi didn't hunt this past season; it would have been her eleventh. She had some great middle years sharing time with Molly, doing delicate work none of the other dogs could do. She struggled through her tenth season, putting in only an hour at a time, still doing superb work on singles and running coveys. In New Mexico, she was the only one of the four dogs who handled blue quail with any consistency. But her hearing had all but left her by then. I'd blow the whistle and watch her stop and cock her head to try to home in on the direction. As often as not, she chose wrong and ran frantically the wrong way. A few bad scares in big country convinced me she should retire.

She slipped badly through the following summer and fall. I came home from Kansas in December and found her barely able to get up. Heartsick, I felt sure she was nearly ready for that long one-way trip to the vet. We made the obligatory visit to see if anything could be done. Dr. Lee prescribed a fairly new arthritis drug called Rimadyl and predicted I'd be pleased with the results. A week later she was chasing English sparrows out of the hedges, wrestling with Molly, and boiling out of the dog house to challenge any and all perceived threats to backyard sovereignty. Each Rimadyl caplet should be gold plated for what it costs, but I don't begrudge a penny.

I'm thinking of taking old Heidi along for the ride a few times this fall. She's fine company and loves road trips. She would enjoy the excitement of the roadside rest stops, campgrounds, and motel rooms. She could romp about at lunch or while we put boots on the other dogs. She doesn't go far these days.

And who knows? If the birds are skittish enough...

Guilt

 An obnoxious mechanical roar, distant but closing. After a few minutes, or hours—I'm not sure—the racket seems very close. Right at the edge of consciousness, I struggle to think; I know I'm not at home; but where? Then I feel the coolness on my face, the sharpness of the air in my nostrils. Ah! Deer camp.

Still in my sleeping bag, I crawl to the tent door and peer through the mesh. Nothing. Complete blackness. The roar stops suddenly and I look toward the sky and make out the outline of a ridiculously huge motor home not fifteen feet from my door. I look at my watch and squint to no avail. After a bit of groping about, I find my glasses miraculously intact beneath my sleeping bag. Four twenty A.M. The generator starts again. Time to get up anyway.

But the bag is warm. Trying to ignore my bladder, I lie back and luxuriate, reflecting on the real importance of being on my stand before daylight. This all seemed like a fine idea last night. My bladder settles the argument, and I pull on my down jacket then dig my pants from the bottom of my sleeping bag. Warm pants, frozen boots. I curse myself for not sleeping with my boots, but my last attempt didn't go well. I probably should have knocked some of the mud off first.

Several lanterns are already burning. There are maybe twenty people on this 16,000-acre Hill Country lease, but I know only the father and son I met last night. Lo and behold they have two pots of coffee brewing on their Coleman stove. I pitch my dented, blackened pot back into the cook box and sidle up to say good morning. Right on cue, they offer me a cup, which I gratefully accept.

The father is a security guard, the son a construction worker. The older man calls his son Bubba because a baby sister once had trouble saying "brother." They analyze and argue over the weather and what it means and then go on for five minutes about who is and isn't pulling his weight in camp. "I apologize for this piss-poor coffee," the older man says. "I guess I'd better show the boy how it's done. Hell, Bubba, I could see right through twenty feet of this stuff."

His son pours himself another cup. "By god, you didn't have any problem with me crawlin' out at four o'clock to make it."

The father shakes his head and snorts. "I knew if I didn't start on you early, we'd be here 'til noon. Better look and see what Mama packed us for breakfast. We're gonna all starve to death if you don't get busy."

Acutely aware of my own father's absence, I decline their breakfast invitation.

Low thirties; cold if you're standing around camp, warm enough to raise a sweat if you're walking hard. Since I'm standing around camp, I naturally overdress, never mind that I've been doing this since I was big enough to toddle along behind my father. Long handles, camo fatigue pants, wool shirt, wool sweater, ludicrous plastic blaze orange vest, stocking cap, rifle, flashlight, fanny pack full of unneeded gear, and I'm ready to go.

Five thirty-six. Too early still, but there's nothing else to do. I climb the barbed-wire fence behind my tent, ripping the crotch in my army surplus pants, and head up the first hill. Halfway up something large jumps onto the trail twenty feet ahead.

Resisting the urge to run screaming back to camp, I manage to
get the flashlight on after dropping it in a wild search for the
switch. A large doe stands motionless, staring into my beam.
Sunrise is an hour away, but the doe tag burns a hole in my
pocket. Fearing my weakness, I turn the flashlight off, stamp
my foot, and listen as she crashes through the brush. I see this
as a good omen.

On top, I look out over the 300-acre flat I plan to hunt.
Although it's still pitch dark, I'm tempted to push on to my
ambush spot. I'm too keyed-up and anxious but manage to talk
myself out of stumbling blindly into the mesquite thicket that
yesterday held a small buck and a half-dozen does. Nearly chok-
ing on desire, I sit down on a cedar log to wait for better light.
Sweat runs down my glasses. I pull off the sweater and tie the
arms around my waist knowing full well I'll be freezing again in
a few minutes. Behind me in camp, trucks start and grind away.
A dog barks. Someone laughs. Close by, night things move in
the brush.

***

I had arrived in camp literally sick with work concerns.
Getting three days off to hunt took major negotiation, but I
finally convinced management the situation was so hopeless
that nothing mattered. I had hoped the long drive would pull me
out of it; the breakaway and the initial exhilaration; clear sky
and nothing to do but drive and daydream; seven pleasant hours
along back roads through interesting country; the country
stores and roadside eateries. I went through all my little rituals.
I listened to my favorite Dallas station until I drove out of
range. Then, with both widows down, I sang over and over a
half dozen hymns from my Kentucky boyhood; I sipped coffee,
ate wonderfully greasy cheeseburgers and pickled eggs,
munched antacid tablets, stopped at scenic overlooks and historical markers, talked with other hunters at rest stops, petted
bird dogs at service stations, honked and waved back to several

dozen truckloads of guys wearing orange caps. In short, I did the kinds of things you need to do to get a trip started right. But the funk remained.

I pulled into camp, found a level spot next to a sagging clapboard house, and set up my tent among strangers who seemed to be working hard at ignoring me. I probably appeared too surly to approach, especially after I nearly put my hand on a black widow spider that lived in a small rock pile I had to move to make room for the tent. The temperature was in the mid-seventies, perfect weather for hunting if you're after rattlesnakes, which in Texas are probably as abundant as the four million or so deer. I spoke briefly with the foreman, a shriveled cowboy named Floyd, about my assigned hunting area, which turned out to be the pasture behind my tent. He assured me that I, the new guy and last person to arrive in camp, was getting the prime spot.

I glared at my neighbors and crossed the fence to begin my perfunctory "scouting trip" in the afternoon heat. The pasture looked open and empty, an ocean of waist-high brush. I wondered where a deer could possibly hide. Sweat ran into my eyes. Gnats circled my head. My canteen was in camp. My binoculars, I realized, were on the dashboard of the truck.

I was thinking of work and that I shouldn't have taken the day off to drive out here to this miserable excuse for a deer lease when I heard movement ahead in the brush. I stopped. Something moved again. I took two quick steps, and twenty blue-gray birds flushed with that unmistakable game bird clamor and flew low over the cholla and prickly pear, banked to the left, and disappeared around the base of the hill.

Quail. No doubt about it. But what kind? They certainly weren't bobwhites. The foreman would know. I moved on a bit less burdened, wondering if these birds would behave for a pointing dog. Ahead, thirty or so angora goats halted their brush clearing operation to stare at me. I've always had a soft spot for these tough, raffish, half-wild little trolls. I walked more or less in a straight line toward a two-acre thicket that abutted the barbed-wire fence on the ranch's western boundary. Beyond the fence lay another ranch, strictly off limits. The owners, I was told, had zero tolerance for trespassers. Naturally, the cover on that side of the fence looked infinitely better than the goat-chewed kindling on my side.

I eased into the thicket, which opened up nicely after a few yards. Across the clearing, another covey of quail, loosely synchronized like a school of fish, moved back into the brush. I got a good look this time. They were bluish gray with white crests like mohawks, and distinct, rounded, overlapping breast feathers. They looked slightly larger than bobwhites. I had seen them in magazines and books but couldn't name them. I had read that southwestern quail species are notorious runners, so I ran at them, and sure enough, they disappeared into the brush without flushing. I was wondering about bird dogs again when a fork-horn buck that must have been standing there in the open not ten feet to my left magically materialized, snorted, jumped the fence, and disappeared.

I was alive for the first time in months. Here was a deer, a buck no less. I had gone scouting, made no effort at stealth, and had found him. Or stumbled upon him. No matter. To hell with work and budgets and schedules and suburbs and mortgages and all the things that make you feel like you're dragging a boat anchor. I spent the rest of the afternoon on the hillside above my thicket, watching goats and cattle and the occasional group of deer just up from their afternoon nap. Near dusk, without looking at my watch, I headed for camp.

Back at headquarters, I asked Floyd about the quail. "Goddamn cottontops," he said gravely. "Runnin'est little sumbitches that ever was." He spat in the corner of his little office. "Rurn ye dogs for sure." I thanked him for the warning and walked back to the tent, trying to decide if cottontops would be best hunted with an English pointer or German shorthair.

***

Dawn. Fog drapes the entire pasture below me, including my thicket. You expect heat and aridity here in the southwestern corner of the Edward's Plateau, but not this. My sweat dries, and the earlier excitement subsides. I doze then jerk wide awake at the sound of wing beats. A skein of geese, white-fronts, materializes above me in the fog. They are well above the valley floor, but on my hilltop it seems that I could stand and touch them with my gun barrel. The fog-damped sound of the first gunshot rising up and out of the hills to the south brings me out of my trance. Time to move, fog or no fog.

By the time I reach the bottom of the hill, the sun is on my face. I can see considerable detail through holes burned in the fog. The birds are frantic, making up their late start. A goat coughs somewhere in front of me. I'm late.

Through openings in the fog, I see the boundary fence and my thicket a hundred and fifty or so yards to the south. The wind is in my face, so I move to within comfortable shooting range, about eighty yards away, and sit down under a mesquite tree. Deer are in there, I know, browsing around the clearings, stopping periodically to stand motionless, to listen and check the wind.

My backside says about forty-five minutes. I check my watch. It disagrees. Seventeen minutes and counting. But my backside is more convincing. I get up, stretch luxuriantly, and ease toward my thicket. It takes me nearly twenty minutes to cover the eighty yards. Slow, but not nearly enough so. I stand at the outer edge of the thicket, knowing damn well I'm blowing it but knowing just as surely that something is about to happen. Another step. Snort! Five white flags are flying over the fence. I sprint to the clearing. No antlers in sight. Just the white flags bobbing in the distance. Then silence. No birds. No wind.

Nothing but the pulse in my ears. I'm thankful that deer hunting is a solitary sport.

I exhale, and another doe loses her nerve and flushes twenty feet to my left. She runs along the fence for a couple hundred yards and then veers out into the pasture and stops suddenly to stare back at me. I drop to a sitting position and bring the rifle up, my elbows resting on my knees. Too much brush. I can't see a thing. I ease back to my feet. She's still there. I try to lay the cross hairs on her neck, but it's too thin, and I'm breathing too hard. I move the cross hairs behind her shoulder. An easy shot. I take up the slack in the sloppy factory trigger, take a slight breath, hold it, and squeeze.

She bolts, but I can't stop the trigger squeeze. The rifle bucks, and for a fraction of a second I lose the picture, but I know I've missed. What spooked her? A sun glint off the barrel or scope perhaps? Or did she just lose her nerve? No matter. I've missed a head of big game for the first time in my life. Or worse, I might have shot her badly, although I don't think so. I make a perfunctory search for blood and hair and find nothing. The thought of her lying somewhere gut shot, sick with pain and fear, and waiting for the coyotes, makes me queasy. I promise myself that I'll never take another offhand shot.

***

The bucks hanging from the camp meat pole depress me. But then I don't deserve a deer. Others in camp evidently showed some modicum of discipline. I hope no one heard my shot. "Heard you shootin'," they'll say. "Where's your buck?"

"Oh that must have been over on the Cox place. I didn't see anything worth shootin'. Looked at a smallish six, but I've gotten picky in my old age." Fortunately no one puts me to the test.

The coffee and sausage pick me up a bit, and I decide to stroll over to the check-in shack to see Floyd. He and another man nearly have the hide off of an eight pointer when a red

Suburban pulls into the yard. A grim young couple gets out and walks up over to meet Floyd. The woman is an Hispanic beauty, with gorgeous dark eyes and long hair tied back in a ponytail. Floyd looks at her in the unobtrusive way elderly men admire young women. Her eyes are moist. "I shot a fork horn," she tells Floyd. "I'm sorry. I thought it had more points. I must have been too excited." Shooting forkies is strictly forbidden on this ranch, the idea being that a four pointer could be a high quality yearling.

"This is her first deer hunt," her husband says.

Floyd is enjoying himself. "Jus hold on. Les have us a look." He shuffles over to the Suburban. The couple dutifully follows. The young man drops the tailgate and pulls the head of a small buck out for inspection. Floyd studies the tiny rack. "Got a rang?" he asks the woman. She cocks her head questioningly. "A rang," Floyd says. "On yer fanger."

She pulls a delicate little ring from her right pinkie. Floyd takes it in one hand and carefully adjusts the position of the deer's head. I move a little closer. He places the ring on a small bump on one of the main tines. The ring stays in place due to gravity as much as the size of the alleged point.

"By god, I call that a five-point buck," Floyd says, pointing to the ring. The couple beams. The man puts his arm around his wife and pats her lovely bottom. She claps her hands, skips over to her eviscerated deer, and lovingly strokes its neck just above the bullet hole.

***

Gene Hill wrote that he would support a law that gives his state the authority to strip for life the hunting privileges of anyone convicted of shooting illegal game. He's probably right. For purely selfish reasons, though, I'm glad the state of Kentucky does not have such a law.

I was nineteen years old when I shot a doe, illegally, on family property in the eastern Kentucky mountains. I knew better.

My father had taught me better, but I wanted that deer badly, and in my mind, game laws were like speed limits—It's okay so long as you don't get caught. If you get caught, well, you haven't committed a real crime.

But as that big doe rolled down the hill and came to a stop right at my feet, I knew I had committed a real crime. The four-point buck that followed her to within twenty feet of me and paced back and forth in front of me snorting and pawing, refusing to leave until I ran shouting at him, didn't help matters.

As I cleaned the doe, my first deer, I told myself that I had done no wrong. This deer had, after all, been taken on private property—family property no less. We could do as we damn well pleased on our own property. Besides, my family and I would make good use of this deer. We always ate what I shot. Nonetheless, I was terrified of what my father might say. And there was the buck that I hadn't seen until after I had broken the law.

By the time I got the deer to camp, I thought I had convinced myself that everything was okay and that I was in fact quite the hunter. After all, just getting a deer was quite a feat in Kentucky in the 1970s. Still, I lied and told the two hunters who walked by that the deer they saw hanging from the limb was a button buck. I'm sure they wondered why I didn't invite them in for a cup of coffee and a closer look. And why did I consider cutting the evidence of my crime down to roll it over the mountain out of sight and, hopefully, out of mind?

My partner and best friend, who had shown proper restraint earlier that morning when he hadn't been sure if what he saw was a small buck or merely a doe and wishful thinking playing on the undergrowth, withheld comment when he saw my deer. He withheld it again when the game warden stopped us; again when we were told we were under arrest; and again, God bless his heart, when the cell door slammed shut behind us.

The game warden was courteous, professional, and much to my consternation, downright friendly and pleasant. ("You boys is under arrest.") He could have impounded our vehicle (my uncle's Blazer) and our guns, but he didn't. He did take our rifles as a formality but told us we could probably pick them up in a couple of days. I was indignant nonetheless. "That deer was shot on private property," I said. I'll never forget his reply. "Son, that deer is the property of The Commonwealth of Kentucky. This ain't Europe."

After we'd been locked up for an hour or so, the judge said my friend was free to go and that I would need $500 bail. A few minutes later the jailer brought a telephone. "We're only supposed to let you make one call, but you can go ahead and make as many as you need to," he said. I called my father. "Uh …Dad…you're not gonna believe this…"

While my friend went to get something for me to eat, I got to know my cellmates. Both were in for armed robbery and were awaiting transport to the state penitentiary. Quite a rush for a guy who had gone through high school without being sent to detention hall. The younger of the two, a man in his early twenties with no front teeth, asked me what I was in for. I told my story. He shook his head sympathetically as he rolled a cigarette. "If they don't get a man for one thing, they'll get 'im for somethin' else," he said.

I had been bonding with my fellow prisoners for a couple of hours when my uncle arrived with the bail. The local paper exposed me for the criminal I was—almost: "Henry Chappell— Possession of Illegal Beer—Fined $200." I got off way too easy.

***

Mid-afternoon. Settled comfortably beneath a squat juniper, I watch my thicket, the same one that I blundered into this morning. Either my edge has worn off or my bottom has gone numb; I feel as if I could sit here dozing for hours. A group of twenty or so angora goats wanders past, coughing and chewing the low hardwood. If they are aware of me they show no sign of it. I wonder about their mortality rate. The pasture is littered with goat skeletons. I doze for a few minutes, and when I open my eyes the goats are gone.

My bush shakes violently and I roll away and try to stand, but my legs have gone to sleep. I wallow about and finally make it upright on feet that feel separate from the rest of my body. I stand for a moment letting blood return to my lower extremities. The entire bush shakes again. I cut a wide swath around to the other side and find a wild-eyed goat, its long hair hopelessly tangled in briars. He stands there pathetically and coughs. Coyote bait for sure. I lay my rifle down, grab the goat's horns, and pull.

It suddenly occurs to me that even small goats are quite strong, and that holding one four feet off the ground by its horns might be risky, so I let go and the little ingrate lands on his side, regains his footing, and ploughs off through the brush looking for his compadres. Shaken, I resume surveillance of my thicket.

The sand under my juniper now matches the contours of my bottom. I luxuriate, drowsy again, and watch a porcupine work its way out on a dead mesquite limb. Then I notice the spike buck directly in front of me. How long has he been standing there? He's just across the fence—the fence that separates legal hunting from poaching. I put the cross hairs on his neck. He's as good as dead. Just squeeze the trigger. But no. I won't do that again. The sun hits his eight-inch spikes. Now here's a deer that needs killing. I could drop him in his tracks with a neck shot, pull him under the fence, and no one would be the wiser. Except me.

He's moving along the fence toward the thicket. I'll either get him in the open or forget it. I hear my pulse. Shoot! No! The cross hairs wobble. I take another breath, exhale, and take up the trigger slack. He reaches the edge of the thicket. Some remote corner of my brain becomes aware that it's almost dusk.

I'm squeezing the trigger, yet holding back just enough. My god! It's only a deer—a spike! He steps into the thicket. A neck shot is out of the question now. But I can still make a lung shot. But that might not anchor him. He could run for several hundred yards, and I'd have to cross the fence to look for him. I can't believe I'm having this argument with myself. You weak, greedy bastard! The buck takes another step forward and becomes a shadow in the brush, and the argument ends. I lower the rifle and hang my head between my knees.

The sound of my pulse fades, and I lie back, stretch my legs, and wiggle my toes. It is cooler now, just before dark, the softest part of the day. I am tempted to linger, but I have a long walk to camp ahead of me, and of course my flashlight is in the tent. I'm suddenly very tired.

I walk back up the hill. Small animals move in the brush, and coyotes begin their evening serenade. I am not thinking of deer at all but of pointing dogs stopping and starting and quail running beneath mesquite. I'll hunt deer again someday. Maybe.

photo by Brad Carter

Chihuahuan Desert Duo

The man was short and stocky, about as broad as tall, and wore black, high-topped Converse All Stars and a game belt that looked as if it might double as dog bedding. He pointed out a thick furrow that ran diagonally across his German shorthair's underside and right flank.

The dog, one of the old-style shorthairs, mostly liver and built like a draft horse, stood calmly on the tailgate and seemed to enjoy the attention, although a few minutes before he had nearly dismantled his boss's camper shell trying to get at Brad's young setter Buck, who had sauntered over to get acquainted.

"Goddamned javelinas," the man said. His tall skinny partner nodded in grave agreement. "This summitch ain't got a drop of quit in him, and sometimes it gets him in trouble. He took off down an arroyo, and I knew damn good and well what he was after. By the time I got to him he was staggerin' and bleedin' buckets."

"You ain't never seen nothin' like it," the skinny partner said. "I thought sure he was dead."

The stocky man spat then began a careful examination of his dog's ears. The dog's eyes narrowed to slits, and I wondered if he'd go to sleep standing there on the tailgate. "I picked him up and started for the truck; hell, he was bleedin' all over me. That brother of mine, goddamn him, said I should just go ahead and shoot my dog. I said, shoot the dog hell. I'll shoot you first!"

The skinny friend had been busy trying to pluck an errant fleck of tobacco from the tip of his tongue. He gave up and spat. "By god, he meant it too," he said and then went back to work on his tongue with his thumb and forefinger.

"We finally got him to the truck, and I called my wife from Lewis Flats and told her to call the vet. She found him on the golf course with his buddies. There were five vets waitin' on us in Las Cruces." He held up a spread-fingered hand. "Five vets now—thousand wonders he made it."

He watered his dog from a dishpan while we bared our ignorance of desert quail hunting. We had hunted hard all morning and had four Gambel's quail to show for our effort. Our new acquaintances were both nearing ten-bird limits. The dog finished drinking and nuzzled my hand with his dripping muzzle.

"Hunt around the windmills for blues," the stocky man said. He spread our map on the hood of his truck and circled a half dozen windmill sites with his pen. He evidently sensed our surprise. "Plenty of country and birds for everybody. We ain't as covetous as you Texans. You'll find Gambel's in the arroyos."

The two drove away and went about forty yards then stopped and backed up. "I meant to tell you," the stocky man said, "watch out for rattlesnakes. I know you boys from Texas know about snakes, but I'm tellin' you—watch it." They left again and drove up into the hills.

We found some meager shade beneath a juniper and sat on our coolers drinking Gatorade. I browsed the Audubon Society's field guide *Deserts* and pointed out that according to the range map, we were not in prime javelina country. Brad said that as soon as he got time, he'd breathe a sigh of relief. Feeling better, I dozed, and just as things were beginning to fade out, five shots rolled down out of the hills and behind them a man's voice yelling, "Dead! Dead! Dead Bird!"

photo by Henry Chappell

***

Brad and I had come to New Mexico to hunt desert quail. I grew up quite content with bobwhites, and until I moved to Texas, I was only vaguely aware that other species existed. What's more, everything I read and heard led me to believe they couldn't be worked with pointing dogs which, in my mind, put them in a category with band-tailed pigeons and chachalacas—novelties I might hunt if it didn't cost me any money or much trouble. Then, a dozen or so years ago, on a deer hunt along the Pecos River, I blundered into several coveys of blues. Some ran; some didn't, and the seed was planted. Then I read Tom Huggler's *Quail Hunting in America* and never got over it.

Brad and I had shot a few blues (also known as scaled quail or cottontops) on the High Plains along the Texas-New Mexico border and incidental to bobwhite hunting in the southeastern Panhandle where real blue quail hunting typically involves much driving along ranch roads, occasional sprinting and cussing, and no dog work. But we had never really gone after them, and we had never seen a Gambel's quail. Finally, after two miserable bobwhite seasons in Texas and yet another depressing August census, we began a methodical, scientific study to determine the optimum location for a desert quail hunt. In other words, we made a few calls, ordered some maps, and settled on southwestern New Mexico where a Department of Game and Fish biologist told us we could expect fair to good hunting for blues and fair hunting for Gambel's—*maybe*. The New Mexico summer had been very dry following several poor seasons, but there had been some late rains, and the reports from the field had been encouraging. That's all we needed to hear. We'd take a week off in December, spend a day driving out from Dallas, shoot lots of birds, and eat enough of them in camp to avoid letting possession limits cut our trip short.

***

After fourteen hours on the various interstate highways, we turned south off the pavement east of Deming and promptly got lost. BLM maps, we surmised, are infrequently updated. Our map showed a confusing series of four-wheel-drive trails leading to our objective, the Florida Mountains, which we could see clearly to the southwest. But every trail we tried took us to an unmarked gate or a fence not shown on the map or to someone's stockade or corral. Worse yet, huge tracts of BLM and state land are intermingled with private property, and Brad and I have lived in Texas long enough to be more than a little sensitive to property boundaries. I kept a sharp eye out for churlish ranchers and surly cowhands.

We were alternately looking at our map and the two-track road on the far side of a barb-wire and cedar pole gate, all the while complaining loudly that nothing made sense and that maybe we had overshot New Mexico and were in fact in Arizona, when we realized that a nearby clapboard structure was not an outbuilding but some kind of store. We stepped inside and stood for a few seconds while our eyes adjusted to a dark hallway lined with wooden Indians, dusty jukeboxes, pinball machines, and a single suit of medieval armor. The door to our right led to a little grocery sparsely stocked with staples like pork-n-beans, spark plugs, deviled ham, crackers, and fan belts. We shouted a greeting; no one answered.

Brad said he heard music. Sure enough, George Strait led us down the hall and through a doorway and into a tavern guarded by two huge mongrels that woofed loudly and padded over to give us a thorough sniffing. We stood very still while a very attractive lady behind the bar smiled and studied the scene before her. "You boys are lost, I'll bet."

Her comment woke the single patron, a desiccated cadaver sitting at the end of the bar. "Who's lost?" he croaked. The lady shot him a dark look, and we moved tentatively toward the bar while the dogs continued their olfactory exam. "Just a little lost," Brad said. She put on her reading glasses and studied the map. The cadaver, steadying himself against the bar, eased over to help. "Which way's north?" he gurgled. The lady shot him another exasperated look, and he dozed off again.

After some study, she showed us that we weren't as lost as we thought we were and explained that we had been driving on county roads through public rangeland and could legally go through nearly any of the gates as long as we left them as we found them. "Most of my bird hunters have already quit for the year," she said. "Too dry." We thanked her and started for the door. "*A few* are doing okay though," she said.

Outside, we squinted in the late afternoon sun and reassured the dogs, who were whining and probably wondering if they'd been sentenced to life in a trailer compartment. I wrestled with the limp gate, and we drove south into the desert. The afternoon sun lit the naked West Portrillos. To the west the Florida Mountains cast a shadow over the Chihuahuan scrub.

We found a level campsite near the head of a shadowed canyon on the east side of the Floridas and let the dogs out for a romp while we stretched and watched darkness crawl up the West Portrillos. We put on jackets against the evening coolness and paced around looking things over, giddy the way you are at the beginning of an extended trip into new country. The dogs bustled and snuffled about among the rocks, stopping at times to listen with pricked ears and to sniff whatever strange scents the currents carried. There was only the slightest hint of breeze.

We had just slipped the second tent pole into its sleeve when a huge gust of wind came howling down the mountain and ripped the tent from our hands. I grabbed the tent and held on for dear life while Brad staked and guyed it down. With the sun disappearing behind the mountains, we set the Coleman stove on the ground on the lee side of the truck and hunkered over the skillet to keep sand from blowing into our hamburgers and fried potatoes. Around seven o'clock we gave up and crawled into our sleeping bags. I drifted in and out of sleep as the wind alternately abated and gathered and slammed into the back of the tent. Just after midnight a fiberglass pole bowed violently inward and hit the top of my head. Brad staggered out and secured a slipped guy line, while I spoke passionately of nature's grandeur.

Next morning the truck rocked in the wind as we sat in the cab and sipped coffee and watched the sun come up above the West Portrillos. We decided to concentrate on Gambel's in the arroyos early then move out onto the flats for blues after the wind calmed. It *would* calm, we assured ourselves. Then we jumped out and tackled the tent just in time to keep it from blowing down the mountain. A strategic adjustment seemed in order; we drove into town for ice and groceries.

The grocer shook his head and said no, the wind never blows this hard in mid-December. In fact it rarely blows this hard in the spring, and by the way, I sure hope you boys didn't come far; all reports out of the Florida's are bad; most of the local bird hunters have given up for the year. Just then Brad came in and announced that a plastic bag had somehow opened and our expensive steaks were floating in four inches of bloody ice water. Things seemed to be shaping up about right. We got lost only three or four times on the drive back.

With about an hour of shooting light left and the wind still howling, we cast Dee and Molly up a brushy wash. We were still slipping shells into our shotguns when a nice covey of Gambel's flushed and flew up into the scrub-covered foothills. The singles were wild in the high wind, and we missed badly.

Well after dark we drove off of the desert floor and into a dark canyon, first through creosote, mesquite, cholla, barrel cactus, Mormon tea, and yucca, then higher through ocotillo like sun-bleached skeletons in the headlights and lechuguilla, sotol, and juniper. We found a level campsite and built a little fire out of the wind in a dry, sandy creek and fried potatoes and grilled our wet steaks, which turned out wonderful after all. Then, mindful of flash flooding, we gathered our gear and climbed out of the creek and threw our pads and sleeping bags on a tarpaulin secured at the corners with the biggest rocks we could carry. The tarp edges flapped in the wind, and I went to sleep thinking of the way Molly had swapped ends when a Gambel's flushed from beneath a soaptree yucca.

Next morning the sun cast a rose hue on the Floridas. After breakfast—coffee and cold, dry sweet rolls—we filled our water bottles and sent Molly and Dee across a tobosa grass flat. They ran hard among the barrel cacti and Mormon tea and yucca. Ten minutes into it, sweat ran down my glasses. Molly came in for water and a cussing after a long sprint in pursuit of a jackrabbit.

Brad and I were complaining about the lack of clear objectives when Dee's beeper collar went off in a mesquite flat. The birds held, and we missed four times and watched the entire covey fly over a fence onto a 200-acre block of private land—an island amid several million acres of public rangeland. The dogs came in, finished off the water, had a good roll in the sand, and then laid down, tongues lolling, in the meager shade of a yucca. Brad glanced at his watch and mentioned that we had been out about twenty-five minutes.

Being edge-oriented Texas bobwhite hunters, we couldn't stay out of the dry creeks and arroyos. After cooling a bit, the dogs got birdy in a brushy wash and pointed a tangle of dead catclaw. Brad flushed and shot a single, and Molly brought in the first Gamble's cock I had ever seen close up; pictures had not prepared me. We took a few more singles on our loop back to the truck. Dee, methodical and cautious in middle age, had several productive points while Molly, four years old and out of big-running field trial stock, overran her nose time and again. By noon, when the hunters with the javelina-scarred shorthair drove up, the temperature had climbed to nearly eighty degrees. A bit earlier I stepped within inches of a massasauga. We had already drank half our week's supply of Gatorade, and Molly had chased all of the jackrabbits out of southern New Mexico and now seemed more interested in the shade beneath the trailer than in traipsing around in the desert.

Later that afternoon meticulous old Heidi found several coveys of blues, or at least fractions of the coveys that decided to stop running long enough to be pointed. Later still, as the shadows began to crawl down the Floridas, we moved off the sunny flats and back into the rough foothills and chased coveys of Gambel's through the cholla and creosote. Back at the truck, we guzzled Gatorade while the dogs drank until they flopped down pouch bellied beneath the trailer. In the middle of the night I was awakened by a searing thirst, and the dogs were whining in the trailer. I downed a quart of Gatorade while they lapped up two pans of water.

We fell into a pattern. Out of our sleeping bags, reluctantly, at dawn. Water and stretch the dogs. Breakfast—sausage, scrambled eggs, peppers, and picante sauce rolled up in tortillas; then coffee sipped in the truck cab. Then down out of the confines of the canyon just as the sun rose far enough above the West Portrillos to light the base of the Floridas.

We nearly always found Gambel's first, usually in the brushy creeks or up in the rocky hills in the juniper. The dogs would go birdy, point, then creep or cast about to point again. We got few covey rises, usually just groups of twos and threes and then singles as we worked an area and spread the birds about.

Blues proved much more difficult. We usually found them just as the sun lighted the grassy flats, but they gave us the slip time and again. One morning as we debouched our canyon, a nice covey ran across the road in front of us and gathered in plain sight in the sparse grass on a juniper-studded hillside. We don't road hunt, but we couldn't resist the opportunity. We backed up, put our shotguns together, and cast Heidi and Dee. We shot two birds over points. The rest simply disappeared.

Around mid-morning we'd refill our water bottles and move out into the open desert to hunt the dry creeks for Gambel's and the grass and yucca flats between the creeks for blues. Again, the Gambel's held well for the dogs in the creekside brush, while big coveys of blues often vanished in the desert in front of our frustrated dogs. By late morning, heat and empty water bottles inevitably drove us back to the truck and on to the nearest shade—typically beneath a clump of juniper along a dry wash where we heated lunch, took our shoes and socks off, and shoved our sweaty toes into the dry, shaded sand.

We dozed or sipped coffee and read through midday, occasionally glancing westward toward the Floridas. Late afternoon shadows forming high in the canyons signaled the start of the afternoon hunt. We found Gambel's loafing the afternoons away in the creosote along the creeks, and it was here that we seemed to get the big covey rises. Then we followed the edge of the afternoon shadow as it moved eastward across the desert. Some days Gambel's flushed out of the washes and onto the flats. Then, in hot pursuit, we'd flush a covey of blues. Jogging toward a pointing dog, one of us would ask, panting, "What do you think? Blue or Gambel's?"

Sundown always found us out of water with both dogs working birds. Back at the truck, the sweat dried quickly; chill set in well before we finished cleaning our birds. Afterward we'd luxuriate in our down jackets while we cut boots off the dogs and watched the last sliver of daylight disappear against the West Portrillos.

***

Desert quail are lightly hunted. In an average year, hunters in Texas will take between two and three million bobwhites. In New Mexico, in a big year, hunters will take a few hundred thousand desert quail—blues and Gambel's combined. The lack of interest can be partially explained by the desert species' reputation for running instead of holding for pointing dogs. Also, there's the southwestern emphasis on big game. Mostly though, I think it's the country. Thorny, thirsty country that chews up hunters and their dogs. Molly destroyed four sets of Cordura dog boots in the rocky, snaky-looking draws that Gambel's haunted in the late afternoon after the shadows began to crawl down the Floridas. By the middle of the week she was reluctant to jump out of the trailer, and I resorted to cushioning her feet with layers of gauze. By the end of the week she was yelping whenever I touched one of her pads. I hunted the last three days of the week with dime-sized blisters on both of my big toes. Water is a constant problem; surface water is nonexistent outside of windmill tanks. I started the morning and afternoon hunts with two quarts of water in Nalgene bottles— one for me and one for Molly and Heidi—but inevitably ended up giving it all to the dogs.

photo by Brad Carter

And the desert can grind you down mentally. Harshness is everywhere; the loggerhead shrike's cache of grasshoppers and tiny birds impaled on ocotillo thorns; the cactus wren's orbed nest among the tree cholla spines; the wind; the midday heat that saps the dogs and brings rattlesnakes from their dens; the freezing nights. And desert quail hunting is not a leisurely affair. Stroll up to your dogs after they point and the birds will be long gone when you get there. Run hard and maybe you'll get there in time. Maybe.

Although both species are known collectively as desert quail, blues are primarily a grassland bird inhabiting the shortgrass and mixed prairies on the western edge of the southern Great Plains—western Kansas, Oklahoma, and Texas, eastern Colorado and northeastern Colorado. Along the eastern edge of their range on the mixed prairie, they can be found along with bobwhites. Blues typically inhabit the areas with tighter soils and the associated shortgrasses—buffalo grass and blue grama—along with prickly pear and yucca, while bobwhites prefer sandy upland areas that grow low brush, forbs, legumes, and midgrasses like little bluestem. To the west, they overlap the range of the true desert quail, the Gambel's, in both the Chihuahuan Desert in southern New Mexico and southwestern Texas and in southeastern Arizona in the transition desert grassland between the Chihuahuan and Sonoran Deserts.

Even in the desert, blues prefer flat grassy areas interspersed with desert scrub: mesquite, cholla, Mormon tea, yucca, barrel cactus, and, aesthetics aside, windmills, outbuildings, and junk piles. (A biologist friend of mine dryly refers to rusting, abandoned farm equipment as "blue quail habitat enhancement." Dee, much to his discomfort, trailed a single blue into the middle of someone's honeybee colony.)

Gambel's quail, on the other hand, prefer dry creeks and arroyos, rocky hillsides and draws, and the accompanying tamarisk and tarbrush, although they'll often fly onto the grassy flats when flushed. Like bobwhites, blues and Gambel's will take advantage of surface water if it's present but can make do nicely on moisture gleaned from insects and succulents. I'm told that both species will use irrigated agricultural areas, but I'll take my desert quail in desert habitat, thank-you.

Consistent with the desert quails' lack of popularity with hunters is the lack of interest in, and funding for, scientific research. Like bobwhites, the desert species feed early and late in the day and loaf, preen, and delouse in low screening cover in the middle of the day. Smart hunters take advantage of their quarry's daily schedule, so Brad and I examined the crops of all the birds we shot, but except for the occasional grasshopper or mesquite bean, we didn't recognize a thing. True to form, we bumbled around for a week, *then* talked to several Department of Game and Fish biologists. They admitted that very little is known about the desert quails' feeding preferences, however they were sure that the birds consume primarily seeds and bugs. It always helps to check with the experts.

Finally, Barry Hale, a very helpful biologist out of Las Cruces, sent me a thick paper documenting the results of a recent study on desert quail feeding habits. As best I can tell after browsing about twenty pages of abstruse charts and tables, the birds eat everything. I had hoped to narrow things down a bit. What's more, their favorite food appears to be the seeds of Russian thistle, better known as the tumbleweed, an exotic for godssake. Heavy grazing on delicate desert grassland has been disastrous for desert quail. However, broomweed, which is brought on by heavy grazing, appears to be another favored forb. You have to wonder about the suicide rate among wildlife managers. You also have to wonder if the birds are simply getting by on what they have. Insects, locoweed, crownbeard, pigweed, mesquite beans, and thorn acacia are also important. I'll need to check a field guide before I head back to the desert. Then again, maybe I should just think in terms of seeds and bugs.

Like Texas bobwhites, desert quail numbers cycle wildly with precipitation. Late winter snow and rainfall are critical for Gambel's quail; an early green-up initiates breeding activity. Blues rely less heavily on early rains but require summer rains, as do Gambel's, to provide forage and herbaceous cover for chicks. Winter is the dry season in the Chihuahuan Desert —the dry season in country that averages only eight inches of precipitation per year. On other hand, late summer, when nearly all of the year's rain typically comes, is referred to as the monsoon season. Seriously.

Blues, with their stocky build, lumpen demeanor, and subdued plumage—the overlapping breast feathers or "scales," and white Mohawk—strike me as a desert bird; efficient and perfectly adapted like the roadrunner and cactus wren. The Gambel's on the other hand, especially the cocks with their coal black head plume, face, and beak ("dance hall quail," they're called in far West Texas), the rust colored crown, chestnut and white-streaked wings, seem too delicate and exquisite for the desert. I must have stroked and stared at my first one for five minutes before slipping it into my game bag, and the feeling that I was breaking things small and fragile faded little as the week wore on. But the Gambel's appearance, like that of the delicate blooms atop a barrel cactus, is deceiving. Airborne or running on the ground, they're a gray blur, the running coveys shadows moving in the chaparral. The dogs point, break, catwalk, then point again. You jog up for the flush. Nothing. The dogs raise their heads and flare their nostrils. You blink, wipe the sweat from your eyes. Was that movement you just saw in the brush thirty yards ahead?

***

Friday night December 13, our fifth night of camping. We lay in our sleeping bags and struggled to stay awake to watch the annual Geminid meteor shower. The wind had picked up again as it had every night, and the edges of the tarp flapped noisily around us. The Geminid had built steadily though supper, and the exceptionally slow meteors left long brilliant pale blue streaks in the desert sky, and the peaks above us stood dark beneath the firmament. I pulled my stocking cap down tight to cover the back of my neck and rubbed my palms together in the sleeping bag's warmth and enjoyed their roughness and the fact that it would take a week of desk work to make them pale and soft again.

By eleven o'clock the shower was peaking at nearly a shooting star per minute, but the hours of hustling in and out of arroyos had taken it out of me; the wind and Brad's treatise on synchronous satellites were fading. I searched the sky for the little dipper; then the sun was shining on the peaks above us on the morning of the last day of our hunt.

Dee worked a half dozen coveys of Gambel's before noon, and Buck ran big on the grassy flats, but the blues ran bigger, and back at the truck, he took his water lying on his side. Later the shadows signaled the start of our afternoon hunt, and Molly and Dee quickly found a big Gambel's covey. The singles spread out nicely and held in the tarbrush clumps. As we hunted from one drainage to the next, coveys of both species flushed and mixed and even the blues held in small groups.

My watch showed two minutes before sundown and the end of legal hunting. Brad broke open his gun and walked past Dee and flushed a quail. We couldn't determine the species in the failing light. Brad said, "So they're having a bad quail season in New Mexico." We called the dogs to heel and walked in silence. "You know," he said after a few minutes, "things might get pretty wild out here during a big year."

So Little Time

Outside of waiting rooms with sorry reading material, I cannot remember ever feeling bored. Perhaps I've missed something. Over the last few years, hardly a month passes when I don't come across some article on Generation X and Y disillusionment. It seems a large percentage of our pierced and tattooed baby boomer offspring is so bored and disaffected it can't summon the energy (or sober up long enough) to so much as occasionally raise hell in the name of some misguided cause or other. Life is meaningless, we're told; nihilism and helplessness are the only realities. There are exceptions, of course. The kids who storm university administration buildings at least have an agenda, even if it's merely anarchy and grade inflation cloaked under multiculturalism. Most of them will eventually grow up, hopefully to sue industrial polluters and strip mall developers.

***

As I see it, the question is not, "What can I do?" but "How do I fit it all into a single lifetime?" Or, more realistically, how do I make the best use of the time I have left after duties and obligations have been met? In a perfect world we'd all fill that time with acts of altruism joyfully carried out. Thank God, some people are actually made that way. At the other end of the spectrum are those who selfishly and single-mindedly pursue their passions while everything else, including the lives of husbands, wives, and children, go more or less to hell. Surely each of us has a point of balance between self-denial and self-indulgence. Bored, bitter, miserable (or quietly desperate) people are hell to live with.

"You do not annex a hobby," Aldo Leopold wrote, "the hobby annexes you." Yes, but "hobby" seems a frigid term for Leopold and his sons hunting the Gila and Rio Gavilan with their hand crafted bows. *Passion* seems more apt. A hobby is a frequently enjoyed diversion. A passion is a pursuit that defines a person as much if not more than his occupation, although passion and occupation can be the same. A passion truly matters; not necessarily for its own sake, but for the way it is interwoven with a person's life. My father collected old coins and arrowheads and all sorts of antique chattel. That was a hobby. Hunting quail over his dogs was another matter entirely. Dad was a hunter much as he was a husband or father or

photo by Brad Carter

businessman. If he had not been a hunter, he would have been an altogether different person. Legions hunt and fish. Real hunters and fisherman are relatively few.

On the surface, my close friend John Knox and I have very little in common. He's a city boy. I'm small town all the way. He's a gregarious and well-adjusted father and husband with a successful career in sales; I'm...well...a writer. I played a little college football; he was a utility infielder for the Detroit Tigers in the early seventies. Other than a little dove shooting in Central America during his winter ball days, he has done no hunting and very little camping or fishing. We visit often, work out together, commiserate on being fathers of teenagers, and conspire toward anarchy in our Sunday school class.

I had known John for a long time before I began talking with him about wild places and things; I try not to waste it on people who just won't get it, but when I described for him the first west slope cutthroat I caught on a dry fly or what it feels like to lie in a sleeping bag in a Chihuahuan Desert canyon, it was clear that I wasn't wasting my breath, that he understands that it all matters deeply and why. He understands because he can rhapsodize on the way a hot dog tastes on an August night at the ballpark or the feel of a freshly raked infield. He can tell you about laying a perfect bunt down the third base line and beating Brooks Robinson's throw to first. He can coach a bunch of thirteen-year-olds or play church league softball like a real fisherman can happily jerk bluegills out of a farm pond after two weeks on the Restigouche. He was...no...*is* a baseball player and will die a baseball player and likes it that way. We understand each other very well. I've never asked him, but I know that in his own way he hears the ticking.

***

So you pick and choose and cull and try to decide what matters most. After all, you don't have forever.

***

In terms of my sporting life, I'm an upland bird hunter first and foremost. At this point in my life, I believe I can live without big-game hunting, including turkey hunting, although I still get an occasional itch, especially when the subject of archery comes up. But I'm fighting it, and right now I'm holding my own. Duck hunting I've always enjoyed, but until recently my outings were limited to jump shooting creeks and tanks or an occasional morning sharing a canoe or john boat with a real duck hunter.

But duck numbers are way up. During recent winters, every stock tank and playa in North Texas has been covered with puddle ducks and surprising numbers of bluebills and redheads. This past November an invitation to hunt ducks and geese up on the Llano gave me an excuse to buy a waterproof camo parka and pants and a big ugly twelve-gauge pump (which will be exquisitely nasty once I attach a camo sling) chambered for three-inch shells. My old humpbacked Browning Light

photo by Henry Chappell

Twelve just wouldn't cut it anymore. One needs a real duck gun to hunt with real duck hunters.

Worse yet, I soon found myself becoming quite spiritual about decoy placement. And what could possibly be more manly than breaking ice to kneel alongside a well-frosted Lab in two feet of playa water? Also, I became acutely aware that not only was I the lone member of the party not calling ducks but the only member who didn't even own a duck call. Even more darkly portentous, a Herter's catalogue was in the mailbox when I got home.

Okay, I can handle this. I can find decent duck hunting close to home. A few decoys, a couple of calls on a lanyard (for appearance if nothing else), some new camo neoprene waders, a few square yards of camo netting for the canoe and I'll be in business. Molly will be happy to paddle out and pick up a few ducks. On the other hand, perhaps a real duck hunter needs a real duck dog. I need to think about this.

Incidentally, I don't plan to work in more duck hunting by cutting back on quail hunting. I just plan to work in more duck hunting.

***

I admire naturalists as much as I admire skillful hunters and anglers. Unfortunately, the two are rarely the same. Me for instance. I can identify most of the Southern mast producing trees, because I grew up hunting squirrels. I recognize bundle flower, ragweed, partridge pea, and prickly poppy because quail eat the seeds; aspens because I'm a grouse hunter. I can identify most of the game birds, but only the most common songbirds. I know my accipiters fairly well because they eat quail, but of the beutoes—large hawks that do not generally eat quail—I recognize only the very common red tail hawk. I can identify most of Texas's poisonous snakes because they scare the hell out of me. Of the nonpoisonous species, I recognize only the garter snake and coachwhip. I find this embarrassing and unacceptable.

I own a half dozen field guides which I sometimes take with me on hunting and fishing trips. You probably know how it goes. I should be disciplined enough to leave the shotgun and fly rod at home and go out with the field guides and a pair of binoculars, but I'm not. I've been close a few times, right to the point of pulling out of the driveway, but thus far, I've always succumbed to weakness.

But I have a plan. On every excursion to my tanks I will set aside at least fifteen minutes to study and identify the surrounding flora and fauna, beginning with trees. Should be easy enough. All of my tanks are surrounded by oak trees. I should be able to determine the species with no more than three field guides.

Next comes either birds or birds and flowers, depending on the season. The winter months limit me to birds, and that's okay since the leaves will be off, making for easy birding. I'll keep a list, of course, with date, location, species, and so forth judiciously noted. In fact, my bird list already has an entry: bob-white quail; 23 November 1996; LBJ National Grassland, just beneath Molly's nose; flushed well, flew strongly, sex undetermined.

***

Then there are all those skills lumped under "woodsmanship." And I don't mean building a fire with a bow and drill. I'm talking about the very basic knowledge needed to avoid embarrassment and injury in the field.

For years I let my buddies secure the gear in the back of the truck or on top of the dog trailer for fear of losing gear and revealing my incompetence with rope. Alone, I resorted to funky combinations of half-hitches and granny knots, or when Jane or one of the girls was handy, I'd fall back on the old "Hold your finger right there" trick while I added another granny knot. Tents blew over. Gear shifted dangerously. Then, on a major Dallas freeway, my canoe nearly came off the truck. I decided to learn a few knots, beginning with the taut line hitch.

Then the bowline, clove hitch, and sheet bend. Knot tying has become an end in itself, and I now keep a four-foot length of cotton rope handy in the office. I've tried most of the knots illustrated in E. Annie Proulx's *The Shipping News*. Jane picks up my practice rope occasionally to dust and, if I'm within ear-shot, suggests therapy. But my canoe stays put, and these days I stand around the dog trailer hoping someone needs something tied down. Now if I could just learn the blood knot and the improved clinch knot, I wouldn't lose so many woolly buggers.

I could go on: orienteering, backpacking, Dutch oven cooking, rock climbing, first-aid beyond aspirin and Band-Aids, ax work...I'm literally running out of time.

***

Sloth and melancholy. Edward Abbey called these vices of the romantic realist. Time spent thinking of nothing and everything. To me, both are as essential as love, companionship, and oxygen, although people need them to varying degrees. A few very busy (and oftentimes obnoxiously anal) people seem to require neither. I, on the other hand, have very little difficulty slipping liberal amounts of both into my daily schedule. It's a simple and pleasant matter of separating mind from will, a form of mental rest that can't be gleaned from sleep alone. Occasionally, while sipping coffee just before dawn or while seated on my overturned canoe watching the dogs rid the photinias of sparrows or hunting or fishing absentmindedly, useful thoughts form along with fragmented daydreams and fantasies best shared under a pen name if shared at all. Most often not, however, and that's fine.

Jim Harrison wrote that he has an inordinate amount of time to wander around and think; that poets muse a lot. I like to think that the best poets have their priorities straight. They *make* time for sloth and melancholy.

***

By nature, I am neither an activist nor a joiner. Yet I belong to a couple of organizations whose aims I generally support. I send my annual dues, enjoy their magazines, and occasionally send an extra twenty dollars for some cause or other. I'm copping out, letting other people do the work for me. Some of it is laziness. Some of it is disillusionment. Politicians with social and fiscal agendas I agree with have miserable environmental voting records. And vice versa. The mainstream environmental organizations generally have a friendly or at least benign attitude toward hunting and fishing. At the local level, however, they're often laced with anti-hunting sentiment and social politics I can't stomach.

Sometimes I wish I were either a flaming liberal or stiff collar conservative, or at least a moderate instead of a socially and fiscally conservative anti-development hunter and fisherman with liberal environmental views. Life would be so much simpler. As it stands, I'm usually forced to vote in the interest of damage control.

The various game conservation groups, the Unlimiteds, Federations, and Forevers, with their narrow focus on game probably do more for wildlife than the huge mainstream organizations. Yet at the local level, some of these seem awfully short on biology and maddeningly long on good old boy hokum. My local Quail Unlimited chapter, while it existed, seemed interested only in holding banquets and covering the nearby national grasslands with milo food plots—using hired help of course.

Several years ago, to draw members and raise money, Brad and I organized an informal pointing dog field trial. We negotiated use of a local shooting preserve, got commitments from some big-name field trial judges, made and passed out fliers at gun shows and sporting goods shops, alerted all of the other local hunting and fishing clubs, talked a major mill into donating several hundred pounds of dog food for prizes, and so forth. Our efforts were met with deafening silence both inside and outside of our chapter. We had to call the whole thing off for lack of interest.

So I've been mad and pouting for the past half-dozen years. Good work is going on around me, and I haven't been helping. I need to grow up, get over it, and pull my weight.

***

And there are things I desperately want Jamie and Sarah to know: things I can't simply tell them or even show them, knowledge that can be gained only by being out there. Fortunately it's mostly a matter of taking them, answering questions, listening, and otherwise saying very little. But the competition for their time is fierce. Young ladies should be well rounded, we're told, and then there is my own unwitting selfishness that for some reason I can see only in hindsight when the timepiece ticks loudest.

Somewhere in there are the things Jane and I will do. The trips to Alaska and Europe, the return to the Canadian Rockies, the rivers we'll float, and the camping trips we can't seem to work in these days. And just plain time. Time to dream up more trips to squeeze in. Time to be reminded of why we still actually like each other after twenty years of marriage. I tell myself I can work it all in. Surely. Somehow.

***

Twelve years ago I bought a German shorthair pup and resolved to become a competent quail hunter and dog trainer. I had hunted quail over dogs most of my life, but up to that point it had always been with Dad's dogs and guidance. Somewhere along the way, maybe five or six years later, I realized—not all at once but gradually—that my dogs were at least fair and that I knew where to look for birds and that I could hold up my end of most hunting conversations. I realized that I knew how things

photo by Henry Chappell

should be done even if I couldn't always do them that way in the field.

Knowledge and its proper use, competence, slips up on you that way. Without care, you can forget to enjoy what you do know, especially those things that you know with certainty, and there are so few. I suppose that's one more thing you pick up along the way.

But god, to be ten years old again with just an inkling of life's brevity.

An Evolutionary Product

*"You're a bloodthirsty savage," he said,
"like all boys are bloodthirsty savages..."*
     Robert Ruark, The Old Man and the
     Boy

*However, no one is likely to invent a
     mechanical fox-hound, or to screw a
polychoke on the hound's nose. No one is likely to teach
dog-training by phonograph or by other painless short-
cuts. I think the gadgeteer has reached the end of his
tether in dogdom.*

     Aldo Leopold, "Wildlife in American Culture"

Robert Ruark's *The Old Man and the Boy* is rife with hokum,
hyperbole, and sentimentality. I enjoyed it immensely. Ruark
knew exactly what he was doing. He wrote *The Old Man and
the Boy* to entertain. Yet through the simple stories about a boy
growing up learning to fish under his grandfather's tutelage in
coastal North Carolina in the 1930s, Ruark shows us better
than anyone ever has, the natural development of the
hunter-angler.

     In the young Boy we have the eager, wide-eyed beginner
who quickly develops into the bloodthirsty savage eager for the
kill, who measures his success solely by the weight of his bag

or stringer. By the end of the book, the Boy is an adolescent, deadly, but showing the first signs of the restraint that characterizes the mature hunter. In the Old Man, we have the mature sportsman, also deadly when he chooses to be, but more interested on most days in passing on his legacy than in shooting game. Many of us—many more than we like to admit—never mature beyond the second stage.

There is a parallel evolution, only recently apparent, and like the foregoing, related to maturity. In the first stage, the beginner uses whatever borrowed or inherited equipment he can get his hands on—a single-shot twenty gauge, a cheap spin-cast outfit. In the second stage, dog-eared catalogues accumulate only slightly faster than abandoned gadgetry as the sophomoric sportsman looks to technology—better optics, better ballistics, more horsepower, the latest electronics—to help him to the next level. The hunting and fishing equipment industry depends on this stage of the evolution. I've certainly made my contribution. Prior to the last few decades, a stage two hunter might peak with a fiberglass fly rod, an autoloader, and an outboard motor for his canoe or john boat. Most of the Boy's modern counterparts wouldn't be caught dead fishing in a homemade skiff, or for that matter any vessel unequipped with instruments of electronic warfare. If they can afford it they'll follow Frank and Sandy on an ATV. Unfortunately, they'll affirm their obsession by catching more fish and killing more birds than they did using simple equipment.

Many people never move beyond this stage. Some I've known have simply burned out or gone broke while others have kept going, moving up to laser range finders and battery-operated waterfowl decoys that actually swim and flap their wings. Others eventually tire of the expense and hassle and move to the next stage. They'll refine their technique, making maximum use of a few trusted pieces of equipment; at this stage they are as deadly as they will ever be. They know the lore and their equipment and they know where to look for fish and game. At some point, the real thinkers in this group will begin to ask themselves why they hunt and fish and where they fit in the natural scheme. Perhaps they'll begin to show restraint beyond that imposed by the game warden. Some will go a step further and become students of not only their quarry but its entire ecosystem. They will begin to think of wildlife management as something more than the maximization of the number of legal targets and that red-cockaded woodpeckers, painted buntings, and Cooper's hawks are as important as deer, quail, and turkey.

Finally we have the last stage characterized by the mature hunter/angler who relies on only the simplest tools—a longbow, perhaps, or a muzzle loading rifle, a favorite bamboo rod, a trusted shotgun, and a single, well-trained dog. She gives her quarry every advantage even if it means going home as often as not empty-handed. Although she may occasionally travel for

Photo by Henry Chappell

sport, she most often hunts and fishes her home waters and coverts, which she knows intimately.

I like to think of myself as being somewhere in stage three. I remember stage two all too clearly and wince whenever I think of the crap I hauled into the woods. And I can still be seduced. Not everyone develops along these lines, of course, but the bottom line is that too many of us never mature beyond the second stage, and as a result opening weekend too often resembles a mechanized siege instead of an atavistic escape from the pressures of modern society or meaningful participation in the food chain.

I don't know where to draw the line. I like good equipment, especially high-tech fabrics that keep me dry and comfortable. At this point in my life, I'm not ready give up smokeless powder, Cordura-faced brush pants, or Thermarest sleeping pads. I drive a four-wheel-drive pickup and often rely on it to get me over muddy ranch and logging roads. I fish with a graphite fly rod, wear polarized fishing glasses, and paddle a polyethylene canoe.

Even the great Aldo Leopold used factory-made gadgets, although he asserted that there must be some limit beyond which gadgetry detracts from the outdoor experience. If the "outdoor experience" is largely a matter of aesthetics and aesthetics vary wildly from one person to the next, perhaps the more important question is this: At what point does the use of technology in the pursuit of game become unethical? Not illegal, mind you; unethical. Too often we confuse the two. Of course we will no more reach complete agreement on ethics than on aesthetics, but we had better start working on issues honestly and objectively and irrespective of economics or politics; first because it's the right thing to do; second, and more pragmatically, because the future of hunting and fishing depends on the non-hunting majority's opinion of us. Maybe we could start by asking ourselves how we'd feel if a crew from *60*

Minutes surprised us in the field. Frankly, I'm surprised they haven't.

***

When my daughter Jamie senses that she has a point but isn't quite sure what it is, how to articulate it, or, for that matter, what she really thinks about it, she always ends her assertion with "I'm just saying." Take the time I suspended her driving privileges after she intentionally drove the Isuzu Rodeo into a huge mud hole:

Jamie: Dad, a month is a long time. Besides, the Rodeo came clean.

Henry: Yes, but we ended up burying two other trucks trying to pull it out, and it took me a week to get the mud out of my ears.

Jamie: (Rolling her eyes) I know; I know; I'm just saying.

***

As far as I'm aware, no figure exists for the number of deer shot over feeders in Texas. You can be sure it's a significant percentage of the several hundred thousand killed each season. It's certainly not a wildlife management issue; Texas is home to around three and a half million deer, many of them stunted from overpopulation. In some parts of the state, the herd probably would benefit from a larger kill.

"Feeding" varies from a kid dropping a pocket full of corn beneath her stand to timer controlled feeders preset to dump food at fixed intervals. In many cases the deer are fed over much of the year, and the sound of the feeder dumping will bring them out of the brush. Obviously, the deer quickly wise up after hunting season opens and few exceptional bucks are taken over feeders, but you get the picture. Should hunting over feeders be outlawed? I don't think so; we have more than enough rules already. But it should be scorned within the hunting community. When was the last time you saw an article in a national outdoor magazine encouraging the use of a feeder? It's time we took care of this dirty little secret ourselves.

Apologists claim there's little difference between attracting deer with food and attracting waterfowl with decoys. But there are glaring differences. Decoys are inanimate objects that can't be eaten. Considerable craft goes into decoy placement and calling. Live decoys and baiting with food were outlawed for obvious reasons.

I cringe as I write this. I have always been a reluctant polemicist. Worse, several people I like and respect, including some good friends, hunt deer over feeders. These men are not slob hunters. All of them are kind; they love deer; they never tire of watching deer; they know their quarry and they hunt thoughtfully and kill cleanly. One of these men, a friend who often invites me to hunt quail on his lease, has voiced his ambivalence toward the practice of feeding. But he knows that if every hunter on his lease were to halt the practice, the local deer would all frequent the feeders on adjacent leases. The practice is that widespread. Change, if it occurs at all, will occur slowly from peer pressure. There's reason to be hopeful. Thirty years ago widespread catch-and-release bass fishing would have been unthinkable.

With stands and blinds, it's not so simple. Considerable craft goes into deer stand placement, especially in native habitat, but less so if you're set up over a food plot. The semi-portable elevated blinds so popular in Central and South Texas offend my sensibilities, but only from an aesthetic standpoint. I find them tacky and inelegant, but from any other standpoint, no different from camouflage mesh thrown over a canoe or john boat, which happens to be my favorite type of duck blind.

The semi-permanent elevated numbers with heating and other amenities are a joke, especially when used as they often are: A guide delivers a well-heeled sport before dawn, tells him to stay in the blind until he's picked up, and then watches to be sure he doesn't fall off the ladder. Surely we can distinguish between these and the thousands of functional clapboard stands and blinds built, painted, and thoughtfully placed by members of Texas deer leases. Again, we don't need more rules. We need healthy debate and judicious application of shame without the usual knee-jerk accusations of elitism, snobbery, intolerance, and anti-hunting sentiment.

I was quail hunting with a friend who happens to be an upland game biologist when he mused aloud that deer hunters seemed quick to embrace any new technology that might give them an edge while bird hunters tend to be staunch traditionalists. He has a point, but I think that much can be explained by deer hunting's popularity and the sporting industry's natural tendency to respond with high-tech goodies that a Navy SEAL would covet.

On the other hand, Texas quail hunters have been bouncing over pastures in quail rigs—specially equipped jeeps or buggies bottomed with steel plating—for decades. And lately, I'm seeing more hunters on ATVs following their dogs over terrain that would reduce the standard quail rig to a smoking heap. Pragmatists might argue that buggies and ATVs are simply practical modern versions of the walking horse, but if you've ever been in a saddle for over five minutes, you know that there's more to it than plopping your ass on a cushioned seat and trying not to bounce off and into the cholla when you hit a rough spot. Being a plainsman, I'll leave the quail plantation and mule-drawn wagon business to some iconoclast from the Deep South. Besides, I'm probably in enough trouble as it is.

I realize I'm in danger of treading on motherhood and apple pie here (hunting in the "Texas Tradition" and all that), but I'm not sure if it's motorized quail hunting that offends me or the common ludicrous justification for it. "The Texas plains are just too big and open to be hunted effectively on foot," or so we're told in nearly every magazine article on Texas quail hunting. Let me get this straight. In a good year in Texas, in good habitat, the bobwhite density can exceed a bird per acre and occasionally reaches three or four birds per acre in South Texas. Yet a hunter, on foot, with a couple of decent dogs can't expect to move eight or ten (or more) coveys in six or eight hours of hunting? Brad and I generally move eight to ten coveys per day on heavily hunted public land during mediocre years despite ordinary dogs and a casual (oftentimes lazy on my part) approach to hunting. Maybe the misunderstanding lies with my interpretation of "effective." If you really have to have thirty coveys per day, then you will in fact need a trailer full of big-running dogs and motorized or equine transportation to keep up with them.

Again I cringe. A couple of guides who have been very generous and helpful to me over the years spend much of each hunting season behind the steering wheel of a quail rig. But they have chosen to make a living outdoors with their knowledge of their quarry and their dogs, and they can stay afloat only by giving customers what they want.

As I wrestle with the issue of motorized hunting, I can't help wondering if I'm letting personal aesthetics interfere with objective moral judgment. After all, the people hunting the big spreads in quail rigs usually shoot only covey rises, and there are plenty of pedestrian slobs more than happy to kill every bird in a covey. And as long as well-heeled sports are willing to pay ten dollars per acre for a quail lease or a half grand per day for guided motorized hunting, we'll have wild bobwhites in Texas. I realize too that it's easy to be down on practices other than your own. Yet I also wonder just how much comfort and convenience a hunter is entitled to.

***

Answers seldom come easy. Leopold, always hard on duck hunters for their use of outboard motors, had this to say about fox hunters in his essay "Wildlife in American Culture":

> Fox-hunting with hounds, backwoods style, presents a dramatic instance of partial and perhaps harmless mechanized invasion. This is one of the purest of sports; it has real split-rail flavor; it has man-earth drama of the first water. The fox is deliberately left unshot, hence ethical restraint is also present. But we now follow the chase in Fords! The voice of Bugle Ann mingles with the honk of the flivver!

Fair enough. Now think of a party of hunters riding across the prairie in a quail rig equipped with a grain spreader. (No, I'm not kidding about the grain dispenser; you gotta lure those birds out of the heavy brush. Or so I've been told. My buddy John Hughes calls the practice "chumming for quail.") The hunters and handlers sit in elevated seats to view the work of dogs that have been trained with electronic collars. Perhaps they hunt with electronic beeper collars if not shock collars. All this to hunt an eight-ounce bird. I know it's traditional; I'm just saying...

***

I trained Heidi with traditional techniques and tools—check cord, force collar, and retrieving dummies. I used no electronics; I couldn't have afforded a shock collar if I had wanted one. I was new to Texas quail hunting, but I learned in very short order that I needed help keeping up with her in the thousand-acre mesquite flats and cedar breaks. A small brass bell hung from her collar helped tremendously. Compared to the standard Texas pointing dog, Heidi's range was moderate. She rarely drifted outside of earshot. I simply followed the sound of her bell, and if her nose carried her out of sight before she pointed, I simply looked for her in the direction I last heard her bell. There were occasional tense moments when I searched frantically, worried that she would get impatient and take her birds out, but I always found her in time, and deep down I knew that she would stand her birds for a very long time. Hunt with a dog long enough and you come to know these things. She knew I would eventually come, and I knew she would stand her birds. We were a team. In those first four years very little direction, let alone yelling and hacking, was needed. And the bell's lovely resonant sound, like a small, fast rivulet, fit the brushy draws and dry creeks where she pointed quail and the hardwood bottoms and the upland pine forest where she found woodcock.

Then Brad bought a beeper collar for his Brittany, Dee. I had read about them in the outdoor magazines, and although the thought of a synthetic beep didn't fit my sense of aesthetics, the utilitarian aspects seduced me. I could follow the double beep, not worrying about the dog's exact location—I could just let her hunt. I could daydream, talk to buddies, look for arrowheads, all the while secure in the knowledge that if she pointed, I would be called by the steady, urgent sounding string of single beeps that indicate she has stopped moving. No more frantic searches. Just stroll in the direction of the beep.

Sure enough, it works just like that. Brad left his collar with me one Sunday morning when he had to cut out early for Dallas. I was sold within an hour; completely addicted within a year.

Next season Brad and I were hunting an unusually rank section near Roby, when Heidi disappeared. No beeping. Nothing. Thirty minutes later she appeared out of a mesquite flat and jogged in with a tongue lolling grin as if nothing had happened.

I was petrified. I had just replaced the batteries. I was sure my collar had just quit on me. The wind had picked up, making it hard enough to hear a loud, obnoxious beep, let alone an anemic little bell. In desperation, I put in fresh batteries. It worked.

The day was saved. I could continue hunting. We did well that day, but I couldn't help wondering, had she been on point, out of earshot, or merely off self-hunting, ignoring my calls? Should I get rid of the damn collar or make sure that I always have a spare?

For five years now I've told myself the beeper collar is simply a convenience for me and a safety measure to ensure that I don't lose my dogs in the big country we hunt. But my hunting log shows that I began shooting more birds as soon as I started using the beeper collar. Could be that my dogs and I just got better, that after years of stumbling around, something clicked. Could be, too, that I've substituted modern technology for skill and compromised my sensibilities to boot.

Once I buckled the beeper collar on Heidi, I could just let her follow her nose. In West Texas, where a single pasture may cover 20,000 acres, there is little need for handling. Using the beeper collar, I simply follow her, and let's face it, she was a better hunter at five months old than I'll ever be.

With so little handling, she drifted further and further out. Soon I was hustling a quarter of a mile to get to her, guided by the incessant beeping. Halfway through her first season with the collar, she began ignoring my whistle or at least taking her sweet time coming in. I reasoned that the near constant "movement beeping," a double beep every five seconds had desensitized her to the whistle, so I hung the bell on her beeper collar and dialed in the "point only" mode. As long as she kept moving, the beeper remained silent and I followed the bell. When she stopped to point (or to squat or drink or dislodge a grassburr) the beeping would summon me. This helped. Still, I couldn't shake the feeling that I was training a self-hunter, so I made a point to handle her more, but that was work; it was just too easy to sluff off and stroll along behind her. She found lots of birds, but the sense of teamwork faded. And she continued to drift further out. I would get distracted and realize I couldn't hear her bell. Ten minutes on the whistle typically brought her back, but sometimes the wind would change and I'd hear, very faintly, the beeper calling. How long had she been on point? I had no idea. But she always stood her birds for the five or ten minutes it took me to work my way through the brush to get to her.

I rationalized and continued feeling smug about moving twelve or fourteen coveys per day on public land while the *serious* hunters with leases did only a little better. Then one afternoon, hunting on a huge spread, she disappeared for two hours. Darkness was coming on fast. We had stopped for a rest and a drink of water, and I had turned her beeper off to avoid the incredibly obnoxious beeping that occurs five seconds after she stops to drink or lie down. I must have forgotten to turn it back on when I cast her again. A few minutes later I woke up from some daydream or other and realized that I heard neither the bell nor the beeper. An hour later, hoarse from screaming, temples pounding from the whistle, I was sure I'd be out all night looking for her. A dog out after dark in West Texas is in serious trouble. The local coyotes often kill solitary dogs, almost always at night, and big, empty country presents its own danger. A dog could easily pick the wrong direction and go for days without encountering civilization.

Was she on point, waiting, wondering when I was coming? Just before sundown I picked up the sound of her bell, and she came straight toward my whistle. She broke out into the open atop one of the cedar hills and nailed a covey at the base of a big cedar tangle. I shot a hen, and she brought it to me and crawled into my lap. Brad had been hunting in the river bottom, and I'm thankful I had gotten myself under control before he walked into the clearing and asked me where the hell I'd been. I turned her collar on, and we walked down out of the hills to the truck.

Just how much comfort and convenience is a hunter entitled to? Shouldn't I earn my birds with a little aggravation and discomfort? Heidi is near the end of her career now. She's healthy but can take only an hour or so of work at a time. And her hearing is about gone. Of course hearing loss is inevitable in a dog that lives long enough, but I can't help but believe the loud beeping contributed to her deafness. Often I'll see her stop in the distance to cock her head and listen and look frantically this way and that, only to turn and run in the wrong direction. Do I dare run her without the collar? Old age has taken most of the run out of her; she stays closer now. But there are running coveys and cripples trail. She can still hear her bell though. Its sound can make her young again, if only for a few minutes.

Molly just turned four. She hasn't worn the beeper much. She's cooperative, checks in often, and her constant movement and slashing style make her easy to keep up with. But she runs big when the country opens up...

I'm looking at the beeper collar as I write this. I keep it on my desk so that I'll remember to send it in for repairs; it finally quit on me. Every day I remind myself to put it in the mail, but so far I haven't. It's only July, I tell myself. I have until September or so.

***

A few years ago I was waiting at a traffic light in a small West Texas town, when two hunters in a brand-new black sport utility vehicle pulled up beside me. The SUV pulled a trailer that carried two all terrain vehicles and a deer feeder. Stacked perversely astraddle one of the ATVs were three gorgeous whitetail bucks. People on the sidewalks stopped to gawk. The fearsome hunters looked at the onlookers then at each other and smiled. I took off my hunter orange cap and laid it on the seat beside me.

A Piece of Country

The historical truth that becomes apparent in the end is that the Great Plains have bent and molded Anglo-American life, have destroyed traditions, and have influenced institutions in a most singular manner.

Walter Prescott Webb, The Great Plains

Early on I simply followed my dogs across the broad, often dry river bottoms and through the mesquite and cedar covered hills that form the contours of my corner of West Texas. After all, the quail hunting is good when rain comes at the right time in the right amount, and there are deer—whitetails in the brushy draws and mule deer in the hills—turkeys and wild hogs in the bottoms. People come here from all parts of the country to hunt. Some, like me, hunt on the scant public land; most pay dearly to hunt the big private spreads.

It's good country despite its mistreatment. Not land, mind you. Not property. Aldo Leopold wrote that land is the place where corn, gullies, and mortgages grow, and that country is the personality of the land, the collective harmony of its soil, life, and weather. To me, it's even simpler than that. Land is acreage chopped up, delineated, and subdivided. Land is the subdivision I live in, ranches, farms, city parks. Country is river breaks and low buttes, bison, deer, geese, and alligators, mesquite flats, mountains, and lowlands. People mold and shape land and, to some degree, country. But only country molds people. Thus we have the Texas Hill Country, the South Texas Brush Country, the Upper Middle Brazos Country, and the Caprock Breaks Country. Blindfold a well-traveled Texan, put him in a small town diner in any of the ten ecological regions, pull off the blindfold, and let him look and listen for a while. Chances are good he'll be able to tell you what part of the state he's in. On the other hand, a Chili's in Houston is a Chili's in Dallas is a Chili's in Austin.

The Dallas-Fort Worth metroplex is no longer country. It's merely a geographical area. It does not mold its residents as much as it grinds them into shape, leaving sharp edges. Not that country necessarily molds gently. Country alternately bakes and freezes, feeds and starves, leaving cracks and fissures, soft contours and rough edges. You do not have to live in country to be shaped by it. You need only spend time there, love it, or at least come to terms with it.

I have never lived in *my* country, the southern Great Plains, or South Plains, particularly the southeastern quarter of the Texas Panhandle from the Caprock Escarpment eastward to the Oklahoma border, and from the Canadian River south to the Pease River. I go there to hunt and watch birds, to camp, hike, and explore, to eat at the small town diners and visit with people who actually live there. Actually, I know very little about my country, but what little I know is more than I know about the Dallas area where you tend to know only street names and addresses; where whatever history you can memorize is completely buried by the present and is hard to truly know.

My country is good country, sparsely peopled and still largely grass but with cedar on the steeper hills and tenacious mesquite nearly everywhere else; intermittent rivers—dry at times, torrential at others, but most often broken strings of clear pools, inviting but heavy with salt and gypsum yet perfectly potable to thirsty bird dogs. On the western edge, great red scarps rise to the High Plains Caprock forming hoodoo-haunted canyons of gypsum striped mud stone and Triassic sandstone. Eastward, the plains roll more gently save for the breaks cut by the major rivers—the Red, the Pease, the Tongue, the Little Wichita, and the Canadian—and their major tributaries.

Big, gamey country, perfect for big-running pointing dogs and flat-shooting rifles. Rich country with nutritious grass, cattle, incredible bird life, big bucks, and sometimes a bobwhite quail per acre, and in times past, wild things in unimaginable numbers.

Good country all right. For most, that's enough. But like each of us, country is the sum of everything it has been. Ian Frazier, in his superb book *Great Plains*, called the plains a palimpsest—a perfect metaphor. To understand what is, you must know something of what was.

***

Early on, the hunting was enough. Tenacious juniper grows in the rough, steep breaks south of the Middle Pease in Cottle County. In bitter cold weather bobwhites hunker beneath them and present a near impossible situation for the lone hunter. Pick any approach and they'll just blow out the other side, sometimes right over the dog, to disappear down one of the innumerable brushy draws.

In moderate weather you can cast the dogs southward into the mouth of one of the broad mesquite-choked draws and hunt back toward the head. Cattle graze the draws periodically, thinning the little bluestem and trampling the sandy soil. In good years, when rain comes, ragweed and croton grow thick on the disturbed ground, making these draws lousy with quail in December and January. The low mesquite tangles provide perfect loafing cover amid an ocean of high calorie quail food. The dry sandy creeks that come out of the hills to feed the Pease have islands of stunted plum and ragweed and are nearly always good too.

The creek beds and bottoms of the draws are easy to walk (although the sand burrs are hell on unbooted bird dogs), and it's here that you'll get some of the best dog work and easiest shooting. Some years, sweeping back and forth for a mile or so (or, hopefully the dogs quartering while you pick the easiest walking) until the draw peters out into the hills, you might move a half dozen coveys.

Then, standing near the head of the draw, you hear the singles whistling up in the cedar-studded hills. The dogs know the birds are up there, and before you can decide whether or not they're worth the climb—after all you can finish your limit after lunch in the nice flat river bottom—a pair of copper bells goes suddenly silent somewhere up in the cedar.

photo by Henry Chappell

The singles will be in open areas among thin stands of bunch grass and never far from heavy escape cover. About half the time they'll hold for your dogs. Other times they'll run, and the dogs will point and break and creep up and down the hills, in and out of gullies, until the birds flush wild or finally decide to hold.

Some days in the hills you'll get your birds and other days you won't, but in either case, your legs and lungs will burn. Perhaps when you stop to rest and water the dogs and peel off your long underwear, you'll look back to the north and across the river bottom. If you care about country—and I mean really care about it for its own sake and not for its economic potential or the game it holds—you'll look out over the southern hills and the mesquite flats and the broad, sandy river bottom covered in little bluestem, plum, and chittam, and then the Pease, most likely a string of pools lined here and there with six-foot reeds. And then the red cliffs beyond and above them mesquite again and further still the foreboding northern hills, reddish and nearly bald save for sparse bunch grass and a few lonely mesquite or cedar mottes.

You'll look and wonder. What was this country like before the buffalo hunters and soldiers and Southern yeomanry were drawn by a seemingly infinite amount of land to wear out?

I cannot comprehend geological time. Although I can memorize the ordering and time spans of epochs, I can no more grasp them than I can many of the constants from my engineering days. An electron's charge. Absolute zero temperature. The Triassic period. I simply accept them because their application leads to concepts that do have meaning to me. When I look across the plains I accept the advance and retreat of ancient seas and populations of giant reptiles (or were they primitive birds?), the gradual fluvial buildup on marine rock, and the subsequent erosion east of the High Plains Caprock. For me, meaningful plains history—or prehistory—began a few thousand years after the first hunters walked out of Asia across the Bering Strait and into Alaska to begin their migration down the ice-free corridors to the plains.

***

In his seminal work *The Great Plains*, Texas historian Walter Prescott Webb describes the Great Plains environment: A comparatively level, treeless surface of great extent with rainfall insufficient for ordinary intensive agriculture.

Certainly most of the country between the 98th meridian—Webb's theoretical boundary between the timber country and the plains—and the Rocky Mountains meets these criteria. My corner of Texas, officially part of the Rolling Plains ecological region, is basically flat or gently rolling save for breaks of the rivers, their major tributaries, and the scarp canyons that rise to the High Plains. Rainfall is scant, usually well under thirty inches per year. In relatively wet years this country is classic mixed prairie dominated by warm season midgrasses with shortgrasses in the drier uplands and even tallgrasses like sand bluestem in moist low-lying areas. During drought years, shortgrasses are in greater evidence and flat areas can be almost indistinguishable from the true High Plains shortgrass prairie to the west.

Treeless? Not these days, although the Rolling Plains probably were more so in 1931 when *The Great Plains* was published. Ranchers spend millions keeping mesquite, shin oak, and cedar from overrunning pastures. Fire, the traditional cleansing agent, keeps new brush from becoming established, but nothing short of a dangerously hot conflagration works on mature brush. So ranchers and wildlife managers resort to bulldozers and sometimes chemicals, and, even then, it's mostly a losing battle for all but the richest cattle operations. One well-to-do, brush hating rancher is said to have kept a bulldozer running every day for over twenty years on his sixty-thousand-acre spread near Albany.

But the brush is not a complete curse. Cattlemen hate it, and the deep running mesquite roots abet irrigation in further lowering the water table, but without it the plains would be much emptier today. The true Rolling Plains megafauna—the bison, the grizzly, the wolf—are gone or essentially gone, and other species like the pronghorn antelope and the lesser prairie chicken have been either extirpated or reduced to small isolated populations. In Texas, the pronghorn once ranged as far east as the Dallas area, and settlers encountered prairie chickens in staggering numbers all over the mixed prairie. But the encroaching brush neutralizes the pronghorn's keen eyesight and blinding speed. It crowds prairie chicken leks, provides cover for approaching predators, and interferes with the birds' explosive flush. Today in Texas you can find pronghorns on the treeless High Plains in the western Panhandle and the desert grasslands in the far southwestern corner of the state. Lesser prairie chickens hang on in the shortgrass and sand sage

photo by Henry Chappell

country south of Lubbock and the relatively treeless midgrass and sand sage country in the northeastern corner of the Panhandle.

What hunter, other than the most unimaginative meat hog, hasn't dreamed of being transported back to a time when more bison than people roamed the plains? But a modern quail hunter plunked down in mid-nineteenth-century West Texas could probably shoot a wagonload of prairie chickens for every bobwhite quail. Same with whitetail deer. There probably were few of either outside of the brushy draws and creek bottoms.

When the brush moved in, the whitetails and bobwhites and other brush loving species moved in with it. Today, the Rolling Plains are being touted as the next trophy deer hot spot, and hard core quail hunters don't get excited until bobwhite densities approach a bird per acre. Rio Grande turkeys have expanded their range along with the hardwood brush, and feral hogs, now officially a serious nuisance, grow fat on oak mast, churn up good river bottom quail habitat, despoil ground dwelling bird nests, and terrorize bird dogs.

Good hunting in good country. Still I can't help but wince whenever I see the fuzzy black and white photographs of stern hunters alongside wagons stacked with prairie chickens. Such a waste. And they didn't even use pointing dogs.

***

South Plains, 10,000 B.C. Giant bison graze on a plain just east of a series of great red scarps that rise to an even flatter, less humid plain that stretches to the western mountains. Small family groups are spread desultorily about, calves surrounded by cows, bulls feeding in the distance in small bachelor groups. The grass grows lush and rich in the cool, moist climate. Far to the north, the southern edge of the Wisconsin ice sheet is imperceptibly retreating.

One group feeds near the mouth of a large draw, unaware of the danger lying in the grass forty yards downwind, moving slowly, steadily closer. The wind shifts slightly and a young bull lifts his nose then snorts and shakes his great, shaggy head. The others begin shifting nervously about, alternately testing the wind and staring eastward.

Then a hoarse cry from out in the grass, and a dozen men, naked save for buckskin breechclouts, stand abreast, screaming. The bison wheel and thunder into the narrowing canyon with the hunters in pursuit. As the draw narrows, other hunters in the rocks above stand and shove the butts of their five-foot spears into bone atlatls, draw back and throw, and their long, dark, matted hair falls across their faces. Some of the fluted chert spear tips find their mark in the beasts' sides. Others bounce off the heavy ribs.

At the head of the draw, more hunters wait with atlatl-driven spears, and the confused bison pile into each other; some fall and struggle frantically to get up while others turn back toward the mouth of the draw. The pursuing hunters close the gap to within thirty yards and launch their spears.

Spears rain down from surrounding cliffs. The wounded animals weaken further, and the sweating, screaming hunters run close and thrust their weapons deep into soft organs. Several of the bison are on their bellies, yet their humps still rise above the hunters' heads.

All of their spears thrown, the hunters stand back, exhausted, gasping for breath, holding their atlatls and waiting for the beasts to expire and for the women to arrive to help with the butchering.

In the Caprock Canyon country near Quitaque, Texas, you can stand on a site above Lake Theo where hunters of the Folsom culture butchered a large number of giant bison some ten thousand years ago. That's *giant* bison. *Bison antiquus*. Half again as large and four times as heavy as the modern version, *Bison bison*. Seven feet high at the hump with a five-foot horn spread. Killed with spears.

Other than the Folsom remains in the Caprock Breaks, scant evidence of Paleo-American peoples has been found on the Texas Rolling Plains. But they were there. And when you're sitting back on your haunches up in the cedar breaks, looking out over your country, it's enough to know that Ice-Age people hunted mammoths, camels, and horses, short-faced bears, and giant ground sloths. Hunted them in your country.

About four thousand years ago, the giant game disappeared and no one knows why. Drought probably. Hunting pressure possibly. Whatever the cause, its absence gave rise to the more advanced Archaic and Neo-Indian cultures with their delicate stone tools, pottery, woven baskets, and crude agriculture. In my country, people of the Antelope Creek Complex hunted the modern bison, lived in sod pueblos, and grew corn and squash before drought pushed them out or early Apache raiders destroyed or absorbed them.

In 1541, as Francisco Vàsquez de Coronado and his men crossed the Texas Panhandle, they encountered along the Canadian River a peculiar trail of narrow furrows. They followed the trail to an encampment of Indians, nomadic buffalo hunters using travois pulled by large dogs. By the early 1700s these people, the Eastern Apaches, were well established on the South Plains from central Texas to the Arkansas River. They hunted buffalo, made pottery, wove baskets, planted squash, and traded extensively with the Spanish in New Mexico.

But by the early eighteenth century, the entire Eastern Apache culture had been destroyed. Invading hunters, mounted barbarians like Mongols from the Asian steppes, swept down from the north and burned the Apaches' rancherìas, killed them wherever they found them, and drove the survivors southwest into the Chihuahuan Desert mountains.

A split had occurred late in the seventeenth century among the Wind River Shoshone in the Eastern Rocky Mountains above the headwaters of the Arkansas River. A substantial band mounted on newly acquired Spanish horses left their mountain home and drifted onto the plains, hunting bison from horseback, gaining strength and confidence as they pushed south of the Arkansas, the Canadian, and the Red. They called themselves *Nermernuh* or "People." French trappers called them *Pàdoucas*. The Utes called them *Komàntcia*—those who want to fight me all the time. By the early 1700s settlements in Texas and New Mexico were continually sacked and burned, and terrified Spanish garrisons huddled inside their presidios. *Komàntcia*, on the Spanish tongue, had become *Comanche*.

***

Coronado marched for three months from the Pecos River through the Texas Panhandle to the Arkansas River. He reported his observations:

> On them [the plains] I found so many cattle [bison] it would be impossible to estimate their numbers for there was not a single day until my return that I lost sight of them.

General Philip Sheridan estimated the size of the southern herd at 100 million. The naturalist W. T. Hornady was more conservative estimating between four and twelve million. In any case, the number is academic as Peter Matthiessen wisely tells us in *Wildlife in America:*

> The bison herds were almost certainly the greatest animal congregations that ever existed on earth, and the greed and waste which accompanied their annihilation doubtless warrants some superlative also.

Descriptions of what this dry, dusty country was like prior to settlement varies with the agendas of those who would exploit, preserve, or conserve it. But by all accounts, there was far more grass and less brush than we have today. And along with the grass—little bluestem, buffalo, and grama—tens of millions of bison, the attendant wolves, pronghorn antelope, lesser prairie chickens, and innumerable other prairie fauna.

But forget the popular vision of an unbroken sea of waist-high grass swaying gently in the wind. In drought years, scarce surface water held the bison herds as surely as fencing. They laid the surrounding prairie so bare that army detachments had trouble finding forage for their horses and mules. When the drought broke, the herds moved on and the ravaged prairie began its succession from bare ground to annual forbs and legumes and then on to perennial vegetation until fire, drought, or bison reversed the process.

Continuous, often violent localized change stabilized the West Texas prairies as a whole. Wildfire, started by Indians or lightning and driven by wind, burned hundreds of thousands of acres at a time before being extinguished by rain or contained by creeks and rivers. Unlike today's cool prescribed fires, these hot, wild flames devoured encroaching brush along with nearly everything else in their paths.

Brush and trees—hackberry, elm, and cottonwood—were for the most part restricted to creek and river bottoms. (The Comanches preferred to camp in the open timber along sheltered creeks.) Elsewhere on the plains, young brush that escaped the wildfires was probably trampled by bison or nibbled down by browsers. Prior to the cattle boom, the hills and draws, protected and held in place by grass and thousands of years' worth of organic buildup, were probably more gently rounded than they are today. It's ironic that much of the land feature harshness associated with the Wild West came about long after the frontier had moved on.

Northwest Texas sees an average of only 23 inches of rain per year—much less in some years—but with a complex prairie root system to retain water and regulate its flow, many of the springs, creeks, and rivers now classified as intermittent once flowed year round. Where explorers and settlers heading for

more verdant country saw the Great American Desert, a waste-
land devoid of timber and unfit for human habitation, the
Comanches saw water and grass and an endless source of
hoofed sustenance. Why worry about firewood when dried buffalo dung burns as long and hot as oak?

From 1873 to 1875 about six million bison were killed on
the South Plains. Coyotes and wolves were the short-term ben-
eficiaries of the slaughter, gorging on the rotting carcasses that
tainted the air for hundreds of square miles. But wolfers with
their strychnine crystals came on the heels of the hunters, then
came the bone gatherers, and by the end of the decade the
plains were truly empty in a way they had never been.

So we numbly read the figures and shake our heads and eat
our feedlot beef, but who really gives a damn? What can you do?
Not much, but if you're made a certain way, it all matters even if
you don't understand what you're feeling when you look out
over a piece of country.

You can still see vestiges of the old mixed prairie on some
of the big spreads on the gently rolling plains southeast of my
country. The ranchers have kept the brush beaten back, and
you can look out over thousands of acres of midgrass punctu-
ated only occasionally by an oak or plum motte. Even with the
placidly grazing cattle, these places seem painfully empty, and
in a sense they are. You can look out over several hundred Her-
efords and try as you might, you can't make them bison, not
even for a second.

I'm more at home in rough old river breaks country too
steep for bulldozers and quail rigs. The hundredth meridian and
twenty-inch isohyet of average annual rainfall run almost
directly across my favorite quail hunting grounds. From there
west to the Caprock, the country just gets rougher. Of all the
plains country, the breaks are probably the least changed. There
are quail and turkey and deer there in good numbers now just
as they probably were when the People camped in the open

timber along the creeks. Knowing that makes the country seem a bit less empty.

***

October. The harvest season. As the moon rises over the red cliffs north of the Middle Pease, the Dertsahnaw-yehkuh—the Wanderers—the most far ranging of the Comanche bands, light their fires of buffalo chips, cedar, and blackjack oak. The summer raiding in Mexico was good; over a thousand stolen horses and mules graze in the flat above the river. Stolen Mexican children, under the watchful eyes and sharp admonitions of the Comanche women, hurry about in search of fuel for the fires.

Now back at their winter home in the Pease River breaks, they must prepare for the hungry time ahead. Teepees and brush arbors line nearly two miles of riverbank. Moon up and fires burning, four drummers begin a rhythmic beat, and a half-dozen women with the best voices chant in time. Hunters and women form opposing lines; each woman steps forward to choose a partner, and the dancing begins and builds in intensity. The dancers sweat and laugh, the camp dogs bark hysterically, and the children imitate their elders.

The People dance on, resting occasionally then rejoining at will. There is no ceremony in the dance. Unlike the other plains tribes, the feral, individualist Comanches have little use for religious ritual. Confident that they alone have the favor of the spirits, they dance out of simple joy. Scouts have located thousands of bison two sleeps to the northwest. Hunting camp sites have been selected, scaffolds built, and tomorrow the women and gelded slaves will load the hunting tents, provisions, and butchering tools on mules and follow the hunters to their temporary camp.

The fires die; the Wanderers dance to exhaustion then sit about singing softly before returning to skin lodges that glow dimly from the tiny fires within. Wolves howl from the northern hills, and the camp dogs bristle and answer tentatively. War ponies graze near their owners' teepees while the People sleep.

Sunup three days later, thirty Comanche hunters, naked save for breechclouts and fringed moccasins, sit their spotted ponies and watch the scattered bands of bison stretching to the horizon. The hunters ride bareback; some carry short bows and arrows notched parallel to the heads so that they will slip easily between the beasts' ribs. A few others carry twelve-foot lances. None of the horses is fitted with a bridle. Each riders slips his legs beneath a coil of rope wrapped just behind his pony's forelegs.

A middle-aged warrior whoops, and the riders come off the low hill, riding low and gripping their horses' manes along with their weapons. The riders quickly close to within a hundred yards, and the nearest bands begin to wheel and run; the wave of panic moves forward through the herd and toward the horizon. They ride in among the trailing bison and select their targets before the beasts can get up to speed. Using only knee pressure, the archers turn their ponies and draw to within feet of their prey, running beside the beasts and nocking and shooting arrows one after another. Most of the arrows find their mark in the bisons' sides; some go clean through and into the ground. Others go through one animal and into another. At each *twang* of their masters' bowstring, the ponies, without prompting, draw away to avoid the enraged buffalo's short horns.

The lancers ride alongside their prey and drive their weapons down and in, behind the rear rib and into the soft organs. Within minutes dozens of bison are down, and the hunters ride back to survey the kill, collect their arrows, and begin the heavy butchering. Women watching from the hills jabber excitedly as they start for the killing field. Before they arrive with the horse drawn travois, the hunters have quenched their thirsts with bison blood. The children gather to beg for slices of warm liver seasoned by salty gallbladder fluid.

There will be more hunting in the days to come, but tonight there will be a tongue dance, a celebration by a people content in their own country, secure as few peoples have ever been.

***

When Comanches finished butchering a bison, only the spine, rump, and heart remained. The men bagged the meat—often four hundred pounds or more—in the green hide and loaded it onto a horse or mule for the trip back to the temporary hunting camp. There, the women cut most of it into thin strips to be hung on scaffolds and dried by the sun.

Blood, bone marrow, meat, kidneys, gallbladder were all eaten. Only the heart was left for ceremonial purposes so that the herds might continue to propagate. Paunches made water bags and pots for boiling stew with heated rocks. Sinews from the back were fashioned into bow strings. Hair was twisted into rope. Teepees, clothing, bags, robes, and blankets were made from the hide. Ribs were used as stirring spoons. Hip bones made ideal scrapers. Horns and hooves made cups and ornaments.

General Philip Sheridan understood the Comanches' relationship with the bison. Exasperated with the army's inability to herd the People onto the reservation, he addressed the Texas Legislature:

> White hunters assist in the advance of civilization by destroying the Indians' commissary…Send them powder and lead, if you will, but for the sake of a lasting peace, let them kill, skin and sell until the buffaloes are exterminated. Then your prairies can be covered with speckled cattle and the festive cowboy, who follows the hunter as a second forerunner of advanced civilization.

In 1873, after they had wiped out the bison herds in Kansas, white hunters poured into the Texas Panhandle in violation of the Treaty of Medicine Lodge. The 4th Cavalry—buffalo soldiers out of Fort Concho under the command of relentless Colonel Ranald Slidell MacKenzie—harried an enemy they rarely saw let alone engaged. Then, in October 1874, Mackenzie and his men, aided by Tonkawa scouts, surprised a huge encampment of Comanches, Kiowa, Kiowa-Apache, and Southern Cheyenne in Palo Duro Canyon, killing few Indians but over fourteen hundred of their horses. On June 2, 1875, half-breed Quanah Parker led a starving, demoralized band of Quahadi Comanches into Fort Sill. The Texas plains were at last open to speckled cattle and festive cowboys.

***

In your blaze orange vest and kangaroo featherweight boots, you carry your Italian shotgun and follow your booted dog through the cedar breaks, waiting for her beeper collar to summon you to her point. You walk and ponder the hunters who once laid claim to your country...

***

With the People out of the way, South Texas cattle poured in, the barbed wire went up, and the plains were razed. Fire was suppressed, ground water pumped, and the brush, bobwhites, and whitetails moved in to replace the antelope and prairie grouse. Can you truly appreciate what is without losing sight of what was? The cycles of rain, drought, grazing along with gentler use have brought an apparent stability—and good hunting—to the West Texas prairie.

But the aquifers are going dry despite the inevitable burgeoning water politics. And people are leaving. At present pumping rates the Ogallala Aquifer, the wellspring of the High Plains and the source of the Pease, could be dry in a few decades. Only the most human hating eco-radical (or, perhaps justifiably, surviving Comanches and Kiowa) can take satisfaction from a desperate rancher's busted dreams, but the water is going faster than rain can replace it. So you wonder. When the plains are dry and empty of cotton and cattle, what wild things will move in (or back in) to eat the grass while the resting aquifers recharge? And will we be smarter or all the more desperate the second time around?

***

We're bouncing along a ranch road, the three of us, in a Texas Parks and Wildlife pickup. My companions, biologists Kevin Mote and John Hughes, hope to show me a lesser pinnated grouse, a lesser prairie chicken. Looking out over this northern Panhandle ranch is like looking across two centuries. No mesquite; no cedar. Just an ocean of midgrass and sand sage and low growing sand plum.

I cannot tell you the name or location of this ranch; I am bound to secrecy. Suffice to say it's somewhere north of the Canadian River. As yet, the ever encroaching mesquite is still a hundred miles or so to the south. But it's coming and with it, possibly, the prairie chicken's doom.

But not this October afternoon. We park and John leads the way to a lek. The grass is only knee high, but the walking is deceptively tough, and I wonder how a bird dog would fare. The lek, several acres of gently rolling shortgrass surrounded by taller midgrass, is empty as expected, but John cautions me that adult male grouse stay close to the leks year round.

Two steps into the taller grass on the far side of the lek there is a loud *whir*, like grouse flushing from my boyhood coverts in Kentucky, and the first prairie chicken I've ever seen flushes twenty yards ahead. It flies straight away toward the horizon and disappears as if hidden by Earth's curvature. We all whoop and raise imaginary shotguns, and just for an instant this rough, resilient country seems anything but empty.

Oklahoma

Turn north on Highway 283 at Vernon, Texas, drive over the Red River into Oklahoma, and the road immediately gets worse and the country gets better. Being a hunter, I don't like straight lines, and the land (as opposed to the *country*) around Vernon is laid out per the old Great Plains cadastral grid, squarish, neat, symmetrical, and altogether dull and sterile looking. You expect at any moment to be buzzed by crop dusters. On the Texas side of the Red, you have to drive about 60 miles south of Vernon to the Pease River breaks country or north to the Panhandle sand hills before things get interesting again.

The country just across the Red from Vernon appears less fastidiously kept. With a few notable exceptions, there are less straight lines, more ragged fence rows, more brushy corners. It's country that looks more lived in than lived on. I realize that most extension agents, farmers, and some ranchers on both sides of the Red would point to my "interesting" country as case studies in slovenly agriculture. I'm not qualified to argue from an agricultural standpoint, but I do know that over the long haul, the western half of Oklahoma—the Red Rolling Plains and Prairies—has the most consistent bobwhite hunting in the country. Not the best, mind you; the most consistent. Discounting the heavily managed plantations in the Deep South, the South Texas Plains, in a good year when conditions are near

perfect, will produce more bobwhites than any other ecological region. Densities of four bobwhites per acre were documented during the last boom season. The Rolling Plains around Rotan, Sweetwater, and Albany aren't far behind. I know several guides who claim to have moved over sixty coveys per day on several occasions near Rotan. Scale that figure back a bit in the interest of realism and say forty coveys in a day. You get the picture. On the other hand, after a couple years of drought, the high-powered guides in quail rigs will run a dozen dogs into the ground for a half-dozen coveys.

Quail hunting in Oklahoma, if you believe the informal claims of guides and resident hunters, never gets quite as good or nearly as bad as it does in Texas. Either that or Okies are more truthful than Texans.

***

Early February, gray, drizzly, and much too warm. I turned north at Vernon, drove across the nearly dry Red, a broken string of...well...red pools, immediately hit a pothole and took in the familiar-looking yet subtly different country. Then on to Altus, past the little store where a cashier once spent twenty minutes on the phone running down a nonresident hunting license for me; two cups of coffee before Mangus, then a roadside rest stop to stretch Molly, who immediately pulled up limping with grass burrs, reminding me that I had left her boots at home. Further north still, the Quartz Mountains appeared on the western horizon; under Interstate 40 at Sayre and then the long stretch further north and out of the mesquite to the Washita River and aptly named Cheyenne.

I checked into a little motel, noted the NO DOGS IN ROOMS sign, then stepped outside to meet my host, Steve DeMaso, the upland game biologist with the Oklahoma Department of Wildlife Conservation. We shook hands and he immediately opened the doors on his homemade dog box and introduced me to his dogs, Ella, a liver German shorthair, and Angie, a delicate German shorthair-English pointer mix. In her box, Molly growled her suspicions. We had supper in the adjoining diner, which had windows decorated in a quail and dog motif and columns festooned with posters urging hunters to report the taking of banded bobwhites.

Steve, a Michigan transplant, warned that I should expect mediocre hunting at best and predicted that Oklahoma hunters wouldn't get their normal three million or so bobwhites. We decided to hunt the next morning on some private land with Danny Pierce, a local guide and friend of Steve's, and in the afternoon on some nearby public land. After supper we stepped outside into the darkness and a sudden and surprising, damp coldness; the air felt sharp and metallic in my nostrils. Steve opened his kennel doors, and Ella and Angie jumped off the tailgate and bounced into his room like they knew the drill. I mentioned the NO DOGS IN ROOMS sign and Steve shrugged and said, "I stay here all the time." Following suit, I heeled Molly up the outside steps and past the night manager, a nice lady who smiled and said sonorously, "Pretty doggy."

Next morning Molly and I stepped outside into the darkness and three inches of wet, clingy snow and more falling. I zipped my down jacket, pulled on my stocking cap, and walked Molly across the street to a little patch of grass where before doing her business, she sniffed every blade individually while snow covered my head and glasses and piled up around my collar. Over fourteen years of hunting in Texas, I had never dealt with snow and rarely rain. Brad, I was sure, was not dealing with snow down on the Pease. I stepped into the diner, and Steve looked up from his menu and grinned as if he'd set things up just for me.

Just after sunup we pulled into Danny Pierce's place after fishtailing over several miles of muddy road that contributed to an extra-large cup of coffee being dumped into my lap. Our arrival set off a small army of bird dogs—a scene right out of *Biscuit Eater*—that appeared suddenly from all manner of crates, barrels, and conventional dog houses spread about the yard. Our dogs naturally responded with equal hysteria. Danny appeared and hushed his charges while I banged on the side of Molly's box and threatened to little avail to strangle her if she didn't shut up.

Steve and I consolidated our dogs and gear in my truck then enjoyed another white knuckle drive over the same muddy roads, this time behind Danny, who occasionally slowed to sixty miles per hour to let us catch up. I managed to keep either the grill or tailgate pointed at Danny the bulk of the time, although much to Steve's discomfort, we did lead with the passenger side window more than once. After he'd gotten a particularly close look at a roadside embankment, Steve allowed as how we'd gotten another inch of snow since breakfast.

We slid to a stop at a pasture entrance gate, and Danny jumped out and announced that he'd just seen a big covey run into a plum thicket twenty yards away. He shoved three shells into his Browning Sweet Sixteen while Steve and I frantically put together our over-and-unders. "I'll be shootin' birds while you boys are standing there with empty guns," he said. "A gentleman's gun for a gentleman's bird," I replied. Danny snorted, said something I won't repeat, and cast his big lemon and white pointer Ruff into a gorgeous section of western Oklahoma quail country.

It was still snowing hard, but I could see thick, dark stands of ragweed interspersed with shin oak mottes, plum thickets, and little bluestem. Before I could get my gloves on, Ruff and Molly were making game in the plum thicket. The mostly white dogs were barely visible against the white background, made even whiter by the snow sticking to my glasses. The falling snow and the dogs' snuffling seemed much louder than the tinkling of Molly's high-pitched bell.

The dogs came out the far side of the plum thicket, and sixty yards further on, a huge covey flushed and banked sharply out of sight behind a big motte. Danny said, "There go your gentleman birds."

We found several members of our unruly covey in snow-draped plum thickets or buried in the snow under clumps of little bluestem where they had to literally be kicked out. We moved three more coveys in another two hours of hunting and got some nice work from Molly, Ruff, and Danny's promising pup, a pointer-shorthair mix named Eva. In nearly every case, single birds held nicely and coveys and groups of twos and threes ran like deer.

Around mid-morning Molly's beeper collar went off, and we found her in the middle of a half-acre oak copse. Danny stood on one side of the thicket while I worked my way around to the other. As I crouched looking for a way to get to Molly, a small covey nearly ran up my pants leg. They flushed straight up like woodcock, and I missed with both barrels.

By late morning we were soaked, nearly hypothermic, and stopping every five minutes to wring melted snow from our hats and gloves. We loaded the dogs and drove just across the border into Texas for an early lunch. The little diner's parking lot was full of dog trailers and pickup trucks carrying dog boxes, so we parked across the road alongside more dog trailers and pickups carrying dog boxes and went inside to a sea of orange caps, chaps, brush pants, and dog whistles. Business cards for dog trainers and guide services covered the cashier's counter. Coffee consumption would have been best expressed in gallons per second. We sat down next to a table of hunters, more of Danny's clients, who gleefully reported that they had found five coveys to our four. Danny countered saying that we'd been running a pup. That settled things, but then the waitress showed up with the coffeepot and asked how we'd done.

In this day of destination hunting trips and scores of outfitters promising "the gunning experience of a lifetime" with plush accommodations, gourmet meals, and matching prices, solid, Spartan operations like Danny's are in short supply. If you want to be pampered, check one of the various "approved" lists of guides and outfitters. Danny, on the other hand, specializes in competent guides, good meat dogs, and most importantly plenty of chances at wild birds at reasonable prices. If you're big on cuisine, he'll run you into Wheeler for a cheeseburger.

After lunch Danny went to check in on some other clients, and Steve and I drove up to the Black Kettle WMA, which is part of the larger Black Kettle National Grasslands near Cheyenne. Steve put Ella and Angie down in one of his favorite areas, a big, rough unit studded with plum thickets, shin oak, and cedar. The hillsides were thick with ragweed while the more level areas held healthy stands of little bluestem and other native grasses—in short, everything bobwhites need.

Steve didn't expect the birds to move much with four inches of snow on the ground. And even though the snow had stopped falling, the temperature was dropping fast and the northwesterly wind had picked up. Naturally the hunting would be excellent during the thaw that would come after I had left for Texas.

Sure enough, despite his dogs' best efforts, we turned up nothing in some of the best-looking quail cover I've seen. Then Steve wrenched his knee sliding down a steep hill to get to some birdy-looking creek bottom cover, so we packed it in early. We were a hundred yards or so from the truck and had just unloaded our guns when Angie locked up along a brushy fence row. We took a few steps forward groping for shells, and a fifteen-bird covey flushed and disappeared into the hillside cedars.

On the way back to town, Steve pulled off the road into a small parking lot with a shelter overlooking an expanse of hillside prairie. He said, "I thought you might want to see this." I followed him down a narrow path to a monument overlooking the Washita battle site where Colonel George Custer, despite a U.S. government promise of peace, attacked a Cheyenne camp, killing Chief Black Kettle and his wife. Just a modest little monument denoting ostentatious treachery. You look at the bluestem- and snow-covered hillside and tree-lined creek and try to reconcile the incongruity between what you see and what happened 130 years ago when a few Cheyenne warriors and army troopers slaughtered each other over an egomaniac's ambition.

Back at the motel, I cleaned my birds on the tailgate during what passes for rush hour in Cheyenne. No one gave me a second look other than the manager, who asked for a trip report. Later, in the motel diner, Steve said that he enjoyed getting out of Oklahoma City and coming to these little prairie towns where he's just another hunter instead of the state's upland game guru. We got up to leave and a man wearing brush pants sidled up and said, "Hey, aren't you Steve DeMaso?" I paid and stepped outside to wait for Steve, who was by this time surrounded by a half dozen blaze orange caps. Outside, it was pitch dark and snowing again, and hunters were slipping their dogs into motel rooms.

***

Born and raised in Kentucky, I identify with Oklahomans. Barefoot hillbilly jokes, rarely malicious, are a normal part of my life in the glorious suburbs. There are times, though. On a business trip several years ago, a Newark, New Jersey native seated next to me on the plane asked if I had considered toning down my accent for professional reasons. I was too young, insecure, and flabbergasted to think of a suitable comeback; everything that came to mind contained "goddamned Yankee." I can't remember what I actually said, but we didn't talk much afterward. Likewise, Oklahomans put up with nonresident writers commenting on the condition of their highways and Okie jokes from xenophobic Texans fond of referring to "that third world country just north of the Red."

(Have you noticed that when a radio or television comic tries to act like an imbecile, he inevitably falls back on a poor imitation of rural Southern English? The up side is that he usually *does* come across as an imbecile, though not in the intended fashion.)

All harmless enough and generally inaccurate. New Yorkers are not all rude; Californians are not all weird; we Kentuckians wear shoes and socks, even on the beach.

***

The serious hunting ended when Steve wrenched his knee, so we made the short drive the following morning from Cheyenne to the Packsaddle Wildlife Management Area which serves as the research area for an ongoing bobwhite telemetry study. The snow had ceased by then; it was cloudy, windy, and bitter cold. We pulled into the yard, and Molly bounded off the tailgate to introduce herself to the office cat, who cooled relations immediately by puffing herself up to three times her normal size. Obviously hurt, Molly hopped back into her box and glowered out the open door.

photo by Brad Carter

In the office, among specimen jars full of seeds and other quail crop contents, wildlife technicians Scott Cox and Scott Perry explained telemetry basics. Coveys are trapped using bait and call boxes, and two or three birds in each of the coveys are fitted with tiny radio collars consisting of a sealed electronics module, which fits under the bird's beak, and a wispy antenna, which runs down the bird's back. The radios, they assured me, interfere very little with the birds' flight. The released coveys are then located and tracked, using a directional receiver with a variable attenuator. The operator turns the attenuator to the maximum setting then scans 360 degrees, gradually decreasing attenuation until a signal is picked up. Coveys are then pin-pointed in a similar manner with fine attenuator adjustment. Low-tech electronics; high-tech packaging.

Biologists divide quail research history into two eras. BT and AT. Before telemetry and after telemetry. Prior to the early 1980s, before radio technology reached the point where quail could be safely fitted with radio collars, researchers relied on bands, tags, dyes, hunter surveys, and plain old legwork to track quail movement. Legendary Texas biologist A.S. Jackson literally camped out with bobwhite coveys for days at a time to track their movements. Researchers on the Matador Wildlife Management Area in West Texas dyed a covey orange. Seriously. Amazingly, the biologists were right far more often than not. Imagine what Herb Stoddard could have done with today's technology.

After groundbreaking successes at the Tall Timbers Research Station in northern Florida in the mid-1980s, telemetry came into wide use and biologists were able to look at the bobwhite's life with striking clarity. Long held beliefs were suddenly cast aside while many of the suspicions held by biologists and experienced hunters were confirmed. We're now sure that bobwhites do the damnedest things for reasons known only to them, and that it's best not to scoff openly at homespun wisdom.

Biologists have the maddening habit of couching their statements. "Our data suggests that..." or "based on the evidence, it's conceivable that..." I like pat answers, but the experts couch with good reason.

Bobwhite quail are homebodies, we've always been told. Except for the spring breakup and the fall shuffle they live out their lives within a square mile or so. Every hunter knows that. We've heard it and read it time and again. Yet the latest evidence *suggests* that we *might* be mistaken.

In October 1991 the boys at the Packsaddle began a study on the effects of supplemental feeding of wild bobwhites. Quail were trapped and three to four birds per covey were fitted with radio collars. Predictably, the researchers found that feeders are of little benefit to wild bobwhites although by concentrating the birds, they sometimes make things easier for predators and lazy hunters. The surprise came when birds began to disappear, radio and all. At first the researchers assumed the radios had malfunctioned or had been destroyed or carried away by predators.

To make sure, they made concentric searches around the perimeter of the research area hoping to pick up signals but found nothing. The following spring they flew over the country-side in an airplane and found their birds anywhere from six to thirty-five miles away. The birds moved in all directions, but most moved north to northeast. Nobody knows why. In most cases the birds moved to habitat that was no better than what they left, and in some cases they moved into inferior habitat. Movements of a mile per day were typical.

Then there was the legendary Bird 908 that moved six miles in one day, four miles the next, then fell into a regular pattern of six miles forward and six miles back. Certain that the radio was traveling in a coyote's stomach, the researchers got permission from the landowner, walked into the pasture, and flushed the bird—a single male.

I find the idea of migratory quail intriguing, but Steve, in the tradition of cautious wildlife experts, brings me back to earth. This behavior might not be typical across the bobwhite's range; there may be something unique about the Packsaddle area that causes the birds to move around so much. But just think...little columns of bobwhites marching forth to fill up every available acre of habitat...my habitat. For some reason, I never picture them leaving my coverts. I suppose further study is called for.

***

Smelling a shot at a magazine cover photo, I talked Steve into putting on his vest and carrying an unloaded shotgun in pursuit of radio collared bobwhites by promising him slides for his upcoming presentation at the annual Tall Timbers quail symposium. The logic was faultless. We'd know the birds' exact location; we'd simply lead the dogs directly to the covey; they'd point; I'd get into position and take several photos of Steve limping up to flush the birds. Then I'd get the mythical photo of wild bobwhites flushing in front of three staunch dogs.

We piled into the trucks and ground off in the direction of a known covey home range. Within minutes we had a covey pin-pointed in a big plum mott. The dogs whipped in from down wind and were just beginning to glide into a stylish high-headed point when the covey ran out the far side of the mott and flushed. Steve shrugged and suggested that all the handling and flushing probably had affected the test coveys' behavior. They seemed pretty normal to me. But then my birds see a lot of dogs over the course of a season.

No matter. The covey flew a couple hundred yards then banked into a draw and out of sight. We sent the dogs ahead, and with the two Scotts' receiver chirping away, we shuffled in pursuit through the six inches of snow while I wondered what *Animal Agenda* would pay for a shot of Oklahoma's upland game biologist, in full hunting regalia, accompanied by technicians carrying telemetry equipment. Down in the draw, the dogs dashed about animatedly, their tails whipping furiously. Nothing. They stayed at it for a another five minutes or so until we ran out of patience and tried to help by stomping around in the bunch grass. I suggested that the birds had flushed before we arrived. Scott Cox, who'd been quiet for several minutes, looked up from his receiver. "Uh...boys...we're right in the middle of 'em."

Three experienced dogs amid radio collared bobwhites and we couldn't get a productive point. If you've spent much time after singles on heavily hunted public land, you're probably not surprised. Neither were we, really, but it was strange knowing we were within a few feet of quail we couldn't find. Makes you wonder how many coveys you miss over the course of a season. Finally, Ella locked up on a clump of shin oak. I snapped off several photos as Steve walked in and kicked the brush a half-dozen times to no avail. Then someone moved and birds flushed all around us.

We had slightly better luck on two other coveys, and I got just enough photos to adequately support an Oklahoma quail hunting article with a few slides left over for Steve's presentation. (Yes, we outdoor writers often use staged photos.) The two Scotts found the remains of a dead quail they determined to be the victim of a mammalian predator. Avian predators pick the carcass clean and then defecate all over the kill site while mammalian predators generally leave little more than feathers and a chewed radio, if they don't swallow it. The tiny radios often work their way through predators' digestive systems. Much to his delight, Scott Cox, in search of missing radios, has dug up more than a few transmitting snakes. I wonder how the average freshman biology student pictures her future job.

Back at the office the two Scotts spent an hour or so recounting close encounters in tight spaces with large reptiles, and Steve outlined a planned chick mortality study involving even tinier transmitters. The chicks are the missing link in quail mortality research. Presently, when a brood suddenly disappears, researchers can only guess at what happened. The tiny transmitters will go on five-day-old chicks.

Through the study of radio tagged adult hens, the Packsaddle researchers have already documented double brooding and, more interestingly, polygamy. They use the name "gypsy hen" to describe hens that leave their clutches with males then pair up and nest again with another male. So much for political correctness and the bobwhite's alleged gentlemanly propriety.

***

I followed Steve back to Danny's to pick up my Coleman camp stove, which I had accidentally left during the equipment consolidation the day before. Steve's knee was feeling better, so he decided to hang around and see if any of Danny's unguided clients had gotten in over their heads and needed some help.

I started home over thawing roads that were if anything worse than the day before. By the time I made it to the pavement, my windshield and everything in the bed of the truck was covered in mud, but of course my wiper fluid was still frozen. I started to look for a service station but thought better of it and got out and scraped off the bigger clods. I drove out of the snow around Mangum. Just south of Altus, the wiper fluid started flowing again, and just in time. The sun peeping through the clouds made driving with a muddy windshield a bit chancy. I had already crossed the Red and had just pulled out onto the four-lane before I wondered how Brad had done down on the Pease.

Winter Apparitions

In mid-November woodcock begin dropping into my East Texas coverts. They come down the central flyway from the upper Midwest and alight in our young pine plantations and hardwood creek bottoms virtually unnoticed. Most Texans are distracted by deer, quail, or waterfowl.

Bobwhite quail command most of my attention throughout autumn, but starting with the first full moon in November, I imagine my coverts filling up with woodcock as they pour in just ahead of the freezing weather that follows them down the flyways. By Christmas I need a break from West Texas dust and wind and wild coveys and wilder dogs, so I head southeast for the Texas Piney Woods.

To me, bobwhites seem a natural part of their landscape like little bluestem or prickly pear cactus. Woodcock, on the other hand, appear; then, just as suddenly, they're gone. Other migratory birds do the same, of course, but woodcock drop in at night, unseen, into near impenetrable thickets of pine and blackberry and cat briars. You don't see them sitting out on the impounds or perched on telephone lines. One day you and the dog push through a covert and find it empty. The very next morning, you step in amongst the briars and vines and your eyes jump to whitewash on the pine needles and bore holes in the loam. If you're lucky, the birds are spread nicely about and your dog works from one to the next and you stand waiting to be called to action by the beeper collar or suddenly silent bell. Then you pull your cap down tight and, with your gloved hand before you, pare your way through the thicket, sweating, cussing, fighting panic, running into solid walls of briars, constantly changing routes, all the while talking to the dog to let her know that you haven't forgotten her.

Beside her at last, you adjust your sweaty grip and shuffle forward. If all goes well, you hear the shrill twitter, and your eyes pick up the long bill and peculiarly canted posture against the sky. Or, just as likely, you hear the twitter and jerk the gun up and frantically search for a shooting lane that doesn't exist.

If they're really stacked in your covert, your normally well-mannered dog might be reduced to a slobbering, wild-eyed, bloody mess, on overload, trying to point while bumping three birds at a time. After a few minutes of this, she'll probably give up and clean your covert out in one mad dash while you scream yourself hoarse. But even this is a good sign—you'll probably be into woodcock all day long.

Other times you end up completely skunked and exhausted, your brush pants reduced to rags, your hide covered with puckered furrows. You talk to experts, study the lore, look in all the right places, and find nothing. Perfect habitat, ideal weather, and the woodcock choose to be elsewhere. Then, as you drive back to camp after dark, a half dozen birds flush from the roadside ditches and flutter like moths before your headlights. Woodcock are that way.

***

As I write this, I have on my desk a January 1975 issue of *Sports Afield*. The cover art features a soft-eyed, white and orange Brittany holding a woodcock. Most of the issue is devoted to gun dogs; on the cover next to the Brittany is the familiar quote, "If a man can't find something to like about

almost any dog—especially his own—there's probably something wrong with the man."

The year 1975 seems anything but distant, but the magazine and a little arithmetic remind me otherwise. I remember
the afternoon my father bought the magazine. I was just shy of
fifteen. After basketball practice, Dad and I took my beagle
Zeke to the veterinarian and then, as was the tradition after
annual trips to the vet, we went by Coyle's Drugstore to the
section that offered among other things castration tools, nose
rings (for hogs not teenagers, although the distinction can be a
little fuzzy at times), bag balm, and dog collars. Dad paid for the
magazine along with Zeke's new collar, and that afternoon and
evening I sat at the kitchen table and read for the first time
"The Old Maid," by Havilah Babcock, "The Best Hound in the
State of Vermont," by Jerome Robinson, and a profile of a bird
dog breed I hadn't heard of, the German shorthair.

(I see also, as I thumb through the magazine, that I clipped
out a request for information on a taxidermy course. I don't
remember, but I suspect I was later shocked and disappointed
to learn that the course wasn't free and that I wouldn't be stuff-
ing squirrels within a few hours of receiving the information
packet.)

I also read a short piece entitled "Old Tom" at least a half
dozen times that night and noticed that it was written by a man
named Gene Hill. Until then I had taken no note of authors no
matter how much I enjoyed their work. I started looking for
Hill's writing. I followed him from *Sports Afield* to *Field &
Stream* and bought his books as soon as I could afford them. I've
read all of his early stories several times, but to this day I love
his woodcock stories most. "Woodcock Dogs"; "The Woodcock
Gun" my favorite, I've read it at least twenty times; "Voices
From Woodcock Country"; "The Woodcock Letter." I practi-
cally memorized them.

In "Voices From Woodcock Country," Hill wrote that he hears voices from a time that he lives in all alone. I think I know what he meant. At twenty, I longed to wear leather-topped rubber L.L. Bean boots through alder bottoms. I wanted to "gun the flights" with a Smith or a Parker or a Greener over a close working Belton setter. Instead my beagles pushed up an occasional woodcock along the wooded Kentucky cornfield edges. If I happened to knock one down with my humpbacked Browning autoloader, I had to sprint to it to keep Fellar or Zeke or Sam from eating it. Even more insulting, Dad's setter Toby, an immaculate bobwhite retriever, preferred rolling on dead woodcock to retrieving them. Dad fried them like quail, and we gagged them down for the sake of propriety.

Years later, during a period of obsessive deer hunting, I noticed whitewash and bore holes in an East Texas clear cut. Until then the idea of woodcock hunting west of the Mississippi River, in Texas especially, would have been unthinkable. Big running pointers and unplugged autoloaders didn't seem to go with woodcock hunting, and I had trouble picturing a motorized woodcock rig. But the sign was unmistakable. The clear cut was coming back in young hardwood brush—good whitetail habitat—so I sat with my back to a loblolly and watched the area for the rest of the afternoon. At dusk woodcock flew in like bats and lit in the open spots to feed. I seem to remember a couple of deer at dusk; then again maybe not. That was a long time ago. But I remember the woodcock.

In 1989 Heidi and I were suffering through one of the worst bobwhite seasons on record when I ran across an old *Outdoor Life* article on East Texas woodcock hunting. A dozen or so calls put me in touch with a woodcock expert from Conroe, who seemed taken aback to be talking to someone who shared his interests. He was free with his advice and actually suggested specific Forest Service pine plantations. No, I'm not going to tell you *which* national forest. Naturally, the Piney Woods were then hit with a horrific freeze that sent all the woodcock to coastal areas tied up in waterfowl leases.

I waited the freezing weather out then headed southeast, having been told that woodcock sometimes move north again after a thaw. I hunted hard in the rain from dawn to dusk, slogging through two inches of water. Standing at the truck just before dark, casing my gun and feeling a little silly, like I had been chasing ghosts or yetis, I heard the unmistakable nasal song of a woodcock male somewhere across the flooded clear cut. That night I reread "The Woodcock Gun" then started George Bird Evan's *The Upland Shooting Life*.

Two years later in January, Brad, Jay, and I, acting on a tip from a biologist in Lufkin, followed the dogs into a head-high stand of pines and started moving woodcock. Lots of them, more than we could count, although we heard far more birds than we saw. We staggered out of the pines at the end of the day, briar-torn from head to toe and as wild-eyed as the dogs. We had less than a half dozen birds between us, but we were onto something and we knew it. Public land, lots of birds, and not another soul in the woods. We did eventually run into a group of rabbit hunters, who regarded us with obvious suspicion. Remembering how we looked, I can't blame them.

***

Texas woodcock hunting is so...well...nontraditional. In the Texas Piney Woods, woodcock are hunted in December and January, and that's fine; we don't have the October foliage you see in Tim Leary's photo essays. Short leaf and loblolly pines are green year round. Alder bottoms are few and far between. There are no fall pippins, northern spies, or pound sweets on the hillsides, and thus far I've been unable to locate a stone fence. I suppose you could lean against a couple of strands of rusty barbed wire while you eat your store-bought Granny Smith.

With few exceptions, magazine editors have been uninterested in articles on East Texas woodcock hunting. Too localized, I'm told. Too narrow a focus. But *Vermont* woodcock hunting, that's different. Give us a new slant on the same old stuff. New England hunters showing remarkable restraint in old coverts that used to be stiff with birds; hunting the Little Russet Fellow with spreader loads; mythical flights, Gypsy Moon and all that. To be fair and honest, most of the traditional New England bird hunting literature is very good, and I still can't get enough of it. I've read Sidney Lea's *Hunting the Whole Way Home* three times.

And I understand the northerners' concern about the birds being hammered for two months after they're concentrated on their wintering grounds. Most of North America's woodcock end up stacked in Louisiana's Atchafalaya Basin in January, but good numbers spill into East Texas most winters. If hunters in Texas and Louisiana went after them with the same zeal they reserve for quail and waterfowl, shooting might be a real factor. But they don't and likely never will given the nature of the hunting and the small bag limits.

I've long harbored the suspicion that much of the northern purists' problem with southern woodcock hunting comes from the thought of *their* birds being flushed by a nondescript hound and dropped by a load of number four shot from a Piney Woods cracker's full-choked, bolt action twelve-gauge squirrel gun. George Bird Evans wrote in *The Upland Shooting Life* that woodcock should not be harassed on their wintering grounds. For reasons both selfish and logical, I have a problem with that position. Does the same reasoning apply to waterfowl? No one seems to have a problem with the birds being pounded all the way down the eastern and central flyways where they might have only a few days (or hours) to rest and feed before pushing on to stay ahead of freezing weather. There was a time, however, out of pure altruism (of course), I would have voted for a moratorium on woodcock hunting within a 100-mile radius of Old Hemlock.

***

Inevitably, on the first morning of my annual January woodcock hunt, I have trouble believing they're really out there. Even after Molly's bell stops tinkling for the first time, out of sight, somewhere ahead in the tangles, I still can't believe it. So it seems quite miraculous when I actually hold a woodcock, still limp and warm, in my hand and stoke the cinnamon breast feathers and wipe the moist loam from its long, prehensile bill. The picture just doesn't seem right. Pine plantations; seed cuts; *clear-cuts* for god's sake; towering long-leaf, short-leaf, and loblolly pines; sandy loam and pine needle carpet; the tea-colored creeks. Woodpeckers certainly, but surely not woodcock.

But, as an East Texas biologist once told me, forget about the literature; it's the stem density that matters. Woodcock need the same things north or south: overhead protection from avian predators, forest openings for courtship, open areas at ground level for easy movement, and an accessible supply of invertebrates in general and earthworms in particular. So you make the substitutions: Pine plantations, head high to about twelve feet and hellishly grown up in briars for Aspen coverts; young clear-cuts coming back in blackberry, southern wax myrtle, eastern baccharis, and head-high hardwood brush replace alder bottoms in the picture. You'll find bore holes right in the middle of pine plantations, but winter woodcock generally loaf during the day then feed through the night in fallow fields, roadside ditches, and new clear-cuts.

But if you want to keep things as simple as possible, just look for briars. The wickeder the better. If you come through a day of East Texas woodcock hunting and don't look as if you've been hand washing barn cats, you probably won't have any birds to show for your efforts. If you and your dogs are nice and bloody, you still might not have any birds, but you probably at least heard a few flush while you were trying to rip yourself or your shotgun free from some nightmarish tangle or other.

I got a call a few years back from a man who had read a woodcock article I had written. He said that sitting in his deer stand late in the day, he had seen several woodcock flying out of the woods and into fallow fields but added that he and his buddies had been unable to find a single bird with their pointers during the day. I asked him where he had been looking. "Thickets," he said. I did my best to stress the pain and blood loss involved. "Yeah, there were some briars," he said matter-of-factly. I don't think he got it.

I have no useable shell loops on my hunting vest. They were reduced to tatters after about a half-hour of woodcock hunting. Regardless of temperature, I wear buckskin gloves, heavy canvas shirt, long underwear, and heavy brush pants. And I still end up bloody. If I were adequately protected, I wouldn't be able to move let alone mount a shotgun.

Ask me to show you a real East Texas woodcock hunter and I'll point to Jay Chesley: about six foot two and two hundred thirty pounds, in heavy canvas overalls, disastrous sweat stained Fedora, carrying a riot gun, and following in the wake his huge, close working shorthair Shatzi makes through the briars and saplings. Jay (yes, we call him Jaybird, or simply, The Bird) grew up hunting desert quail in southeastern Arizona, picked up bobwhite hunting when he moved to Texas, then went unaccountably nuts over woodcock. Picture this large, normally reserved man letting go a war whoop and holding his riot gun over his head in triumph and shouting "Fetch Shatzi! Fetch! Fetch! Fetch! Fetch!"

And she does fetch, often unprompted. I shoot; the woodcock flies away; I issue appropriate commentary then move on. Minutes later Shatzi nuzzles one of us from behind and held gently in her great jaws is a dead woodcock, ostensibly the one

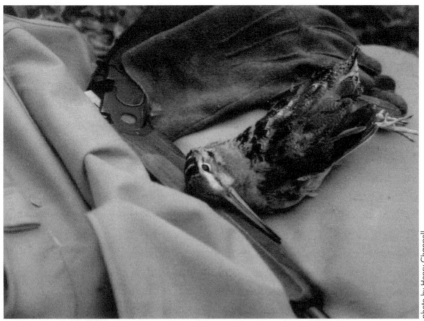

photo by Henry Chappell

whose ancestry I insulted moments before. Like her boss, she's a real woodcock hunter. She quarters just beyond shotgun range and checks back often while my two wild-eyed West Texas bobwhite dogs rip the foliage to shreds a half-mile beyond beeper range. At the end of the day Jay is ready for a nice relaxing evening of sylvan bliss—roaring fire, gallon of Wolf Brand chili, box of Cheezits, and six-pack of Caffeine Free Diet Coke—and I'm in serious need of a really stiff drink and a throat lozenge.

***

There might be fifty woodcock hunters in Texas, counting Jay and me. (Brad considers himself a quail hunter who occasionally hunts woodcock.) If you're serious about East Texas woodcock hunting, you will eventually know of Dr. Monte Whiting. If you're very lucky, you'll get to hunt with him, but you'll have to get in line. Monte is a professor of Wildlife

Management at Stephen F. Austin University in Nacogdoches and the undisputed authority on Texas woodcock hunting. I've shot exactly one five-bird limit of woodcock in ten years of hunting, and I got it while hunting with Monte. We must have flushed fifty birds that morning on a quick hunt squeezed in before Monte had to be back at the University to teach a late morning class.

I envy Monte not so much for his knowledge, although I envy that too, but more for the way he makes the Piney Woods a part of his everyday life. When he's not holding class in the woods, he's doing research there or hunting there. Ducks along the creeks or on the big impoundments. Turkeys in the hardwood bottoms. Deer, woodcock, and quail in the uplands. He can tell you where to find a good supply of fatwood, show you a tiny hidden pond that once supplied cooling water to lumber trains. He can show you the best place in the woods to learn song bird identification, point out where the old loggers used crosscut saws, show you how to tell that a piece of woods burned thirty years ago, tell you why a certain hump is a *little* too grassy for woodcock. He's a teacher with a hunter's eye for the world. He's always teaching and, in one way or the other, hunting. Little wonder his students line up to hunt with him. He'll take them to a spot in the woods and say, "Okay, look around and tell me about this place; tell me what happened here." I fill up a pocket notebook every time I hunt with him.

Follow him into the woods, and you'll struggle to keep up. He's a big man with long legs. Watch him plow through the briar walls, and you'll understand the disastrous hunting coat and heavy chaps that look as though they've been run through a chip mill.

Cody and Pax, his white and liver Brittanys, will be bustling about in the briars forty or fifty yards away while Monte gives a treatise on this or that and points out all manner of things you wouldn't notice on your own. Directly, he'll stop and listen for the dogs. If their bells are still tinkling, you'll either follow or Monte will redirect them to another more hellish island of briars. Eventually the bells will go silent and the two of you will crash off in the direction you last heard them. You might find the dogs right off, but more likely you'll have to get down to dog level and peer through brush and vines until you spot a stationary patch of white. Then you'll wonder how the hell you'll ever get to the dog.

Chances are good that by the time you've tried and abandoned a route or two, you'll hear Monte's voice coming from where the dogs are pointed. "You stand right ovuh theyuh, and I'll flush this bud fo ya. You whoa now, Pax!"

Get into position in the little clearing, and Monte will either kick the bird up or throw his cap at it; or maybe he'll have Cody or Pax flush it. In any case, you'll hear that brittle flushing twitter and the bird will likely fly right over your head, and as you fight off panic and try to cover the bird, you'll wonder how Monte knew it would fly your way.

Back at the truck, Monte will whip out his pocket scales and record the weight of every woodcock in the day's bag, partly in the interest of scientific method and completeness, but mostly to help in his battle with the U.S. Fish and Wildlife Service. If a hen weighs more than 220 grams, he'll carefully draw the bird and there's a good chance he'll show you egg follicles.

Conventional wisdom and the U.S. Fish and Wildlife Service hold that woodcock nest on their traditional breeding grounds in the northern United States and southern Canada, and that southern breeding is so rare as to be trivial and unmeasurable. Monte and his students, who have spent hundreds of hours in the Piney Woods documenting breeding, nesting, and brooding activity, assert that in some years fifty percent of all woodcock in North America nest in the South.

The difference is important and the implication far reaching. The USFWS reports a two percent per year decline in woodcock numbers in both the eastern and central flyways over the past decade. That's quite believable given the rate of suburban sprawl, aging woodland, and anti-logging sentiment and the trend toward the use of rank domestic grasses for pasturage. Correspondingly, in 1997 the USFWS reduced the bag limit from five to three birds per day and shortened the hunting season by fifteen days along the central flyway. The same reductions were made years ago along the eastern flyway, even though the party line has been that gunning pressure is not a factor in the birds' long-term decline. And it's probably not a factor, given that woodcock numbers have continued to drop despite the fact that both hunter numbers and annual kill have steadily decreased as well. You have to wonder if perhaps the bag and season reductions are symbolic; we must, after all, do *something*.

Fair enough, you say. We can't afford to gamble. When it comes to a species' well-being, conservatism is called for. But what if woodcock aren't doing nearly as badly as the USFWS data indicate and all that's really happening is that hunter interest and—let's be honest and pragmatic here—funding for research and management is being squelched by the reduced bag and shortened season.

Farfetched? Consider this: The USFWS estimates are based on counts of courting males on traditional northern breeding grounds: the Great Lakes states eastward to the Atlantic Coast. Monte and several other southern researchers, who aren't nearly as bold with their assertions, believe that there has been a shift in breeding range over the past forty years due to changes in land use. Southern forestry practices, as unpopular as they are with most environmental groups, generally produce excellent woodcock habitat. In recent years nesting woodcock have been documented as far west as Central Texas and as far south as Galveston. So it appears that the USFWS is sampling a very small percentage of the woodcock's current nesting and breeding range. The long downward trend might simply be the result of inadequate sampling due to shifting habitat.

We aren't likely to get an answer anytime soon since the USFWS seems unwilling to seriously consider Monte's theory despite considerable evidence—February hunting in Louisiana was halted because hunters were flushing nesting hens. John Bruggink, eastern shore and upland game bird specialist with the USFWS, told me in a phone interview that although he's sure Monte knows what a woodcock chick looks like and he's willing to concede woodcock might occasionally nest in the South, the USFWS doesn't believe southern breeding and nesting are significant. Monte concedes there is much he doesn't know and that he desperately needs funding for research, particularly telemetry-based research. But if history is any indication, the money won't be forthcoming. Woodcock aren't one of the South's glamour species. Monte was recently granted a quarter million dollars for eastern wild turkey research and consulted on a huge bobwhite telemetry study funded by Temple Inland, the giant forest products company. In contrast, he has managed to scrape up a meager $20,000 or so over the past fifteen years for woodcock research.

A few years back I was working on a magazine article on southern woodcock hunting. Naturally, I phoned Monte for input, and just as naturally he expressed quite strongly his frustration with the USFWS. I asked him for a summary quote. "The USFWS is clueless about woodcock nesting in the South, and their singing ground data are worthless," he suggested.

I wince at his terseness, but I hope he's right.

***

I love woodcock so I worry about them. They aren't prolific breeders, and they don't suffer the October to April carnage that gallinaceous birds do. Oddly, hunting provides the surest relief from my worry. Woodcock *do* show up in my East Texas coverts each winter, often in good numbers, though I rarely take more than a couple of birds. And there are the local breeders.

In late January you might hear the nasal *peent* late in the afternoon. At dusk, if you're lucky, one of the males will move into an open area in the big timber to begin his courtship sky dance—the ever narrowing corkscrew ascent to an apex above the treetops followed by an abrupt vertical descent and a lovely, liquid chirping song.

You watch the dance with your gun broken open and your dog sitting at heel with her ears pricked at sounds coming from the darkening woods. When the dance is finished, you walk to the truck in the dark, hoping—praying perhaps—that these winter apparitions will always haunt our southern woodlands.

Roughing It

We pulled into camp after dark, cold and tired with maybe a half dozen birds between us. We lit the lanterns and fed the dogs, and while Brad built a fire, I set the Coleman stove atop the dog trailer and started supper. A few minutes later we had a fire going and pork chops and a skillet full of potatoes frying on the stove. Brad suggested that a pan of beans would go nicely. He lit our spare stove, dumped a can of VanCamp's into the aluminum pan, and while he was at it, started a pot of coffee. Feeling much better, we put on our down jackets and stocking caps and took in the night sky and sized up our neighbors' camps.

We were set up in the hunter campground on a large West Texas wildlife management area. Actually "campground" is a euphemism for a barren, windswept pasture usually carpeted with sand burrs, ten acres upon which the Texas Parks and Wildlife Department happens to allow camping.

It's not a bad place for hunters with motor homes and campers; they need only a place to park. But it's a bleak spot for tent campers. Most nights high wind makes fire building a risky proposition, and the dogs, on a two-minute potty run, become pitifully festooned with sand burrs.

But in a way, I've always seen the camping policy as an example of correct prioritization. A wildlife management area is for wildlife. Not one acre of useful habitat should be wasted. We humans can camp on whatever desolate hardpan happens to be left over. It doesn't hurt us to occasionally take a back seat to wildlife. Probably in response to loud and indignant whining, TPWD recently added a very nice tent camping area in a nearby mesquite flat. The camping there is much more comfortable, but I don't feel nearly as righteously hard-core when I stay there.

But that night we were definitely camping on hardscrabble. We filled our plates and ate by the fire, then while we waited for the dishwater to get hot, we sipped coffee and watched the other camps clustered eighty yards away around the outhouse and the water spigot.

I much prefer wilderness camping, or at least unrestricted camping in remote areas. But once I accept that I'm restricted to a campground, especially a hunter campground, I can actually draw comfort and a mild feeling of fraternity from my neighbors as long as they aren't right on top of me. The distant fires, the occasional whine or bark of an anxious bird dog, and the indistinct sound of other hunters' voices become atmosphere instead of noise.

State parks, unfortunately, tend to be magnets for inebriated college kids, who always manage to camp within a hundred feet of me. A few years ago Brad and I tried a state park near our favorite quail hunting spot. We had a nice sheltered campsite complete with a picnic shelter and a view overlooking an 80-acre lake. We thought we were on to something. Then about ten o'clock that night a dozen or so youngsters pulled into a nearby site. Smashing Pumpkins, Hole, and the standard drunken raillery kept us awake until midnight. We dozed through a short lull only to be awakened around 2 A.M. by loud and protracted retching and vomiting. Then one of the girls started crying, and as best we could tell, someone kept passing out on the steering wheel, thus serenading us with sporadic two-minute horn blasts.

So we were back in our old hunting camp, less cushy for sure, but far more peaceful. By the time the dishwater was hot, my eyelids were drooping and the cold had seeped into my legs and bottom despite the hot coffee, fire, and heavy clothes. We hurried through the dishwashing, watered the dogs, and crawled into our sleeping bags.

I woke just before midnight to the sound of a motor home grinding just south of us across the pasture. They stopped, and I heard them letting their dogs out and going about setting up their camp. No problem. I've pulled into lots of campgrounds in the middle of the night. I dozed off again. Then their dogs started barking. Lots of dogs. And they continued, except for occasional five-minute intermissions, through the wee hours of the morning.

I might have slept an hour the rest of the night. I thought about walking over and asking them nicely to quiet their dogs. I also thought about banging on their door and asking them what the hell their problem was. But it was cold outside and warm in my sleeping bag. Instead, I burrowed further into my bag and wrapped my parka around my head. Surely, I reasoned, the owners would eventually get up and take care of the problem. After all, what kind of idiot lets his dogs bark all night long in close proximity to twenty other campers not to mention himself? Surely the people camped right next to them would ask for quiet. But bird hunters as a group are tolerant and easygoing. The dogs barked on.

Dawn broke slate gray and bitter cold. The dogs had finally stopped barking around five in the morning, so we took advantage of the silence and slept an extra hour. Everyone else in camp appeared to be doing the same. It was spitting snow by the time I crawled out and pulled on my parka, frozen brush pants, and boots and staggered out to start the coffee water while Brad stretched and watered our dogs. A sharp, damp wind blew in from the northwest.

The Coleman stove hissed comfortingly. I put the coffeepot on, zipped my parka up to my chin, and headed across the pasture to visit a new friend we had met the day before. I thought his coffee might be ready.

Our friend hadn't emerged, but as I approached his camp I noticed the motor home that had pulled in the night before. Then I noticed a very nice eight-hole dog trailer in tow. But the dogs—seven Brittanys—were chained out in the open nearby. After barking themselves to exhaustion, they now lay in seven pitiful, shivering, tightly coiled bundles on the frozen ground. And not a food or water pan in sight. Their owners' RV was still dark. A man from one of the other campsites walked over with his lemon and white pointer bitch whipping her tail furiously and straining on a lead. He said good morning and looked at the pitiful string of Brittanys. "Left them out like that all night," he said. "Hell I'd bark too."

You have to wonder. Were the dogs' owners really that callous and inconsiderate? I watched the dogs shiver and thought about it. The day was shaping up gloriously: a plummeting barometer, snow, and shortly, hot coffee and sausage and eggs back in camp. No, I decided, they're probably not callous and inconsiderate, just too stupid to know any better.

***

I'm a firm believer in low-impact camping, but I've left my share of blackened fire rings. Some I left in the ignorance of my youth in places they shouldn't have been left; most, I think, have been appropriate. I'm embarrassed to admit it in this day of high-tech wilderness camping, but I probably prefer a solid camp in a national forest, remote, but outside of fragile wilderness areas, where I can feel good about gathering plenty of firewood for a nice big fire pit. I'll take a roomy cabin-style tent that I can leave in place for a week without fretting over impact. All the better if the site has been lovingly used before by kindred souls. Of course fire rings and other camper impacts are

photo by Henry Chappell

ugly blights in the wrong places. But in a well-used piney woods clearing, they can be a welcome sign, especially if a predecessor left the site clean with a nice pile of firewood.

I come honestly by my affinity. To my father, hunting for a campsite meant scraping the underpinning of his heavily laden Ford station wagon over various two-track roads leading to Green River Reservoir until he found a nice gravel bank with a pristine site back in the hardwoods. Once we chose a spot, he laid siege with his ax and saw, carving civilization from Kentucky hinterland.

We erected and entrenched the big canvas cabin tent; drove nails into trees for hanging lanterns, shaving mirrors, and cooking utensils; set up at least two camp tables; dug a large fire pit; and hung clotheslines. With camp in place, my dear fastidious mother set about keeping house. After everything was ship-shape, we would drive to the boat dock. Dad, brother John, and I would bring the boat around to our camp, and Mom would return in the station wagon.

We camped for two weeks every June. Midway through the first week, John and I would stop whining about bugs and lack of air conditioning. Whatever the temperature happened to be was what it was supposed to be. Bugs and grit were just there, no more noticeable than the air around us. Shirts were off by ten in the morning and stayed off until dark. Shoes were a distant memory. We swam, fished, hiked, and ate—fried chicken, steak, tomatoes, cantaloupe, beans and green onions from the garden, sausage and eggs or country ham in the mornings, and a fish fry every few nights.

We had miles of shoreline to ourselves and caught scores of bedding bream with night crawlers if we had them or pieces of bacon and bologna if we didn't. At dawn, with fog on the water, we'd throw surface plugs at schooling bass. Just before dark we'd bump plastic worms slowly along the bottom of our cove.

Dad might bounce up the road and into town to check in at work or to pick up my grandmother and various aunts, uncles, and cousins for a raucous few days of laughing, fighting, and gluttony. Mostly though, Mom worked on her tan and Dad relaxed around camp, making further "improvements" or watching John and me lose his good bass plugs to underwater brush. At night during the cooking and eating, we'd listen to Loretta Lynn and Conway Twitty ("Hello, darlin'...") on Mom's portable radio. After a week with no air conditioning, the June nights seemed downright chilly, and the summer sleeping bags (on cots, of course) felt just right.

Two weeks every summer. I took them completely for granted. And some kids have to get by with Disney World.

About the time I hit my early teens, the Corps of Engineers, citing trash problems, restricted camping around Green River Reservoir to designated campgrounds. They probably were afraid Dad would defoliate the entire shoreline. We tried the public campground one year; someone stole our cooler, and Dad and Uncle Johnny nearly came to blows with a carload of local thugs who yelled obscenities at one of my older cousins. That was our last family camping trip.

***

When Brad and I started hunting together, we fell into the habit of staying in cheap little West Texas motels. We both enjoy camping, but setting up camp takes time—time that might otherwise be spent in pursuit of quail. Those were good days.

An Indian family owned our favorite motel. The patriarch, a gracious little man we called Swami (I know, I know, and I'm sorry), went to great lengths to ensure that we had extra blankets and always reserved for us *the choice room*, which was said to have the best heater. We'd roll in from Dallas about midnight, ring the bell, and old Swami would stagger out in his pajamas, cheerfully hand us our key, and assure us that our extra blankets would be waiting in our room. We could settle up after the next day's hunting.

The price was right and the rooms were comfortable, assuming you could ignore the occasional large rodent and the loud popping of the ancient wall heaters. And you could get a good breakfast at 5:30 A.M. at the little diner up the street.

Swami's parking lot could be a festive place on Saturday nights during boom seasons, full of hunters and dog trailers from all over the country and bird dogs tied out on every square foot of available grass. On mild nights doors would be open much of the time while hunters continuously carried gear in and out. We'd set our camp stove on the dresser and heat up a couple cans of chili. Outside, someone would be standing at their tailgate, barbecuing hamburgers or venison sausage on a hibachi. Inevitably the pointer from Alabama would shake his chain and barge in to visit the hunting party from Lubbock.

The dogs always were hyper the first night, jumping from bed to bed, getting in the trash, and lapping from the toilet. By the second night we'd have to drag them from the beds, and we'd be too tired to notice the popping heater or the braying donkey in the nativity scene across the street.

We've stayed at motels all over Texas and Oklahoma, some of them real death traps with Rube Goldberg wiring and plumbing. You look at the ancient gas wall heater and wonder if it'll quit working before it kills someone. The pilot light is burning, but what the hell is that odor? Check the sheets for spiders. I once shook out a brown recluse. Okay, forget the heater and roll the sleeping bags out on the beds.

A few years ago I called, expecting to hear the Swami's voice. It was late September, but we were expecting a big season and I knew the rooms would go fast. An unfamiliar voice told me he'd bought the motel and had turned it into a respectable business. And by the way, we were out of luck; he was booked solid through the end of December. We stayed there once late that season. Brad said that must have been one expensive coat of paint the new owners had slopped on; the price had gone up by a third. Or maybe it was the American ownership touted on the sign out front. We decided we'd better start camping.

Last season I noticed signs at the motel citing an ordinance against dogs outside of their boxes. I gather that hunters are now supposed to haul their dogs beyond city limits to let them pee.

I wonder how old Swami is doing.

***

By the time I was in my early twenties, the quail hunting in central Kentucky was all but finished. Dad and John and I took up deer and grouse hunting in the eastern Kentucky mountains. In our first deer camp, we nearly froze to death in our cheap summer sleeping bags. We crawled out of the tent every morning sore and exhausted from seven hours of shivering. I doubt the temperature dropped below forty.

Next year we came back with foam pads and good cold weather bags. The temperature dropped into the low teens, but we slept like logs and got into plenty of grouse. Winter, I decided, is the time to camp; no bugs, very little sweating, and, best of all, the feeling you get from toasting by the fire for two hours then bursting into a frigid tent, frantically changing into clean long handles and dry socks, then sliding in and feeling your body warming a snug sleeping bag.

We had solid camps in the mountains, close to a fast creek with plenty of good oak and pine firewood nearby. When Dad sent John and me after firewood, we knew exactly what he meant: We were to search until we found a dead, uprooted tree then drag it back to camp, using the truck and tow chain if necessary. Dad would douse the root end with Coleman fuel, light it, and we'd move the tent and vehicles back an additional thirty feet. Dad liked big fires, and he tended them constantly to keep them that way.

I last saw our old mountain campsite about a dozen years ago. The fire pit and Dad's improvements were still in evidence. But what had once barely passed for a logging road had been much improved for the sake of coal trucks.

I won't be going back.

***

My camping technique and choice of gear have evolved primarily in response to the West Texas wind. Shortly after we moved to Texas from Kentucky, Jane and I bought a four-pole, freestanding cabin tent for family camping. It served well in that capacity, and I used it extensively in my East Texas deer hunting days. It's extremely light, well ventilated, and tall enough for me to stand in. One person can set it up in about five minutes.

Tall and light with only four aluminum poles. On our first West Texas camping trip, the wind bent two poles and collapsed one side of the tent despite Brad's frantic middle-of-the-night guying efforts. Afterward it was a little warped but still usable. On the very next trip, a High Plains blue quail expedition, a dust storm blew up and finished the job, hopelessly mangling all four poles. A bit of equipment tuning seemed in order.

The following summer we studied various tent designs and finally settled on an eight-pole dome tent and vestibule designed to withstand high winds. According to Jane, it should be a government approved tornado shelter for what it cost. We chose the six-person model assuming it would comfortably sleep two normal-sized men. That autumn we set it up in Brad's backyard, in a brisk wind, then stood around admiring it and making pronouncements like, "This baby ain't goin' nowhere!" It did look stout.

A few weeks later, on the Friday night before the opening day of quail season, we set up our tent, noticed with satisfaction that the wind was getting up, then smugly went to bed. I was nearly asleep when a big gust hit the front of the tent, bowing the fiberglass pole right in on top of us. We jumped up and added a guy line to every point on the tent we could tie a cord to. The tent bucked furiously the rest of the night but held. We arose bleary-eyed the next morning to calmer winds. We cooked breakfast then set up our vestibule, again tying out and staking every point we could. The air was muggy for November and smelled of rain.

We went hunting and found several coveys despite the annoying stiff southerly wind. Right after lunch it really started blowing, this time from the northwest. We gave up hunting and pulled into camp and found the vestibule collapsed. A guy line knot had slipped and a pole had snapped, driving a jagged end through the vestibule wall. I complained, and the manufacturer sent a new vestibule and replacement pole.

A month later tremendous gusts nearly blew the tent, with Brad and me in it, off a New Mexico mountain.

We made some adjustments, and our tent has since worked fine. We've learned that with judicious guying we can make it work, without the vestibule, in even the worst West Texas wind. But in calmer weather, the vestibule has proven invaluable. Without it we would have done much of our cooking in rain or snow.

We've since looked into expedition grade tents, figuring that if they'll hold up on Mount Everest, they should make out fine in a West Texas pasture. But after looking at the prices, we're thinking a 20-foot Airstream might be more economical.

Hard-core winter campers will scoff, but we do camp often in freezing weather. My old Holofil sleeping bag has lost some loft over the years, but with polypropylene long johns, wool socks, and an EcoRag stocking cap, I've yet to sleep cold. Brad has a newer version of my bag with a hood and all sorts of nifty drawstrings and Velcro fasteners. If I need to really seal off my head and shoulders, I cover up with my down parka. Brad occasionally shoves a couple of the chemical hand-warmers into his bag to warm his feet. Naturally I give him grief about old age and poor circulation.

My bag has a comfort rating of -15 degrees Fahrenheit, which probably means that, at that temperature, it might save a dry healthy person from death by hypothermia. I haven't put my bag to the complete test, but I've slept toasty warm in it in twelve-degree weather. Lately I've read and heard a lot about three-season bags and winter bags and summer bags. Undoubtedly some people can afford to specialize, but I like Brad's axiom: Decide how much you can spend on a sleeping bag and then spend at least twenty-five percent more—once. I'll go with the warmest bag I can afford; I can always take off my stocking cap, expose my shoulders, or unzip my bag in warm weather. I doubt anal retentive backpackers will care for my camping advice.

Of course we're always looking for ways to improve "our system." A pair of Coleman lanterns will heat the inside of a tent or vestibule surprisingly well. But what if we came up with attachable aluminum reflectors, beyond the aluminum foil jobs crappie fisherman use, to direct the heat? Or maybe an attachment that will allow a lantern to serve as a hot plate? We can't have all that heat going to waste. Brad, my hunting buddy/ machinist, is looking into it. Misery is the mother of much invention.

***

Most of our really comfortable camps have been in the East Texas Piney Woods. We try to get down there every January for a few days of woodcock hunting. Out of the wind among the short leaf and loblolly pines, we set up a real camp complete with a big fire pit and sheltered cooking/eating/loafing area. Jay, the most maniacal camper I know, declares every East Texas camp "the best camp we've ever had." His enthusiasm is infectious, and I inevitably catch myself prancing around singing and whistling ridiculously.

A few years ago Jay and I arrived to a cloudburst in the Angelina National Forest. I locked in the front wheels, and we slogged along the logging roads toward the designated hunter camp, a camping area set aside for deer hunters. It was a garbage dump; at least fifty cigarette butts per square foot; beer cans, plastic sheeting, fried chicken buckets. I can't begin to describe it. (Why do so many otherwise conscientious people forget that cigarette butts are trash?) Several campers had used roofing felt as ground cloths and evidently felt no need to carry it out when they left.

Fortunately, after deer season, you can camp nearly anywhere in the national forests in Texas. We found a nice secluded spot well off the important logging roads.

The rain had slowed to a drizzle when we began making camp. Heidi, Molly, and Shatzi set off in search of mud holes to run through. We set up Jay's little two-man backpacker's tent since my tent had recently been destroyed by High Plains wind. Jay was still inside laying out pads and sleeping bags when Molly and Shatzi came out of the woods running side by side, growling and snapping at each other. Both are dominant bitches, and each thoroughly despises the other. They ran on, heading straight for the open door of the tent, oblivious to everything except their desire to kill one another. I saw the whole thing setting up, but to save my life, I couldn't utter a word. With a final burst of speed the two wet, filthy hounds ran snarling and snapping into the tent and right on top of poor Jay.

There was a shrill scream of surprise and a sudden bulge at the back of the tent. A peg holding one of the guy lines popped out, and Jay growled with a fervor that could bring tears to the eyes of a displaced Kentucky boy: "Heeeyah, get outta heeyah!" Then came *Whap! Whap! Whap!*

The two combatants rolled out of the tent and scattered into the woods.

Just after dark Jay and I sat at the camp table beneath our nylon tarp. The rain had started again, and we'd periodically stand up and poke the middle of the tarp so the gathered rainwater would gush off the sides. The temperature had plummeted after sundown, but fire building was a hopeless proposition in the downpour. I sat bundled in my down jacket and stocking cap; Jay wore his venerable dusty, sweat-stained Fedora and was still in shirt-sleeves. We had the coffee on, and Jay had already belted down several mugs of hot chocolate and was working on another. Our camp was pitch black save for the stove's two flames; Brad had the lanterns and wasn't due for another two hours.

Jay took a big gulp of the hot cocoa and looked up at the sagging tarp. "You know," he said with contented smile, "I believe this is the best camp we've ever had."

***

But I best remember the bleak camps. On the High Plains or in the Chihuahuan Desert, wind can make a tent more trouble than it's worth. Hunting season in both regions is also the dry season, so you can throw down a ground cloth, pads, and sleeping bags and sleep under the stars with virtually no worry of rain.

The first thing you realize the next morning when you crawl out of the sleeping bag is that a tent holds a surprising amount of body heat; getting dressed out in the open at daybreak in January is a chilly affair.

But tentless camps are marvelously simple, and at the right place at the right time, lying in your bag and looking up at the

photo by Henry Chappell

firmament, it's hard to imagine camping any other way. The wind's more or less steady moan is vastly more conducive to sleep than incessantly flapping tent walls. You go to sleep looking at the heavens, and if you position yourself right, you open your eyes to the sun rising over distant mountains or prairie horizon.

We camped tentless for five nights in a desert canyon a couple of winters back. The wind battered us constantly in some of the bleakest, starkest, most God-forsaken and beautiful surroundings imaginable. A few months later Brad and I sat at his kitchen table looking at slides from that trip. He handed me a slide that showed me hunkered over the Coleman stove, stirring something in my iron skillet. I was sitting on a dog food bucket, and the stove sat out of the wind against the front driver-side tire. The background was completely dark; the only light came from a pair of lanterns: one on another dog food bucket, the other on the ground next to me. I had on my old army surplus wool sweater and stocking cap pulled down over my eyebrows. My face and hands looked shockingly pale in the lantern light.

I held the slide up against the late afternoon light streaming through the kitchen window, and Brad said, "That slide pretty well sums it up, doesn't it?" I nodded and thought, That was the best camp we've ever had.

Snipe Hunt

 As always, a touch of relief comes when I turn right onto the unpaved road. The moon sits high and nearly full in the eastern sky tonight, five nights before winter solstice. In the rearview mirror, I see the new subdivision entrance, bright, brash, neat, and sterile on what had been native blackland prairie. Before me, though, elms form a tunnel over the narrow road, and fog from the creek bottom hangs low over the hay fields to either side.

Over the creek, past the interesting stone fence along the road to my left, up the hill, finally, to the wooden steps that go over the old barbed-wire fence. Just ahead, a locked gate bars entrance into the back of yet another subdivision. I ease the truck off the road, find the flashlight and leash beneath the passenger seat, and step out into the fog—cool, wet, and heavy against my face and in my lungs. I smell wet, earthen decay. Heidi and Molly whine and beat their docked tails against the sides of their kennel and frantically paw at the doors.

Heidi first. The instant I free the latch, she noses the door open and dances, every muscle quivering, onto the lowered tailgate. Two unsuccessful tries at slipping her bell collar over her bobbing head, and I snap at her. The gentle lady's tail slows a bit; she holds her head perfectly still. I slip her collar on and lay my face against her graying muzzle. Her bell tinkles softly as

photo by Henry Chappell

she sniffs my hair. I'm forgiven. She hops lightly off the tailgate and sits, ears pricked toward the creek bottom.

The suburban tension, bordering on despair, that nearly kept me home is with me still. The kennel shakes. I brace myself for Molly. She explodes from the door, all chest, neck, and rippling flanks, eyes looking past me through the fog. Expletives are useless. I grab the hide on the back of her neck and force her bell collar over her head. She wags her tail furiously even as the collar pulls her facial skin so taut that her eyes become slits. Collar in place, she leaps from the truck, bowls Heidi over, and then sits smartly while I fasten the kennel doors. Both dogs' tails sweep back and forth in the gravel.

On the release command they bolt under the fence and sprint up the hill to the north, running more than hunting. I climb the wooden steps and start up the hill. I can feel the coolness of the wet, ankle-high prairie grass through my leather topped rubber boots. My jeans will very shortly be wet above my knees. Brass dog bells tinkle a hundred yards away on the hilltop. Even under the full moon, I can see no more than twenty yards in this dense, cold, wet fog. I draw as much as my lungs will hold and try to ignore the hysterically barking dog and the spotlight in the backyard across the road. The creek bottom looks dark and inviting.

We are on a hundred acres of blackland prairie owned by a local conservancy and left accessible to anyone who will treat it with care and respect. Bounded to the north by a golf course and the south and east by an expanding subdivision, this tiny plot is a peephole into North Central Texas's prairie past. A flowing creek along the western boundary provides swimming depth pools for the dogs. Shelter belts of elm, bois d'arc, and honey locust provide edge habitat, shade, variety, and shield the eyes from the putting green and spanking new two-story homes across the northern fence. Few people know of this place. I'll do my part to keep it that way.

Bells come at me out of the fog. Then pounding paws, breath, and frantic snuffling combine to sound like *chuff! chuff! chuff!* Both dogs fly by me and down the hill toward the golf course. I whistle and direct them westward toward the creek bottom. Can't risk marring that perfect fairway.

Down the hill, through the shelterbelt, and into the flooded bottom. The dogs are out of sight ahead of me in the fog, splashing in an inch of water. Suddenly, both bells go silent. I whistle, assuming they've stopped to listen for me. Nothing. Perhaps they have found a roosting covey of bobwhites on the dry ground along one of the edges. I hope not. Scattering quail after dark, separating them from the life preserving body heat of their covey mates puts the individual birds at great risk, especially in this wet bottom.

I probe back and forth with the flashlight beam. Nothing but fog, brown grass, and water. I move ahead thirty yards and try again. The beam sweeps across Molly frozen on point, her stub tail straight up, quivering like a tuning fork. She rolls her eyes up at me as I walk by. Ten feet in front of her there are wing beats, a flash of gray feathers, then silence. A meadowlark? I tell Molly to go ahead. She takes a stiff half dozen steps and locks up again. I take another step. *Skrrrt!* At least three more birds flush into the fog. Snipe. No doubt about it. Heading for the coastal marshes, they've stopped in this bottom to rest and feed. Molly moves up and points again. The entire bottom is covered with snipe.

I flush Molly's bird and then sweep the beam looking for Heidi. After five frantic minutes I find her on point near the middle of the field. Two birds go up. She snuffles ahead twenty yards and points again. I realize that Molly's bell has gone silent again as well.

For the next half hour the dogs point and I flush. Snipe are normally impossible for pointing dogs to handle, but tonight they seem reluctant to flush in the darkness and fog. I lose

photo by Henry Chappell

track of their numbers and the number of points. The bottom is ghostly white—fog and grass and water under moonlight. The dogs fly over the grass between points. Steam rises from their wet fur. Nostrils flare; flanks and forelegs tremble under the tension. The little brass bells, surreal, stop, start, fade in and out.

There are just too many snipe; the dogs' nervous systems are on overload. They no longer hear me. I try to call them in and then give up and put them each on a lead and start for the truck. But they are wild-eyed and near uncontrollable. Leashed, they continue to point snipe. I drop their leads and flush the birds and then jerk the dogs back to heel. Finally out of the flooded bottom, we climb the hill toward the entrance. Mud spattered, soaked to the bone, panting happily, tongues lolling from the sides of their mouths, the dogs regard my laughter quizzically. I'm not sure why I'm laughing or what I'm laughing at, but I'm sure I'm going home a changed man. Changed for a few hours at least.

Back at the truck, Heidi and Molly dance and sneeze, shake their heads, and sniff my face and ears. A ring of dried slobber shows white around Heidi's dark brown muzzle. Both dogs flop down in their box and thump their tails against the fiberglass sides. I start for home, soaking wet to my waist, sweating, glasses fogged.

Brightly lit yards. Garish Christmas lights. Are there desperate people behind those windows? Do they know what is outside their doors? Does anyone care about moonlight and fog, wet prairie and snipe? About sanity?

Winging It

The Coleman lantern was the center of my universe, a point of light and heat in the brittle-cold darkness. It warmed my hands and face as I hunkered over it but did nothing for my feet or for my bottom planted on the five-gallon dog food bucket. Despite long underwear, two pairs of wool socks, heavy canvas pants, and hunting boots, the earth was sucking heat from every point of contact with my body. I stamped my feet and watched the coffeepot for the telltale plumes of steam from the spout and the hole in the center of the lid where the glass percolator knob had been before it disappeared in the bowels of my cook box. The camp stove flame did little toward heating the inside of the ice-encrusted tent vestibule. I pulled my stocking cap further down the back of my neck and zipped my down parka clear to the top so that only my eyes and the bridge of my nose were exposed.

Two hours earlier, at four A.M., Brad awoke and announced that we had forgotten to check out after the previous day's quail hunt at Fort Riley Military Reservation. I said something, probably incomprehensible, and dozed off. Then I heard him say, "I guess we'll have a search and rescue fee to pay." I woke up. Brad offered to drive back to the fort and leave a note if I'd get up and get the coffee going. The deserted little state park where we were camped is only a fifteen-minute drive from the fort recreation office, and since the water in the coffee pot was frozen solid (we had filled it the night before knowing full well the five-gallon water jugs would be frozen by morning), we reasoned that he would be back about the time the coffee was ready.

We stepped outside and took in a world covered in ice. We disconnected the dog trailer, and Brad swerved away in the pickup. I had already drank the first pot of coffee and had another going by the time he slid back into camp.

After gorging on sausage and eggs, we appeared promptly at the recreation center to take our lumps. The boys behind the counter laughed, thanked us for the note, and admitted that all that business about search and rescue fees was basically a scare tactic to encourage people to sign out. "We'd have left you out there for a night or two before we'd have sent someone looking for you," one of them said.

Much relieved, we headed for a series of food plots near the fort's northern boundary. The sun was out; the morning was still fresh. Full of fat and cholesterol and wired on coffee, we began to feel that old anticipation creeping back. Then, about five miles up the road, we realized we had forgotten to check in.

***

At some point, or over a stretch of years, perhaps, most of us decide what kind of hunter we'll be. For some, the realization comes gradually in the form of philosophical progression and maturity. For others, it's purely a matter of peer group, economics, and opportunity. There are shooters (as opposed to hunters) who get in line to pay several hundred dollars per day to ride around in a mule-drawn wagon with Spud or Slim or Shorty and shoot liberated bobwhites. A few shooters with real money and connections opt for bona fide quail plantations with wild birds, topnotch dogs, and for all I know, black dog handlers who sing to their charges and staff who address their male guests as Cap'm. If you believe much of what has been written on the subject, this is the ultimate, the pinnacle of upland gunning; for the shooters anyway. Hunting in the grand tradition and all that. I wonder.

The more pragmatic types (or maybe they haven't read Nash Buckingham) opt for a Texas quail rig, guide, and army of big-running dogs. Also, there are the travelers ever keen for world class sport, and then variations and hybrids of all of the above. Well down the socioeconomic scale are the season lease hunters, the preserve hunters, the day-lease hunters, and somewhere near the bottom, my group—the hard cases, broke, cheap, or both—who hunt on public land and shamelessly impose on friends and acquaintances for free access to private land.

And beyond economics, some of us prefer to yell at our own dogs, clean our own birds, sleep on the ground, cook our own meals, and wash our own dishes. The Charlie Waterman fans among us know we're in good company.

At times, though, guides can be indispensable, especially the good ones who genuinely like people and who not only are willing to find targets for you but to teach you as well. I would be a better fly fisherman if I would occasionally hire a competent guide instead of flogging the water in various rivers and putting down fish because I'm too pigheaded and cheap to take advantage of available local knowledge.

What makes me shun guided hunting? Insecurity, mostly. I feel pressure to perform when someone I'm paying gets me into birds. No one wants to be an incompetent sport. And this: No matter how solicitous a guide might be, he's not your buddy. Yes, friendships can and do form between guide and sport, especially if the two hunt together often. In general though, being nice to you is the guide's job. He might love his job; he might genuinely like you. But the fact remains: *You* are his job for the trip. He's there because you paid for his services.

And that's perfectly fine. For me though, that financial relationship tends to form a barrier and a distraction. Of course that's my problem not the guide's, but there it is.

Then there are the financial realities. I can make a couple of guided hunts per year or I can hunt whenever I have time or even when I don't have time but want to bad enough to go anyway. But I can't do both. I would probably shoot more birds on two or three guided hunts on private land than I do in an entire season of public land hunting. Same with fishing. But if pounds of meat per outing were the objective, I'd hunt at a shooting preserve. I did that once, but that's another story.

Somewhere along the way my close circle of hunting friends and I settled into a regimen of public hunting mixed with the occasional day lease or invitation to hunt on private land. We're homebodies basically; we hunt quail in West Texas and woodcock in East Texas, unguided and over our own dogs. A few years ago Brad and I began a yearly tradition of a freelance adventure into new country after unfamiliar birds.

Kansas seemed like a sure bet. Pheasants and greater prairie chickens and our ace-in-the-hole bobwhite quail. We are, after all, adopted plainsmen. Still swaggering from our success in New Mexico, we made the calls, ordered the maps, made a few contacts. A guide? For a pair of pompous, minimalist hard cases like us? Forget it. On the day after Thanksgiving 1997, we loaded dogs, gear, and a week's supply of artery blockage and headed north for the Flint Hills.

***

THE PLAN: Leave home at the crack of dawn; drive six hours north to Wichita; then a few miles east to El Dorado WMA; set up camp; hunt quail that afternoon and all the next day. Then on to Council Grove WMA for a day or so of pheasant hunting before heading north to Manhattan and Fort Riley Military Reservation and several days of quail, pheasant, and prairie chicken hunting. If time allowed, we'd head west to Glen Elder WMA for some really serious pheasant hunting.

Well planned and airtight, we said. All of the wildlife management areas had been highly recommended by a Kansas Wildlife and Parks small game biologist, and according to the literature, spring and summer nesting success had been phenomenal. Our only concern was the Kansas possession limits, which seemed a bit meager by Texas standards. We'd hate to cut the trip short because of a full bag.

***

First stop, El Dorado WMA. Lots of grass, most of it woolly and waist high. A few mature trees and very little low brush that we could see. Of course we were nearing the eastern edge of the tallgrass prairie; we had noticed the increase in tree-lined drainages as we came off of the Oklahoma mixed prairie and into Kansas. But Kansas quail and Texas quail have the same

photo by Henry Chappell

needs, we reasoned. Brad rubbed his beard. "This is supposed to be good, huh?"

"Uh... relatively good, I guess."

"I wonder what *good* is on public land up here?"

"I didn't think to ask."

Brad allowed we could make Council Grove before dark. We picked up Highway 177 and drove into the Flint Hills.

Through Cassoday, the self-proclaimed prairie chicken capital of the world; then into Chase County and over the creeks and by the places William Least Heat-Moon eternized in *PrairyErth*. Roniger Hill; Bazaar; Gladstone; Cottonwood Creek; Strong City. Signs along the road said, KEEP THE GRASSLANDS FREE in opposition to government purchase of Chase County lands for establishment of a tallgrass prairie preserve. Brad grunted at the first sign. But at the second: "Let's unload the dogs and guns and head out across one of these pastures and see just how free these grasslands are now."

The flat-topped Flint Hills rose on either side of us, their shallow soils and plow-breaking Permian shale ensuring the survival of this six million acres of tallgrass prairie, the only sizable expanse that remains of what was once 240 million acres. But in December the tallgrasses (big bluestem and Indian grass) were in little evidence; the uplands looked comfortingly like my familiar mixed prairie with its bunch grasses and ample bare ground. The draws held cottonwood and hackberry and bur oak.

The first thing we noticed about Council Grove WMA was the NO CAMPING sign. Second, the hundreds of acres of milo. Throughout the week hunting in and around milo food plots, I would think of Vance Bourjaily's observation on Iowa hunters in *The Unnatural Enemy*: "Iowa hunters are obsessed with corn. If there are no birds in the cornfields, they consider the situation hopeless." All that standing milo was a bit disconcerting to a pair of rangeland bobwhite hunters, but we reasoned that the birds would be in the milo early and late and would loaf in the bordering woods. Yes, bobwhites are bobwhites. The pheasants would be either in the milo or the really thick stuff along the creek. We'd concentrate on the thick stuff since two hunters couldn't hope to pin a pheasant in 500 acres of row crops. Feeling better, we drove into town for a pizza. Still, I yearned for a nice weedy sage flat, some prickly pear cactus, and a sand plum thicket.

The Corps of Engineers campgrounds around the reservoir were closed for the winter. We considered camping there anyway but decided against risking arrest so early in our trip. We looked the local bed and breakfast operation over but didn't see a good way to slip the dogs up to our room. Fortunately we found a cheap little rat hole that catered to hunters. Brad pitched a squeaky toy for the elderly owner's friendly Chihuahua to fetch while she rang us up and summarized the local pheasant situation: Word was, the management area had been shot out, so perhaps we would be interested in some preserve hunting. Brad and I looked at each other and nodded knowingly. We'd heard that said before in our country. The locals had undoubtedly pronounced the area shot out after a few unsuccessful drives. We thanked her but declined.

Just before bedtime Molly and I were outside looking for a patch of grass, when I noticed a man unloading gear from the storage compartment of an exceptionally nice dog trailer. He said he and his partner were from Michigan and had been coming to the Flint Hills to hunt quail for the past fifteen years. Ruffed Grouse Society and Quail Unlimited decals were prominently displayed on the back of his trailer. He said they hadn't done well the past three days—two or three coveys per day on private land—and they had only moved one covey that day because they had spent the afternoon in an unsuccessful search for a lost dog, a German shorthair bitch. I said I was sorry and wished them luck with their search. The temperature had dropped into the low twenties. I shuddered thinking about a dog out there after dark, alone, hungry, cold, confused. He said, "Hell, I'd have quit looking a lot sooner, but my buddy is attached to that dog. I figure there's no shortage of good dogs."

He went back to his unpacking, and I stood there for several seconds trying to decide if I'd really heard what I thought I heard.

Back in the room, Brad and I studied the ancient gas wall heater. "What do you think?" he asked. "Too early in the trip to die of asphyxiation," I said. We turned the heat off, rolled our sleeping bags out on the bed, put on our long handles, and turned in.

We walked into the local diner the next morning, and there sat the two men who had lost the dog. The man I had spoken with the night before smiled pleasantly and greeted us. I nodded. Brad regarded him coolly and said nothing. We finished our hotcakes and sausage, and on the way out the man wished us luck. I thanked him and hated myself for it while Brad regarded him with an expression most people reserve for pimps and dope dealers. His partner didn't seem to know what to think of us.

Back at the public milo field, we unloaded the dogs, Dee, Buck, and Molly, and like good Texas bobwhite dogs they set off for a thorough search of promising cover in the immediately surrounding counties. A bit of coaxing (ardent whistle blowing and Anglo-Saxon oaths) brought them off of the adjacent private property and back onto the management area.

The weather was perfect: overcast, high thirties, damp. We hunted the edges, the woods, the hills above the creek, and the milo rows parallel, perpendicular, and diagonally. We didn't get so much as a flash point. Our opinion of the local word on pheasants rose considerably.

That afternoon we drove in silence toward Manhattan. After a while Brad said, "At least we didn't have to mess with dog boots."

***

The lady at the Fort Riley Natural Resources Office was apologetic but firm. She couldn't sell us the $13 hunting permits we'd need. We would have to wait until the next morning and buy them at the recreation center, which was closed on Mondays. I said that this restriction wasn't mentioned in any of the literature they'd sent nor in any of the several conversations I'd had with various Natural Resources Office personnel including her. Recent change, she told me. But we could look around if we wanted to as long as we displayed a registration card on the dashboard.

Fort Riley Military Reservation, or simply "The Fort" to locals, was founded in 1853 and is home to the combat units of the Fifth United States Army. Driving along the main drag is like driving through a good-sized town. There are homes, barracks, big stone administration buildings, grocery stores, gas stations, convenience stores, schools, churches, apartment buildings, athletic fields, restaurants, a small corralled bison herd, and, in Junction City just beyond The Fort's southern boundary, an excellent assortment of topless bars. In short, all things required for the fighting man's physical, emotional, and spiritual well-being.

About 68,000 of The Fort's 110,000 acres are managed for multiple use including wildlife management and hunting. Located in the northeastern Flint Hills, The Fort's landscape—rolling mid- and tallgrass hills cut generously with hardwood lined drainages and brushy draws—is varied, interesting, and in some places, ruggedly beautiful. In season you can hunt ducks, deer, doves, quail, pheasant, greater prairie chickens, turkey, wild hogs, and even elk if you draw a tag. There are several hundred acres of wildlife food plots and a couple dozen ponds stocked with bass, bream, and catfish.

The Fort is a godsend to local outdoor types. Unfortunately word has gotten out, and nonresident hunters like me are pouring in by the thousands. Restrictions are surprisingly few: You check in, find out which units are open to hunting that day, follow the state game laws, then check out at the end of the day. You're required to stay at least 200 meters from any soldiers you might encounter in the field, and whatever you do stay out of the *Impact Area*. No problem. For the benefit of the duller sorts, all written warnings concerning restricted areas end with YOU COULD BE KILLED!

We went scouting. To the north we found mostly grass, much of it very thick. To the south, mostly woods. There were some birdy looking draws but nothing I could look at and say with confidence, "There'll be a covey in there." A bobwhite is a bobwhite, I repeated. It struck me that some probably live a lot better than others.

It was nearly dark and spitting snow by the time we started driving tent pegs at deserted Milford State Park. We had found a pleasant spot close to the reservoir with a nice belt of cedars shielding us from wind coming off the water. We were wrestling with the rain fly when the park ranger pulled up to check on us. We expected him to be incredulous that anyone would be tent camping on the Kansas plains in December (we encounter that attitude frequently), but he was pleasant and interested in our little expedition. And he was a bird hunter and Weimaraner man. Better yet, he told us we were camped next to a huge Corps of Engineers wildlife management area and that if we would stop by the office one morning he'd get a map out and put us on birds.

Feeling better, we inhaled two cans of stew, let the dogs run around for a while in violation of the park leash law, then went to bed.

***

Next morning we jumped out of the truck as soon as they unlocked the recreation center doors and ran in to buy our permits. The man behind the counter, a civilian, went over the rules and gave us a few pointers. Hunt the northern half of The Fort for pheasants, the southern half for quail. Always check out at night or be prepared to pay a search and rescue fee. And one final unpublished but inviolable rule: Stay the hell away from The General's horses!

We headed for the southern hills toward a spot that looked promising on the topo map. Brad mused aloud that convoys of HumVees carrying grim-looking camo clad young men leaning on 30-caliber machine guns tend to make one more than a little sensitive to Fort rules and regulations. We parked and let the dogs out just as an M1A1 tank came rumbling up the tank trail that ran parallel to the main road. The commander looked up from his map and waved. We put the dogs on leads, waited for a convoy of camo trucks to roar past, then walked across the road and cast Buck, Molly, and Dee down the hill into a labyrinth of brushy draws and drainages. The light drizzle that had been with us all morning turned into a cold, steady rain. The fusillades on the Impact Area sounded and felt ominously close; I would have sworn that the hills shook whenever the big tank guns fired. Even now, that morning hunt seems a bit surreal.

Almost immediately Molly jumped a four-point buck and took a gleeful ten-minute side excursion. She settled down after being reminded of the local abundance of good switches. The draws had plenty of good bobwhite loafing cover—low briars, blackberry, sumac, plum, and standing herbaceous cover— but I saw very little native food outside of oak mast and occasional patches of stunted ragweed. The open hillsides and flats were covered with bluestem and switch grass too rank for foraging. We found no food plots, lots of deer, and no birds.

The rain picked up further, and we ate a soggy lunch in the truck and watched columns of armored personnel carriers roll by. Another tank stopped in the tank trail. At a range of about forty yards we watched with morbid fascination as the crew slewed the big gun in our direction, the elevation perfectly adjusted to send a round through the passenger window. The turret turned slowly; the muzzle came into view. Was there an instant of hesitation in the slewing, just as we were looking directly down the barrel? Another ninety degrees and the gun pointed directly down the trail. We sat and smiled. I still think they did it for the pure hell of it.

More of the same that afternoon hunting in the hills along tank ruts and among cut-out plywood houses used for ranging practice. Molly pointed a bedded doe but remembered the switches and broke off her chase after a few carefully worded threats from her boss. Water squished in my boots as we circled back to the truck. Neither of us noticed the check-in station on the way out.

Back in camp, the dogs showed little interest in coming out of the trailer. We shoved their food bowls into their compartments and shut the doors. After getting into dry clothes, we huddled in the tent vestibule, wolfed down skillet fried hamburgers, and crawled into our sleeping bags before eight o'clock. The warm bag and dry wool socks felt heavenly. I pulled my stocking cap further down the back of my neck and draped my down parka over my upper body for extra warmth. The low tapping of rain became the solid tick of ice against the tent's rain fly.

***

I sat up at the sight of three bald eagles—two adults and a juvenile—perched in the top of a tree near the road on the shore of Milford Lake. I had been slouching, fighting off drowsiness when I should have been navigating. The park ranger had given us detailed directions to several spots on the management area he said should hold birds. But Brad's truck was warm and my belly was full of a half gallon of the tomato soup we'd had for lunch after another birdless half-day death march at The Fort. The windswept lake looked foreboding as big waters do in winter, and the three inches of snow added very little cheer to the picture. But the sun was out, and the temperature had risen into the low thirties.

We found our first spot, a wind-hammered series of half-acre milo plots along the banks of a big cove. Stands of pines provided a windbreak in places, but the bulk of the time Brad and I had to shout at each other against the wind. And it was a cold wind that hurt my teeth whenever I opened my mouth to shout directions at Molly. But the place looked birdy and, judging from the empty shotgun shells laying about the food plots, really had been at one time.

We hunted anyway. The food plots, the head-high cattails near the water, back in the pines, in roadside ditches, on grassy hillsides. We did manage to flush a few rabbits; the last two tempted me sorely. I love fried rabbit, gravy, and biscuits, but I worked long and hard teaching Molly to ignore bunnies.

As we walked along muddy road back to the truck, Dee began cat-walking toward an open grassy area between two islands of pine. Our shotguns jumped off our shoulders; then we saw what Dee smelled: A line of hunters—four of them I think—walking abreast across the opening. Then we noticed a man a hundred yards up the road standing next to a pickup. He waved. Molly ran ahead to get acquainted. We asked if they were getting any pheasants. He held up a scoped bolt-action rifle. "Deer hunters," he said. "Sometimes we push up a few pheasants. You're welcome to walk along with us. We're driving the pines. They say there are deer in there." We thanked him, declined, and called the dogs to heel.

Just before dark we slogged through ankle-deep mud in a big food plot bordering a brush and timber lined creek. No birds in the brush; none in the milo. The crystal clear sky held little of the day's earlier warmth. I had trouble feeling my gun's safety. Buck and Molly found a nice deep pool in the creek and jumped in for a swim.

We felt better once the potatoes and pork chops were frying. Two lanterns and both camp stoves warmed the vestibule so that we could unbutton our coats and eat in relative comfort. Eight thin breakfast pork chops, dipped in milk, floured, and fried; a skillet full of potatoes, and a pan of beans all washed down with a scalding pot of coffee. After the dishes were done, we let the dogs in for some attention. Brad lit the stove again, and in a few minutes we were scratching the dogs' ears and sipping hot apple cider. Brad said he thought he was good for at least another month of Kansas bird hunting, but he was thinking seriously of firing his guide.

I climbed into the truck and drove off to look for a phone.

***

We planned to hunt greater prairie chickens on Saturday, the last day of the trip, with Chad Richardson, a young biologist and animal damage control expert with the U.S. Department of Agriculture. We hadn't met Chad, but a mutual friend, Texas Parks and Wildlife biologist John Hughes, had asked him to take Brad and me on a chicken hunt at The Fort. I had thought about calling Chad, a Fort regular, earlier in the week to try and squeeze out some inside quail and pheasant information. But I felt I was imposing on him already by expecting him to take a couple of guys he'd never met to his prairie chicken spots. But times were grim; I called him at home and shamelessly unloaded the whole pathetic story. He listened patiently then asked why on earth we didn't call the minute we hit town. "Stop by the office first thing in the morning and we'll see what we can do," he said.

Next morning Chad introduced us to his wife, Karen, a biologist with the Fort Riley Department of Natural Resources. As I shook her hand, it occurred to me that I hadn't bathed in five days and that I might smell like someone who had been living outside with wet bird dogs. But as far as I could tell, we didn't make her eyes water. Chad never gave us a second look.

We laid out our map, and he marked the location of a dozen food plots including several familiar to Karen through her game bird research. He also marked several other likely spots, some for quail, others for pheasants. He said he'd come with us were it not for some feral hog business he had that afternoon and then he'd be up most of the night with a pellet gun taking care of a pigeon problem at a nearby refinery.

We found all of the food plots and not a single game bird. But there were other sights. If you can get away from the roads and tank trails and shut out the mortar and artillery fire, you can find images right out of *PrairyErth*. Lots of old foundations, stone houses even, some of them still intact save for missing roofs; tiny dwellings with narrow doors and that flinty hardscrabble pathos. You look out over the Flint Hills and get bitter about what has been and what could be and chafe at the ugly tank ruts and explosions. But then you ponder the necessary evil of it all and the good fortune to live in a country where you can walk around the better part of a major military reservation with no fear of arrest and summary execution. Or, I suppose you could believe that if the United States would simply lay down her arms, the rest of the world would follow. The various expansionist states and third world despots would come suddenly to their senses, and thousand-year-old ethnic hatreds would cool overnight. Most of Earth's citizens lack the freedom to sue on behalf of endangered species let alone publicly oppose military activity. Just how much does the average Iraqi have to say about chemical weapons development or pollution in the Euphrates River? People with simple answers make me nervous.

But we had come to hunt birds. That night we pulled into a checkout station alongside two other hunters. There were six bobwhites laid out on their tailgate. We exchanged pleasantries, and when we were back in the truck Brad said, "I'll bet they shot all six out of the same covey."

photo by Web Parton

***

It was pitch dark and twelve degrees when we met Chad at the filling station north of The Fort. We shook hands and I thanked him for going to the trouble to take us hunting. "No trouble," he said. "About all I do is hunt and fish." This would be the day. No doubt about it. Chad was all over the local chickens. He had been watching them and knew that several birds flew into a certain food plot every morning just after daylight. As we followed him to the chosen food plot, I mulled over my gunning options. Should I go with my old humpbacked Browning Light Twelve choked improved cylinder or stay with my Beretta and screw in the full and modified choke tubes? This was supposed to be strictly a pass shooting proposition. By December greater prairie chickens are gathered in flocks and are virtually unapproachable. I threw ballistics to the wind and decided to go with the Beretta because I enjoy carrying it.

Just as we were coming to stop, a herd of about thirty elk broke into the open on the other side of the road. After watching them disappear in the hills, we hopped out and began pulling on heavy sweaters, camo parkas, and gloves. Chad looked in the direction the elk had gone and said, "Now there's a sight you don't often see around here." Then Brad noticed a pickup in the middle of our food plot. Two hunters were dressing a cow elk right in the middle of our chicken spot.

Figure the statistics. The state of Kansas issues around ten elk permits per year. Maybe half of those are actually filled, yet one gets filled in the middle of *my* five-acre food plot.

Chad insisted that Brad and I each go ahead and pick a corner and take a stand to watch for incoming chickens (strange things do happen after all). He went to help the hunters load their elk. I went to a back corner, kneeled, cradled my gun, shoved my hands in my parka, and waited. After about fifteen minutes Brad walked over to help with the elk. Feeling guilty, I got up to do the same, but they shooed me away saying they had it covered. Five minutes later two chickens appeared on the horizon, heading straight for us, heading straight for us. I watched, didn't move. A hundred yards out they veered sharply away and into the hills. I stood up and stomped some feeling back into my feet.

Back at the truck, Chad wiped the elk blood from his face and suggested we put the dogs down. He knew the location of several leks and we might actually get lucky. In any case, the time for pass shooting had...well...passed. We put Dee and Molly down and headed for the first lek, a nondescript few acres in the open grassy hills. After some walking, Chad announced that we were close, and sure enough, Molly pointed. Within seconds a half dozen greater prairie chickens were up and gone before we could get within fifty yards of shotgun range. Molly ran up the hill and pointed again with the same result.

I got on the whistle determined to keep her close despite all her genetic predisposition. She swung around nicely and pulled up hard forty yards in front of us. We walked past her, and a large brown game bird flushed right at our feet. I mounted the gun, dimly aware that Chad was screaming Hen! Hen! Hen! But my mind was screaming Chicken! Chicken! Chicken! Swing! Swing! Swing! Fortunately your faithful and experienced outdoor reporter made the connection between the bird's long tail and Chad's desperate warning and stopped his swing, if not his trigger pull, in time to avoid killing a pheasant hen.

More leks; more chickens; all of them way out of range except a pair that flushed twenty feet away alongside a cock pheasant as we staggered along a set of tank ruts with our guns resting on our shoulders.

At one point we saw a coyote, gorgeous in his winter pelage, loping unhurriedly along the spine of a hill. We stopped and watched him, and he looked back over his shoulder at us. Chad didn't have his predator call with him, but he dug though his vest and produced a turkey call. He popped it into his mouth and let go a loud cluck. The coyote stopped in his tracks and turned and stared. Another cluck. We didn't move. The coyote was a statue 150 yards away, burning a hole in us with his stare. After about thirty seconds he turned and casually galloped away without looking back as if to say, "yeah, right!"

After lunch we drove to Chad's secret pheasant hot spot, an out-of-the-way corner of The Fort. On the drive, Chad told me that he grew up in Ohio, joined the army after high school, and fell in love with the Flint Hills while he was stationed at Fort Riley. After serving, he earned a degree in wildlife biology at Kansas State University in Manhattan. "I love these Flint Hills," he told me. "Whenever I've been away, I always start feeling good when I see these hills and the open spaces again. This is my home."

Chad hunts deer, ducks, pheasant, quail, and turkey in season and fishes for walleye the rest of the year. I said that Karen must be an understanding woman. He smiled and said she really didn't know any better. Her father was a government trapper and a maniacal hunter and fisherman. Chad normally hunts with his wachtelhund, Foxy, but felt that a flushing dog might cause a problem among three pointing dogs. Brad and I were disappointed; we had looked forward to seeing our first wachtelhund, which we learned is a versatile German spaniel resembling a Boykin spaniel.

I noticed his gun, a no-nonsense Remington 870 Express chambered for three-inch shells and mostly devoid of bluing and finish. We've all heard the axiom "Beware the man with only one gun." I would add to that: "Beware the man whose one gun looks as though it often doubles as a canoe paddle." I was beginning to feel like a rank amateur.

We stopped at the end of a muddy two-track next to a house with a backyard menagerie—homing pigeons, ducks, geese, emu, guinea fowl, and goats to name a few. Buck bounced out of the trailer and up to the emu pen, tail up and ears back. The huge bird sauntered over to the fence and regarded Buck from a yard away. Buck's tail dropped a bit, and he looked back at Brad for further instructions.

Brad managed to get Buck's attention off the emu and sent him down the hill into a bottom full of reeds and thick grass. Molly had already disappeared somewhere ahead, and Chad, carrying his personal howitzer, jogged ahead to act as a blocker. Several hens and at least one cock boiled out. We had no idea if the dogs flushed them or if they flushed wild when they reached the end of the heavy cover. Chad reported that we pushed out a half dozen cottontails as well.

We pushed on along a brushy creek. Molly pointed a few times, and all of the dogs got birdy, but the birds, including several cocks, flushed well out of shotgun range and, as far as we knew, flew out of the country.

For the final push, Molly and I hunted back to an old railroad bed where we would wait and act as blockers for Chad and Brad as they worked a strip of briars and scrubby trees. Molly sat at heel and shivered and whined as we watched a half dozen cocks flush out of everyone's range and fly across the bottom and over the hill. We could have pursued, but this trip was finished. Finally, Chad dropped a cock. Its momentum carried it over a fence and onto private property, but Dee scooted under the fence and brought in his first pheasant.

Back at the truck, the three dogs pointed a half dozen overstuffed pigeons scratching around in plain sight in the middle of the drive. Brad made sure all three were steady then walked in and chased the birds into something resembling a short flight.

We said our good-byes as darkness came on. Brad gave Chad a set of dog boots to use on his upcoming trip to hunt with us in Texas. We watched Chad pull out onto the highway, and Brad sighed, still leaning on the truck. "Well..." he said, "I guess we'd better get busy cleaning all of these birds."

***

Halfway to Wichita we were well into planning our next adventure. We had narrowed it down to chukar hunting in Idaho or grouse hunting in the southern Appalachians. Brad had never seen a ruffed grouse, and neither of us had seen a chukar, but we had a couple of books and some magazine articles. We'd spend the summer poring over maps, making phone calls, and explaining to incredulous acquaintances that it's no big deal and that we really don't need a guide. By November we'd have our hunting area narrowed down to a few hundred square miles. We figured that should be enough for a good week's hunt.

photo by Henry Chappell

Prairie Grouse,
More or Less

I cannot see them—it's dark still—but I can hear them: *whoom*-whoom-*whoooom*. Even above the wind. *Whoom*-whoom-*whoooom*. The wind abates. Tail feathers rustle, fanning open, shut, open. Then *cack-cack-cack-cack* and the sound of beating wings.

Nor can I see my companion for the morning, a Canadian birder who arrived at the blind fifteen minutes ahead of me. But I can hear him too, whispering that he is working on the gallinaceous birds, that tomorrow he will head southwest for Texas and Davis Mountains State Park to look for Mearns' quail. After that he'll be heading for the Ruby Mountains in Nevada to look for Himalayan snowcock. I've already decided that I like him.

Whoom-whoom-*whoooom*. Like air blown across the mouth of a jug. Or like a bullfrog? I squint, looking through the little window. It is nearly sunrise but overcast and cold on the eastern edge of Kansas's Flint Hills this April morning. The light increases, slowly, imperceptibly, and at last I can see something out there in the bluestem. Opening my day pack, I realize that I left my binoculars in the truck. My new friend hands me his binoculars, and I get my first dim look at *Tympanuchus cupido*, the greater prairie chicken.

Erect pinnae, jet black; jaunty yellow eye combs; inflated air sacs, yellow, ringed with orange; wings down, nearly dragging; black tail fan open like a turkey gobbler's; white pantalooned legs; dark chevroned breast and back. Feet stamping, he moves forward like a wind-up toy. His neck jerks forward; the neck sacs collapse. W*hoom*-whoom-*whooooom.* Another cock flies in from the horizon. They boom and strut then ignore each other. Finally they square off, and I slide forward on my seat, ready for the fight. But where are the hens they're fighting for? A foot apart, the cocks eye each other and posture, stamp their feet five times per second, then about-face as if dueling. "Damn," my Canadian friend whispers. "I thought we were about to see a good scrape."

I glance aside to see my companion for the first time, a short, tanned, fit, middle-aged man who reminds me of a fishing guide. He points out the main lek, or booming ground, sixty yards distant beyond a barbed-wire fence. Sure enough there are nearly twenty birds there—fourteen cocks and three hens as best we can count—and the cocks at the center of the lek are sparring in earnest. The birds right in front of our blind are obviously subdominant; probably chased off the lek by stronger cocks.

Hens come and go, appearing and disappearing on the horizon. A hen joins our two nearby cocks, but after a few minutes she leaves, probably unimpressed. My companion and I pass his binoculars back and forth. The booming seems more urgent now.

A harrier appears over the lek.

I suck in a breath; she hovers just above three birds, dips and misses, wheels, and tries again. The grouse seem completely unconcerned, casually ducking at the last second then continuing the business at hand. After several minutes the frustrated harrier, an elegant female, alights amid her would-be breakfast and is accosted forthwith by three raffish cocks. My

Canadian friend speaks for the harrier: "Hey, I'm here for breakfast not sex."[1]

She drives her suitors away and stands watching. Scheming? *All this poultry! Surely there's a way!* "I'll bet she's whispering in their ears," my friend says. "Just want you all to know I'll be eating your kids in a few weeks." The booming continues. The little hawk swaggers among the grouse, looking them over like a rancher at a cattle auction.

***

Prairie chicken. What an unbecoming name for a grouse. Willa Cather notwithstanding, prairie homesteaders probably had little inclination toward poetry. Imagine someone calling a ruffed grouse a woods chicken. Think about it. *New England Woods Chicken Shooting. An Affair with Woods Chickens. Woods Chicken Feathers.*

Both lesser and greater prairie chickens are also called pinnated grouse because of their pinnae, the thick black neck feathers the cocks hold erect during the courtship display. That's a much better name, far less suggestive of filthy, flightless, hilariously stupid barnyard fowl. Try to approach a pinnated grouse and see how much they remind you of a domestic chicken. You might get within fifty yards before the bird flushes and flies out of sight.

I probably rolled my eyes years ago when I first read George Bird Evans complaining bitterly about outdoor writers calling woodcock timberdoodles. Now I understand. One of *my* birds has a stupid name. "Timberdoodle," at least, sounds cute. Unfortunately, I've called the birds prairie chickens or simply

---

1 Perhaps I seem unnecessarily prurient here. It's possible the cocks were trying to drive the harrier away. Yet considering their arousal, I doubt they were capable of that kind of discernment. Some of you, I suspect, will understand completely.

"chickens" long enough that "pinnated grouse" sometimes sounds pretentious.

***

Of the game birds I've hunted, pinnated grouse most epitomize wildness. John Madson wrote that in all of modern America there is no more lost, plaintive, old-time sound than the booming of the native prairie chicken.

Pinnated grouse are grassland birds in the truest sense; you won't see them hanging around backyard bird feeders. Nor will you find their fat, genetically deficient kin at game farms or on shooting preserves. In general, they fare poorly near human enterprise. Therein lies a serious problem. Unlike pheasants and bobwhites, pinnated grouse can tolerate only moderate grazing and very light agriculture, two of today's most glaring oxymora.

Historically there were two pinnated grouse species and two related subspecies in North America: the greater pinnated grouse or greater prairie chicken (*Tympanuchus cupido*) of the tallgrass prairie and the lesser pinnated grouse or lesser prairie chicken (*Tympanuchus pallidicinctus*) of mixed and shortgrass prairies of the southern Great Plains. An eastern race of the greater pinnated grouse, the now extinct heath hen *(T. cupido cupido)*, lived on the eastern coastal grasslands of New England south to Virginia, while the coastal race, the Attwater's prairie chicken *(T. cupido attwateri)*, inhabited the Texas and Louisiana coastal prairies in staggering numbers.

By 1791 relentless gunning pressure had made heath hens scarce enough on Long Island that hunting was prohibited between April 1 and October 5. But heath hens were tasty, and the demand in the eastern population centers continued. The last heath hen was seen on the mainland in 1869. By the turn of the century only 100 remained, all on a preserve on Martha's Vineyard. The population rebounded slightly only to be beset by a disastrous spring fire in 1916, a wave of migrating goshawks the following winter, and the inevitable genetic problems that go with a tiny population. By 1932 they were gone.

The Attwater's prairie chicken has been in serious trouble for more than half a century. Officially listed by the U.S. Fish and Wildlife Service as an endangered species in 1967, the birds have slid further into the extinction vortex with each passing year. By 1996 there were only forty-two birds left in three isolated populations in Galveston, Colorado, and Refugio Counties in southeastern Texas. No amount of knowledge or modern technology can replace coastal prairie buried under Houston suburbs. Dramatic successes in captive breeding programs at Fossil Rim Wildlife Center, Texas A&M, and the Houston Zoo offer a glimmer of hope. Amazingly, a few carefully conditioned, pen-reared Attwater's hens released in 1996 survived to hatch eggs in 1997.

Still, the birds need a place to live. Small, isolated habitat fragments mean small, isolated Attwater's prairie chicken populations highly susceptible to genetic problems, disease, or a sudden concentration of predators—a wave of migrating hawks, for instance. Habitat problems are being addressed with landowner incentives. By maintaining Attwater's prairie chicken habitat (by not overgrazing or paving or otherwise destroying coastal grassland), a landowner can receive state funds for brush control while remaining free of any responsibility for the birds should they increase in number or move onto the land. More landowner stewardship, I suppose. Drive a species into the extinction vortex then take credit for not finishing it.

Captive breeding probably will save the Attwater's prairie chicken from extinction. Maintaining a truly wild, genetically diverse population is altogether another matter.

***

Greater pinnated grouse are tallgrass prairie birds and as such are holding their own in the one remaining expanse of tallgrass prairie, Kansas's Flint Hills. Holding their own meaning they aren't in serious trouble despite a generally downward trend over the past several decades. They are also hanging on in remnant patches of tallgrass prairie in Oklahoma, Iowa, Illinois, and other eastern prairie states. Sketchy nineteenth-century records suggest that the homesteaders' inefficient agriculture benefitted the birds much as the small patchwork of farms did bobwhite quail, ruffed grouse, and woodcock in the East. The small, scattered fields and inefficient harvest provided winter forage yet left the grasslands effectively unbroken. Greaters appear to have spread northward and eastward into the Dakotas, Ohio, and Indiana, and the transition grasslands of Wisconsin and westward onto the mixed prairie to overlap lesser pinnated grouse range. Their numbers probably peaked around 1880.

Prairie literature is rife with tales of huge flocks of greaters. Homesteaders ate them in lieu of their own domestic chickens; artist George Catlin wrote sheepishly of his participation in a piggish massacre; George Armstrong Custer, predictably, slaughtered the birds with zeal. But with ever increasing human population on the plains, continued market hunting (much intensified due the disappearance of the heath hen in the East), and more efficient agriculture, the bird's range and population had slipped significantly by the turn of the century. The downward trend along with ever more intensive agriculture has continued with disastrous lows during the 1930s drought and occasional modest gains after ideal nesting conditions. Today in the Flint Hills the birds are threatened by excessive burning and double stocking of pastures and general loss of habitat due to development. While fire has always been an important ecological agent, annual burning of pastures to improve grass production for cattle destroys the residual tallgrass nesting cover. Biologists generally recommend burning every third or fourth year.

Nevertheless, greater prairie chicken hunting can be very good in the Flint Hills—emphasis on the word *hunting* as opposed to *shooting*. Finding a flock is one thing; putting a two-bird limit in your vest is another. Modern hunting mortality appears to be in the noise and almost entirely compensatory. But you can bet that if the assault on their habitat continues to the point that the birds get into serious trouble, sport hunting will be held up as the culprit. Legal hunting will end to a huge collective sigh of relief; the assault on the tallgrass prairie will continue, and a mildly interested public and various groups hot on the heels of their next conquest will look back and lament the birds' lack of recovery.

***

On a mid-April morning in 1998, my friend John Hughes, a biologist with Texas Parks and Wildlife Department, pulled off a gravel road and onto a two-track ranch road. Two hundred yards along, he cut his headlights, stopped the truck, and rolled down his window and motioned for me to do the same. I did and the sound that wafted through the open window was unlike anything I had ever heard. *Thoo-up*; *thoo-up*; *thoo-up*; a liquid sound, like water from a leaky showerhead. The birds were very near. We sat in the dark at the very edge of the lek—their courtship display ground—listening to the fanning tails and beating wings. The sky lightened so that we could make out the tops of the Panhandle sandhills and, gradually, the display before us: the bright orange tympanal air sacs filling and collapsing; *Thoo-up; thoo-up*; the dragging wings; the posturing and sparring; the sudden drumming of wings and *cack-cack-cack-cack*; the hens coming and going, scratching unconcernedly about, plucking the occasional seed.

John made his count: twelve cocks and three hens. As we drove to another lek, I thought of the Kiowa-Apaches whose sun dance rituals mimicked the lesser pinnated grouse's courtship display.

***

The lesser pinnated grouse, the greater's western cousin, inhabits the southern mixed prairie in West Texas, western Oklahoma, and Kansas. Shin oak, sand sage, and a mixture of tall-, mid-, and shortgrasses characterize its habitat. Lessers also can be found in pockets on the High Plains shortgrass prairie in West Texas and eastern Colorado and New Mexico in places where the more common tighter soils give way to sandy ground, sage, and shin oak. Lessers feed on insects and greenery, shin oak mast, the seeds of various forbs and legumes, and domestic grain when it's available near habitable grassland.

Like the greater prairie chicken, the lesser benefitted from the homesteader's primitive agriculture, peaking in number around the turn of the century. Railways offering special fares carried chicken hunters into the Texas Panhandle, and ice-cooled railroad cars loaded with obscenely large kills returned to eastern population centers. Light grazing and sparse human population left the grasslands effectively intact, and grain sorghums, stacked and shocked, provided the birds with accessible winter forage. But the trains also brought more settlers and more efficient tools to pulverize the topsoil. Then the dirty thirties brought drought, and millions of tons of flour-fine topsoil left the south plains for the Atlantic Ocean. The true grasslands were disappearing and lessers were shot wherever they were found. In his 1963 *Journal of Wildlife Management* article "The Lesser Prairie Chicken in Colorado," Donald Hoffman brings the 1940s mind set into focus:

> A flock of 17 prairie chickens was observed in the early 1940's by a resident of Las Animas, Colorado, near the site of Keller, located approximately 3 miles east and 2 miles south of Las Animas in Bent County. This flock was reportedly shot out by hunters and none have been reported in this area since.

By 1937 the birds were all but gone in Texas, and the state legislature halted legal hunting. A two-day season was opened in 1967 after surveys indicated the population had rebounded sufficiently in a few Panhandle counties, but the birds have never really recovered in any sense of the word.

As I write this, the U.S. Fish and Wildlife Service is considering a petition by the Biodiversity Legal Foundation out of Boulder Colorado to list the lesser pinnated grouse as a threatened species. Most of the principals believe the petition is a shoo-in. Although Texas has a stable population in the northeastern corner of the Panhandle, and the 1998 surveys showed a significant gain, the birds are doing poorly over most of the rest of their range. New Mexico and Oklahoma have already suspended their lesser prairie chicken seasons. If the USFWS rules in favor of the petition, all legal hunting for lessers will be suspended, even though there appears to be no scientific reason to suspend hunting in Texas.

From a broader perspective, a threatened species listing could force the U.S. Forest Service and other agencies to take the prairie chicken's needs into account in their grazing plans. Countless species, game and non-game alike, would benefit. And the attention drawn by the petition alone will undoubtedly benefit the birds across their range. All things considered, a suspension of a two-day, two-bird-per-day season seems a small price to pay for the benefits gained from a federal listing. Push me into a corner and I'll admit that I support it, very cautiously.

Yet there's a gnawing concern among hunters and wildlife managers that some so-called conservation groups are loudly backing the petition because they see it as a tool for ending lesser prairie chicken hunting. Even more troubling, some mainstream conservation groups normally unopposed to legal hunting seem to believe that a moratorium on hunting will help the birds significantly. Should the birds eventually recover, the most militant and litigious groups will fight delisting to the bitter end. And for one reason: They don't want the birds hunted.

Lessers are in trouble because their habitat has been chopped into small parcels. They're big country birds; you can raise a covey of bobwhites on your back forty, but you'll need around 5,000 acres to raise a small flock of prairie chickens. Ending Texas's two-day hunting season will accomplish nothing.

Still, I hunted lesser prairie chickens this past October with mixed emotions.

***

There are three methods for hunting pinnated grouse: pass shooting birds as they fly into leks or grain fields, hunting on and around leks, or simply covering ground in likely habitat. The latter is a needle-in-the-haystack proposition. Last season a good friend of mine hired a quail guide and spent a day riding

photo by Henry Chappell

photo by Henry Chappell

over the plains in a quail rig looking for lessers. The guide ran eleven pointers into the ground in about eight hours. They moved over thirty coveys of bobwhites and no grouse. Late that afternoon my friend shot a lesser hen as it flew into a milo field. The guide had seen a few lessers around and evidently thought he could find them by simply covering ground. Possible perhaps, but not likely given a density of several hundred square miles per bird.

Pass shooting grain fields can be effective if you've done your homework and know which fields the birds are using. I suspect that most of the chickens taken each year are shot as they fly into grain fields or leks.

Conventional wisdom holds that pinnated grouse can't be worked successfully with pointing dogs, and like most conventional wisdom this particular piece is only partially valid. I've found that late in the season greaters will often hold for pointing dogs but will flush out of shotgun range. I saw the behavior time and again hunting with Chad Richardson in Kansas. Molly would point, the birds would hold; we'd start toward her only to have the birds flush before we got within fifty yards. I find that surprising; it seems to me that given the constant coyote threat, the birds would be especially sensitive to the presence of any canine. Monte Whiting suggested that adult birds might not consider a coyote, or any canine for that matter, a serious threat. Humans afoot definitely spook them. A close working pointing dog or a flushing dog might be more effective, although I suspect that if the dog stays within shotgun range, the birds will hold for neither dog nor hunter.

But young prairie chickens will hold, I'm told, and Kansas has an early greater prairie chicken season for the benefit of pointing dog people. In recent years the season has run from mid-September to mid-October, and I've been sorely tempted. But thus far the thought of hunting juvenile birds in miserably hot weather has kept me away. Then again, many of the bob-whites I take every November, especially after late summer rains have broken a drought just in time to salvage the year's quail production, are peepers only slightly larger than an English sparrow. If only legality solved ethical conundrums. Hopefully I'll have this sorted out before September.

In any case, if you're going to hunt your birds as opposed to pass shooting them, you had better know the location of a few leks. Pinnated grouse cocks, both greater and lesser, are tied to the leks year round. Hens and juveniles are much more widely disbursed outside of the courtship season. Lesser pinnated grouse leks typically are open areas, islands with tighter soils which favor shortgrasses as opposed to the surrounding sandy uplands which favor mid- and tallgrasses. Greaters use similar areas—open hillsides and swales—on the tallgrass prairie. The birds are typically on or near the leks early and late in the day. Here's the rub. When the birds are exposed on the open lek, they can see you coming and aren't about to hang around while you stroll into shotgun range. But if you can catch them in the taller grass just outside the lek, you have half a chance. Sometimes.

***

Kevin Mote and I had just let Molly out in a sea of sandhills just north of the Canadian River in the northeastern corner of the Texas Panhandle when she locked up on a shortgrass flat that to my eye wouldn't hide a grasshopper. Kevin and I started after her at a jog while I groped in my vest pocket for shells. It was mid-October and cold; Molly's breath formed a cloud around her head as she stood her birds. We were still forty yards away when I closed my over/under and three crow-sized grouse flushed cackling and banked with the wind, their pale undersides whitened by the sun as it cleared the low hills.

Two of the three flew until they disappeared miles distant; another seemed to alight behind a nearby sandhill. We followed, and just beyond the hill, Molly pointed a tangle of sand plum. Kevin went left, I went right, and a huge covey of bobwhites, still two weeks out of season, blew out of the thicket. I mounted my gun without thinking while Kevin, a biologist with the Texas Parks and Wildlife Department yelled, "Don't shoot!" I didn't, and Molly, wild-eyed, foaming, and oblivious to my whistle, snorted off into the hills to look for the singles. We never found that other prairie chicken.

We had given up on that first bunch of grouse and were on our way to another lek when Kevin suggested that I try running Molly without her bell or beeper collar. I did and we started getting shots all of which we blew miserably. Lessers are deceptively fast, and even when they hold, they still flush well out of improved cylinder range. Kevin and I were both carrying our light bird guns, mine a twenty-gauge Beretta with the full and modified tubes and Kevin's a Remington 870 choked modified. A twelve-gauge choked improved modified or full with a heavy load of number six shot would have been about right. I lost a cripple and still cringe when I think about it, and Kevin's yellow Lab, Lorie, brought in another hard-hit bird only after a desperate chase.

By late morning the temperature had risen into the sixties. Molly was gimpy from a high-speed collision with a barbed-wire fence. The cottontail made it under; Molly didn't. We were working our way across a lek that happened also to be a prairie dog town, the perfect place for prairie rattlers. Molly had her head in a prairie dog burrow when two chickens flushed at the edge of the lek. We emptied our guns then watched the birds disappear on the horizon. Kevin said we must have been distracted by thoughts of rattlesnakes. A few minutes later, after Molly pulled up high and hard on a box turtle, I began to suspect that she had lost a bit of focus.

Of all the ranches I've hunted, this one, a huge Hemphill County spread, most exemplifies landowner stewardship. And it's a working ranch complete with cattle and gas and oil wells. Many of the leks we hunted were documented in the 1940s; who knows how long they've been used? Perhaps the Kotsoteka—the Buffalo Eaters—the Comanches, who for two centuries laid claim to this country just north of the Canadian River, once listened to courtship booming on these same leks.

Once when we stopped to admire a nice stand of sand bluestem—the predominant sandhills tallgrass—Kevin swept his hand across the horizon and said that what we were looking at was probably as close to pre-settlement mixed prairie as any rangeland left in Texas. Sand bluestem and Indian grass grew in the swales, little bluestem in the sandy uplands, and buffalo grass and gramas on the tighter soil. Early and late in the day columns of pronghorn antelope sauntered along the fence lines, and harriers hovered just above the grass while the larger raptors worked the prairie dog towns.

By the time we finished lunch, rattlesnakes were lying in the roads, so we left Lori and Molly whining in their box and struck out across the hills for a remote lek that Kevin was sure would hold birds. I followed stiffly and tried to ignore the dime-sized blisters on my big toes. I have no idea how he found the lek without a GPS. For that matter I've never understood how anyone finds the same place twice in the middle of an ocean of sandhills. The lek was empty, but we began flushing chickens in the surrounding midgrass. Kevin flushed a pair along the top of a low hill and dropped a beautiful fully pinnated male. Thinking that the birds might be holding around the hilltops, Kevin offered to switch places with me. I went high; he went low, took about ten steps, and flushed and dropped another chicken. Kevin was pocketing his lesser and apologizing when I flushed two birds, missed, and watched them fly a half mile to alight on a sage covered hillside.

We were walking along the hillside, sweating profusely, when Kevin pointed out a racer coiled about the base of a clump of sage and mentioned that we were in a fine place to find a rattlesnake. I was too hot and tired to care. I had just eased my gun into a nice comfortable cradle carry when a chicken flushed right at my feet and flew straight away. I'm sure I looked a little spastic, but I caught him with the second barrel. Kevin ran up the hill and picked up my bird, a male with exceptionally long pinnae. We stroked the bird's dark chevrons and fingered the orange air sacs, and I felt I was holding something from another time and that something very real and important had just passed.

Next morning broke sunny, windy, and cold. I left my gun in the truck and carried a camera. The plains were making weather; the gusts laid the grass nearly flat, and a sullen band of clouds formed on the horizon to the northwest. Lori flushed a bird from a hill above a big lek. Kevin dropped it cleanly and Lori brought it to hand. The sun was barely up, and though we had planned to hunt the rest of the day, there was finality in Kevin's last shot. He unloaded his gun and announced that he had shot enough prairie chickens for one season. A few steps later, we flushed three more birds from a hillside and watched them bank and glide and finally disappear among the grassy contours.

***

Turn north on U.S. Highway 83 in Childress in the southeastern corner of the Texas Panhandle and drive parallel to the Oklahoma border. The country you will see on either side of the road is primarily rough, badly overgrazed mesquite and cedar uplands with much snakeweed and very little grass. Continue north. Cross the Salt Fork of the Red River. You'll see more of the same. Northward still, you'll drive out of Collinsworth County and into Wheeler County, through the little town of Shamrock then across the North Fork of the Red. Shortly thereafter but prior to the town of Wheeler you will drive abruptly out of the mesquite and into a country of rolling midgrass hills and modest buttes, true mixed prairie, the country most likely to be the lesser prairie chicken's last stronghold.

But the mesquite line is creeping northward. Lessers once inhabited the entire rolling plains ecological region, parts of the Edwards Plateau (Central Texas), and the western Cross Timbers region—basically the entire Panhandle plus the remaining northwestern quarter of the state perhaps as far east as Fort Worth and as far south as Austin. Then came the mesquite invasion, which probably played as big a role in the lesser's extirpation as unscrupulous hunting and conversion of rangeland to cropland. Today in Texas, of the original 50 million or so acres of lesser prairie chicken habitat, no more than 800,000 acres remain in scattered parcels in the northeastern corner of the Panhandle and another 350,000 acres remain on the southern High Plains near Lubbock. The High Plains population is dwindling as the local agriculture changes from grain sorghums to cotton.

The popular explanation for the mesquite invasion is that the seeds were carried out of South Texas by longhorn cattle and disseminated in their droppings on the long drives to Kansas. Perhaps. Kevin, who did his graduate work in range management, tells me that mesquite was probably present on the South Plains all along but was kept in check by fire, bison activity, and the large numbers of browsers. But with settlement came fire suppression and heavy cattle grazing, which raised the soil temperature and abetted germination of the mesquite seeds.

In any case, lesser pinnated grouse cannot survive on mesquite and cedar infested prairie. Although they require some low brush—preferably shin oak or sand plum—for screening and thermal cover, mesquite and other invaders overrun leks, provide approach cover for predators, and interfere with the birds' explosive flush.

On the other hand, pastures can be too immaculate. Those soothing unbroken bluestem pastures come at a high price, both in the chemicals required to remove the sand sage and the lessers that lose this essential screening and thermal canopy.

If lesser prairie chickens eventually dwindle to captive-bred populations, ignorance, greed, and our own lack of resolve, rather than hunting pressure, will be the culprits.

***

In the Texas Panhandle, there are two names synonymous with game bird management in general and lesser prairie chicken recovery and management in particular. Pick up any highly regarded paper on South Plains game bird management and you will see their names; if one or the other is not the author, then their work will be sited in the bibliography. The late A.S. (Jack) Jackson and Richard DeArment, both field biologists throughout their careers with Texas State Game, Fish and Oyster Commission (known more recently as the Texas Parks and Wildlife Department), were there in the beginning when no one really had any idea how many prairie chickens were left in Texas. And it was their survey data that justified the reopening of the two-day October hunting season.

I had seen their neat, accurate lek survey maps: A.S. Jackson's 1941 sketch on onionskin and Dick's later map sketched on the back of a Commission sign warning polluters of a $1,000 fine for allowing waste oil to collect near watercourses. Somewhere in the files at Canyon or Canadian, I'm told, is another of Dick's lek survey maps, this one sketched on the back of a wedding invitation. Most of the leks are still active. When Texas Parks and Wildlife Department renewed its survey efforts in response to the threatened species petition, these half-century-old maps guided biologists two generations removed to birds most lifelong South Plains residents never see.

A week ago I had the privilege of spending most of a morning with Dick DeArment at his home in Wheeler. John had described him as a lovable bear of a man; an apt description of Dick, now seventy-nine with a full head of white hair and dark eyes and those huge hands and the thick neck and shoulders suggestive of a man quite powerful in his younger days. We sat in his living room, and between assurances that he'd get to the *really good lies* directly, he summarized his life from his days as a bird loving Pennsylvania boy locked in grim combat with the English sparrows that were forever trying to take over his bluebird houses, to his first two years in the wildlife management program at Texas A&M; then World War II and his stint as a B-24 pilot making bombing runs into Austria and southern Germany; then two more years at A&M on the GI bill; and then a masters degree at Oklahoma State. He went to work for the state of Oklahoma and then in the mid-1950s Texas got a real bargain.

"I knew the boys in Texas; I had been doing prairie chicken work in western Oklahoma," he said. "They offered me a fifty-dollar-per-year increase. I said 'I'm your man!'"

I asked him about his efforts to reestablish a prairie chicken hunting season.

"We caught a lot of flak early on from the bird lovers. I'd have felt the same way if I hadn't been a wildlife man. [Throughout our talk he never once referred to himself as a biologist. He and Jack were 'wildlife men.'] But we showed them the census data and we never had a bit of trouble after that. We always emphasized that any game animal has a surplus that can be safely hunted and that prairie chickens are no exception. The hunt went fine; we had check stations and really worked those birds over; weighed and sexed them; opened their crops and took food samples; got all the data we possibly could—far more than we'd have ever gotten otherwise. We showed the Auduboners the data and they supported us."

I asked him about his association with the world's most famous bird lover.

"Roger Tory Peterson...a wonderful, wonderful man. He wanted to see a lesser prairie chicken. I took him out to the West Ranch[2] and he brought autographed copies of his books and gave them to all of us. Oh the Wests were thrilled. He sketched the chickens and made notes on their colors. He was a remarkable person."

Dick still occasionally takes people out to watch the courtship display. "Oh I still get calls from all over occasionally from as far away as Europe," he said. "But what amazes me are all the people right here in Wheeler County that have lived all their lives surrounded by prairie chickens and have never seen one. I'll take them out and they're absolutely astounded; they'll say they never would have believed it if they hadn't seen it with their own eyes."

He launched into an imitation of a prairie chicken cock, stamping his feet and dragging his arms. "Those males will spar

2   I've changed the name here for the sake of the rancher's privacy and the birds' security.

and bluff and strut, but you let a female fly into the lek and they go crazy, just working and working and fighting. 'For god's sake lady will you please pick one us?'" He laughed. "But in the end the females do all the work, laying and incubating the eggs and raising the broods. All the cocks are good for is strutting, fighting, and breeding."

How do the hens pick a mate?

"It's those bright yellow eye combs. The hen will stare at those eye combs, and finally the old cock will wink at her." He laughed again. "I have no idea how they pick them. Nobody does. I guess they pick the one that struts the best."

What about the ranchers and farmers he worked with?

"I was never refused access. And I made so many friends over the years. I count the ranchers and farmers among the finest people I've known. The really good ranchers, those closest to the land, were always good wildlife people. I'd ask, 'Do you know how many fawns an antelope typically has?' He'd say, 'I'm not sure but I've noticed that they usually have twins.' Or a rancher would say to me, 'You know I think there must be more chickens and deer this year than last.' And I'd say, 'You're right; production is up this year.' I never met a landowner I didn't like."

Dick's wife, Jerene, came in and brought an 8 x 10 black-and-white photo of Dick, middle-aged and sweaty in his uniform, cooling his feet with water from a garden hose. A typical day at the office. The subject turned to A.S. Jackson. The mirth left Dick's eyes. He stared out the window and sat forward on the couch and rested his big hands on his thighs. "Jack was a special man; a brilliant field man and a superb writer. He looked small and frail, but he could walk the pants off you and enjoyed doing it."

Did he ever outwalk Dick?

"Absolutely not! I would never have let that happen. But I nearly died a few times keeping up with him."

Then the stories poured out: the years of literally living in the field with their birds; their failed attempt at establishing red legged partridge in Palo Duro Canyon; the thousands of hours spent in prairie chicken blinds and the things they'd seen; the bulls that warily sniffed their blinds while Dick planned his escape; the rough camps in remote country and Jack's battered tent and sleeping bag that he refused to get rid of.

His favorite bird?

"Oh I loved them all," he said. "But the lesser prairie chicken is the most unique; it's a wonderful, wonderful bird."

***

My new friend the Canadian and I pass his binoculars back and forth. The cocks are still booming although they seem less frantic now in full daylight. The harrier goes aloft and tries again for a grouse breakfast. She hovers and lunges, misses and tries again, but the grouse casually avoid her. After a few more unsuccessful tries she alights again among them. The birds are barely moving now, standing as if exhausted from the morning's exertion. Even the harrier stands torpidly.

For the first time I notice the water tower a mile or so distant and beside it mercury vapor lamps still burning at what appears to be some kind of industrial or commercial site. I worry for these birds; however, it's not the harrier that concerns me.

A Chronicle

The green hanging folder is labeled "Dog File" in my mother's handwriting. It was one of the few files left intact after burglars took a crowbar to my father's locking file cabinet. They took his coin collection, my grandfather's pistol, and a bit of cash my mother had locked up for safekeeping. They also stole my father's guns from his gun cabinet: a twelve-gauge Browning A-5 chambered for three-inch shells, an old .300 Weatherby Magnum that he carried all over North America, a twenty-gauge model 1100 he bought for my mother, and another half-dozen or so guns given him by family and friends. They would have taken his battered, blueless Browning Light Twelve, his bird gun, had it not already been stolen from the cab of my brother's pickup.

Thieves took a good portion of the material things left over from an important slice of my father's life, but they really didn't get much. The stories are still there, many of them recorded unselfconsciously in the Dog File, a chronicle more accurate than any shooting log because it was never meant to be read. Mom kept it because Mom keeps things. You never know when you might need a letter written to a dog trainer in 1957.

The stories are there all right, in yellowed photos and bits or correspondence, pedigrees, and registration slips. But some fill-in is required, so I take the stack as it was gathered from my

mother's den floor after the break-in and arrange it in chrono-
logical order....

***

I'm about to step into a minefield. Perhaps you're already
cringing. Edward Abbey wrote that there is a kind of poetry in
simple fact. My father's papers represent simple facts, but like
Abbey's desert, even the smallest slice of a complicated man's
life spreads far beyond the limits of language. Yet a writer tries
nonetheless. If something matters, then it's worth some risk.
And if a piece of a man's life doesn't matter, then what does? I'll
take my chances.

***

Dad started poorly. The envelope at the top of the stack is
postmarked March 8, 1956. Addressed to J. F. Chappell Jr.,
Harlan, Kentucky, from a Weimaraner breeder in Texas, it holds

pedigrees with stout German names and two pages of the kind of rubbish that nearly discredited the entire breed:

> ...the most exclusive, smartest, kindest most adaptable and best all purpose dogs in America today... have proven outstanding on waterfowl, also as trail hounds, seeing-eye dogs, cattle dogs... "vacuum cleaners of the field..."

Then there are quotes from proud owners:

> ...at six months he pointed anything with feathers ...at seven months he was the best gun dog I ever saw ...

You wonder how many gun dogs he'd seen. There's more:

> ...took my five month old pup to the field just for the first outing... he picked up signals and commands by watching the other pointers... is worth more as a gun dog than all of my high-bred pointers combined ...the pointers literally turned the retrieving over to Axel [the pup]... is staunch on point and is a finished dog already.

My father was a trusting soul. "Had to have him one of them German dogs," my mother says. The AKC registration certificate for a silver behemoth named Duke is dated November 20, 1956. The very next piece of paper in the folder is the name and address of a professional trainer in London, Kentucky, followed by letters from the same, expressing doubt about Duke's potential as a gun dog. Dad never shot a bird over Duke, who spent his life as a beloved pet, napping, terrorizing the help at drive-in restaurants, and resting his muscular seventy pounds against my mother while she picked beans in the garden.

I have no recollection of Duke; he was four years older than me, but I know him through the stories and old home movies, one of which shows me at three, pulling with all my might to free my Easter basket from a gentle gray dog with shoulders high as my head.

***

Next, a paperback copy of *Practical Education of the Pointing Dog*, by J. A. Sanchez Antunano. Price $2.50. I'd give twenty bucks just for the photos and captions: the author in his white jacket, bow tie, and Panama hat educating one of his "apt pupils"; pointers dropping to their bellies at the flush; pointers and setters sitting to deliver Yucatan quail, after they've been properly force-trained to hold a corncob; and page after page featuring an "educator" wearing a jacket, tie, and Fedora and demonstrating the proper use of the famous JASA force collar. A good book, probably as good as anything out there today. (The author gets on my good side right off the bat by referring to long-tailed pointers as "American pointers.") I have to smile at the quaint photos and genteel prose (there's a chapter entitled "Implements Necessary for Training") and I wince at the harsh methods, but I wonder what Señor Sanchez Antunano would think of so many of today's allegedly finished dogs wearing shock collars in the field.

***

My mother is certain that two registration certificates are missing, probably lost in the aftermath of the break-in. She is certain because as a newlywed, she had the pleasure of sharing her bed with two pointer puppies. She assures me in no uncertain terms that she is not imagining this. My parents married in August 1957 and moved into the third floor of the Central Kentucky Motor Lodge where they lived for four months while their house was being finished.

About two weeks after their wedding, Dad slipped up the fire escape with a brace of just-weaned pointer pups. A bit later, with my mother finally quieted and the pups secure in their cardboard box, the newlyweds turned in for the night. Naturally the pups cried until they were snug between their new owners. Over the next several weeks the pups went to work with my father, who was in charge of the Campbellsville branch of the family dairy. Rank has its privileges. Fortunately, Dad's office was uncarpeted.

Trouble resumed that winter when my father's annual week long bird hunting expedition to eastern Kentucky spawned the incident that my mother refers to as "The Time I Almost Ran Over Your Daddy." Mom, twenty-three at the time and enraged that her new husband would actually leave her for a week, feigned an attempt to run over him with her car. Much to her horror, she nearly succeeded. Dad jumped out of the way at the last second, but his hysterical laughter helped matters none at all.

Undaunted, Mom waited until he was asleep the night before his departure, then removed all of his dress clothes from the suitcase. "You won't be needing these," her note said. Fortunately, Dad and his brother Howard were about the same size so Dad didn't have to wear his brush pants to the better restaurants. Meanwhile, my mother grew more terrified by the day, dreading my father's return, sure that she would be divorced by year's end. True to form, my father found his young wife's antics hilarious. Mom was so relieved and glad to see him at the end of the week that she forgot her outrage. Another bird hunter's marriage was off and running.

***

With Mom resigned to her fate, Dad settled down and got serious about dogs and birds and hunting the hilly central Kentucky farm country. The next letter, from Timber Tuck Kennels in Kannapolis, North Carolina, is dated October 31, 1958, and describes a nine-month-old liver and white pointer pup named Meg's Big Fellow:

...you asked about the pup's tail...he holds his tail up, but not like a poker...he is definitely a bold pup and shows no signs of being timid... "Fella" is definitely old enough to show any signs of being unfriendly. He is not afraid of people...

There are black-and-white snapshots and yellowed copies of pedigrees. One page, a top view drawing of a pointer pup, shows the shape and location of his markings and is denoted "Fella - $150."

The snapshots: Fella's sire, Paladin's Warhoop Sage, and dam, Survivors Doone Meg, on point, high on both ends; a litter of puppies with an arrow drawn to the biggest and an accompanying note, "Fella"; and finally nine-month-old Fella on point with his tail high, but not like a poker.

Then the pedigree. Three generations back are Triple Nat. Ch. Ariel, Nat. Ch. Warhoop Jake, Nat. Ch. Luminary and Double Nat. Ch. Shore's Brownie Doone. Two generations back, Nat. Ch. Paladin and Nat. Ch. Lone Survivor.

Enough. The next item in the file is the Field Dog Stud Book registration certificate for Meg's Big Fellow dated Dec 6, 1958. What do I know of "Fella?" That he was a lot of dog for those small Kentucky farms. And my father's favorite story: Fella pointed a honeysuckle thicket. The birds were skittish and as Dad approached he could see them moving around. Some were directly beneath Fella's nose. Others fluttered from beneath him into the thicket. The dog's eyes were as big as saucers, but he stood his birds until one brushed the end of his nose. He snapped at it, and the whole covey got up while Fella remained steady to flush. Dad always ended the story the same. "I should've have whipped him for snappin' at that bird, but I just didn't have the heart."

Fella had a big-running brace mate. A black-and-white photo shows a pair of five-month-old setter pups standing side-by-side behind a wire gate. Both are strikingly handsome, but the pup on the right exudes a bit more class and intelligence. A note is scrawled on the back of the photo:

> Tobey—pup on right—whelped 1/1/58. White and orange. By far the pick of the litter. Will weigh about 55lbs at maturity and be very powerful. Will have good style.

Next, a letter from Bothell, Washington:

> Thanks for the check... Tobey's sire is 100 percent Llewellin dog line bred back to Ch. Mohawk II, and his mother is a great shooting dog that has proven her ability to handle nearly every species of game... If you have seen some of the little snippy-nosed, runty setters with beautiful pedigrees available from some sources, you will no doubt appreciate Tobey's looks... Tobey has been nominated in the quail, pheasant and grouse futurities.

The registration slip for Destiny King Tobey, the first of my father's dogs that I can single out in memory, is dated June 3, 1959.

Next came two white and lemon pointer bitches, Ariel Luminary Fanny and Sarah (*Siree* in my father's eastern Kentucky mountain dialect), litter mates named after two of Dad's sisters whom he adored.

I was born a year later, and other than my recollection of Tobey, who lived to be nearly seventeen, my memories of those early years are limited to mental snapshots, sounds, sensations, and smells. Whipping tails and lemon and liver ticking, lolling tongues and slobber in the back of the Country Squire station wagon; the delicious grainy smell of dry dog food; the oily, doggy feel on my hands; paper blue Peter's shells; the smell of gun oil and my father's scent on his canvas hunting coat and leather-faced brush pants; the feel of fleece-lined gun gases; the smell of silicone boot treatment; longhorn cheese and crackers; dog whistles; and the homemade dog trailer with those dark, mysterious, reeking compartments that I was bound and determined to explore.

And there is the crystal clear image over the edge of a cardboard box of two white and lemon pointer puppies nosing a ball of raw hamburger. Could those pups have been from Sarah and Fella's litter? According to the Field Dog Stud Book enrollment certificate (two dogs and four bitches whelped August 5, 1962) I would have been only two and a half years old. (Hell yes it matters; it occurs to me too that if you've stayed with me this far you probably agree.)

Naturally Mom saved all of the dog licenses. BREED: *Bird Dog*; MARKINGS: *Black and White Spoted*. The Taylor County animal control office stopped at nothing in its quest for precision. Here's one that lists a dog's markings as black and brown. A Gordon? A tri-color? I have no idea. Neither does Mom. "Lord I don't remember," she says. "You never saw such a pack of bird dogs in your life." The details seem desperately important now.

Other images stand sharp and clear. Before I was old enough to accompany my father, I would stare through the front door, waiting for the station wagon to pull up in the dark. I would meet him halfway up the walk, and shove my hands into his game bag to see what he had. Quail always, sometimes a woodcock or even a rabbit shot while the dogs were distracted by other business.

After a sip of Old Forester, he would take off his shirt and head for the basement with a butcher knife and a pan of water. I sat in my pajamas, on a milk case, smelling the musky sweet bird offal that he tossed along with skin and feathers into a cardboard box. While his thick, brown hands mesmerized me, he told me about places called Marrowbone, Hibernia, Sandy Y, and

Ball Hollow (*Baw Holler*), small farm country, none of it over sixty miles away, but to me, sitting on my milk case, these places might as well have been Thomasville or the King Ranch.

Some idiot shot Fella with a .22 while he was out for a romp, and he died just as he reached the back porch. I brooded over this throughout boyhood, though I never really knew him. But I knew *of* him. The other dogs aged and more memories began to stick for good, but it pains me how little of the actual hunting I recall from that busy period in my father's life. I remember sitting in the backseat of the station wagon with middle-aged Tobey's head in my lap while Fanny and Sarah paced and whined in the back. Dad and his buddies J.D. or Fred or others talked over my head and gestured with big, callused hands that hypnotized me. The roads were narrow and crooked, and sometimes I had to concentrate on Tobey's facial features to fight off carsickness. We drove along miles of grown up fence rows and ragged corn fields with weedy edges and hillsides covered in briars and cedar.

We walked over cornfield clods and along hillsides; the pointers were out of sight most of the time, whipping their tails bloody against the briars. Tobey ran fence rows and looped high headed into the wind, and my daydreaming would be interrupted by a new urgency in my father's stride and we'd go to him. Was he high on both ends? That's the way I like to remember him. There would be the *thump-thump-thump* of humpbacked autoloaders and Dad hollering "Dead! Dead! Dead in here!" Then, as often as not, "Now where'd them two bitches get off to?"

***

The registration certificate, dated November 24, 1962, lists a lemon and white pointer dog whelped six months earlier. The registered name, Son of Fairway, has a regal sound and the accompanying pedigree is rife with champions—several of them national champions. But the familiar left-handed scrawl in the top left-hand corner tells me his real identity: King.

I remember King. He killed chickens while we asked for permission to hunt, ate stainless steel buckets, foiled every attempt at his confinement, chewed the leather buttons off of my new winter coat, and often tried to run through barbed-wire fencing. He had nose, drive, and bottom but never pointed a bird although he could find quail with the best of them. So, after six seasons, my father finally put him to good use. He gave him to Uncle Smitty.

For over twenty years my mother's older brother and my father engaged in no-holds-barred competition at all mutual interests. Uncle Smitty had seen all of Dad's better dogs work but knew nothing of King. After a quick sob story about too much work and not enough time for dog training, Dad sent King to Mississippi for a new life as Smitty's shooting dog.

Anxious to show off his new blue blood dog from Kentucky, Smitty immediately organized an outing with several of his area's best quail hunters. Picture northern Mississippi in 1968: Three stylish dogs are on point in the sedge among scattered pines. The hunters approach casually and fan out as they approach the dogs. Only the matched mules and Democrat wagon are missing. Suddenly there are footfalls from behind followed by "Whoa! Whoa! Whoa goddamnit!" That night on the phone, my father weeping with laughter and my mother listening on the other line, Uncle Smitty allowed as how he wouldn't do such a thing to his worst enemy. No one seems to know what became of old King.

***

The seventies. Kentucky's quail population plummeted. The dogs aged and died. My father worked long hours at a new business, while I moved into adolescence and took up rabbit hunting. Other than a registration slip for a beagle, another Fella, a 1971 birthday gift from my parents, the dog file shows no new dogs joining the family during this decade. Until I was old enough to drive, my father hauled my friends, our beagles, and me wherever we needed to go. He answered our questions on guns and dogs but stayed out of the way and allowed us to grow up.

I've wondered about his apparent loss of interest. I had assumed he was just too busy, but as my own dogs age—the first really good dogs I've owned and trained myself—and middle age approaches and the years take some of the edge from my own desire, I am beginning to see where he was. I cannot imagine life without bird dogs and shotguns and hunting, but sometimes you get damned tired and the single-mindedness wanes like it did finally in Faulkner's Ike McCaslin. But you hunt anyway. You come for the hunt if not for the hunting because that's who you are and what you do. You'll come, always; "if only to go back tomorrow."

That's what my father did in those years. He came and sat and waited and listened to the things we told him had happened. He'd occasionally bring his shotgun and shoot a dozen doves with eighteen or twenty shells, remarking always that what we really needed was a dog to pick up our birds and that he guessed he'd better get busy finding one and that after he did we'd be into birds sure enough. We all listened and nodded and prodded as to when and what kind and allowed as how we'd get bird dogs too and we'd pay farmers to plant lespedeza and hold off on haying until the hens got their broods out of the middle of the fields.

None of us really believed it, of course. I went away to college and took up deer hunting.

***

The last registration slip is for Foots Chappell Smith, an orange and white Brittany dog out of ordinary working stock. The silly name was a concession to my mother, who spotted him when he was a just-weaned pup at a kennel in Louisville in

January 1980. She had to have him, and my father agreed that
Foots would be her dog. That arrangement lasted for about
three hours. Dad knew nothing of Brittanys, but he knew a bird
dog when he saw one. Whatever had been dragging him down
was lifted, and when I think of him these days I nearly always
remember him as he was in the four years he hunted with
Foots.

Six decades of living had softened his approach to most
things, dog training included. Fifteen years before, he'd drag
King by the ears back to some point of infraction, and sounding
for all the world like Yosemite Sam he'd expound again: "When
I say whoa, I mean *whoa!*" Foots, on the other hand, never
dragged a check cord, and although I never remember him
intentionally taking out a bird, he learned exactly how long he
could ignore Dad's whistle before switch cutting threats
became serious. Dad shamelessly overfed him and soaped and
scalded his dishes every night. "Worms'll kill a dog," he'd
respond to my mother's nightly harassment. "You want 'im
gettin' worms?"

Foots started his career hunting what was left of Taylor
County's bobwhites, and he picked up our doves, but Dad was
feeling the pull of his eastern Kentucky mountains. Over the
last five years of his life, bird hunting meant grouse hunting,
and Foots' slow, meticulous style was perfect. We had some big
years while I was in college, and when I think of Foots—or
when I think of grouse—I see a stubby, wet, dirty white tail and
hindquarters quivering just ahead in the laurel along the White
Oak fork of Greasy Creek. It's overcast and snow is beginning
to collect on the rib of my shotgun. My father is breathing hard
from exertion and talking softly to his dog: "Whup now... whup
now..."

"I believe Foots is the best I've had," he'd say. I'd look at
the portly little dog snuffling around some sixty-acre field that
Fanny or Sarah would have cut to ribbons in a matter of

minutes, and I'd reflect on the way age and blind love affects a man's judgment. I suspect now that I didn't understand what he was saying.

I came home from Texas for Christmas, and we drove to the mountains and parked next to the creek and let Foots out to grind off some edge before we started hunting. We'd worn jeans and tennis shoes on the three-hour drive and were standing barefoot in our long handles, about to pull on our brush pants and boots when Foots pointed sixty feet away in a blackberry tangle. Dad, in the strongest language I had ever heard him use, said, "Well shit, he's pointed." He looked at his boots and then at Foots. "Well...well," he said. I made no effort. I knew exactly what was about to happen. He pulled his Browning from its case and tenderfooted it over the creek gravel and up the bank to Foots. As he approached, Foots softened and looked back at him with a "I might have been mistaken" expression on his face. "Ye gods, Foots," my father said softly.

We hunted hard the rest of the day, got soaked in wet snow, and nearly got the truck stuck a half-dozen times. The grouse insisted on flushing from the tops of the pines and we shot none. I went back to Texas, and Dad died unexpectedly two months later.

A few weeks after my father's death, my mother was putting her life back together, struggling with the sudden, numbing loss. She had complained for years about Dad's habit of leaving a blanket in his easy chair after getting up at four in the morning to wrap up and watch Canadian football on the sports channel. She was badly shaken one morning when she found the blanket again piled in Dad's chair. For over a week her scalp tingled and the hair on her arms stood up as she walked into the den each morning to find the familiar sight after she had folded the blanket over the back of the chair the day before. She told no one and had begun to draw comfort from her ghost. Then one morning she entered the den earlier than usual and found

Foots lying in my father's chair with the blanket over him. A few days later Foots disappeared after Mom let him outside. We never saw him again.

***

So a few dozen photos and slips of paper bound in memory form an informal chronicle of my father's sporting life and the most important part of my boyhood. It seems fitting that there are no tallies of shots fired and birds killed; Dad would have found a more formal record pretentious.

Loss and regret mount as surely as the years. So you try to grasp the things that have mattered and hold on for dear life.

Arizona

I pulled off the four-wheel-drive trail, got out, and looked westward over hundreds of thousands of acres of oak- and midgrass-covered ridges, draws, and canyons. Then southward over more of the same in Sonora, Mexico. I had come alone that Monday morning in January to hunt Mearns' quail, and, as always, my aloneness brought succor. On this day, hundreds of square miles belonged to me alone; I could go where I pleased with little concern for boundaries. A Texan doesn't take such freedom lightly.

(Such rugged individualists, we Texans! With all our range and sky and mountains and virtually no access to any of it. Resentful? Frankly yes, at times.)

I checked my watch. Eight-thirty. Early still. I let Molly out of her box, lit my camp stove, and started a pot of coffee. Molly loped down the hill and flushed a dozen mallards from a big stock tank. I put together my over/under, sorted shells, and stuffed extra gear into my game vest: matches, tube of fire starter, stout folding knife, map, and power bar. Were I to break a leg in these remote mountains, I probably would be there awhile. No sense dying of hypothermia. Molly came back up the hill, dug herself a bed in the sand, and lay down in the morning sun to await further instructions.

I poured a cup of coffee and sat on the cooler with my back against the truck and looked again over the country I planned to hunt. These mountains, the northernmost reaches of Mexico's Sierra Madre Occidental range, form an ecological peninsula in southeastern Arizona and southwestern New Mexico known properly as the Madrean Montane Forests, a moist, cool wedge between two deserts: the Chihuahuan Desert to the east and the Sonoran Desert to the north and west. Driving south out of the Sonoran Desert and into the Patagonias or Santa Ritas, you leave the low desert and rise first into the grassy mesquite hillocks then higher until the mesquite thins and the oak mottes thicken and the country steepens to grassy ridges, sheer cliffs, sandstone buttes, and craggy prominences.

Coues deer live in these mountains and here only. And cougar. Jaguar? Hopefully; probably. There have been rumors and sightings recently. *El Tigre* has always engendered rumor. Real or spectral, his presence changes a landscape and brings an edginess to a walk in his country. Alone, you watch a beloved dog disappear amid the oaks and jumbled boulders on the ridge above and from nowhere comes a prickliness and sudden sensual acuity; you strain to hear her; you squeeze the dog whistle between your thumb and forefinger. Then you pick up the faint sound of her bell and then she's snorting back down the ridge toward you. You relax and let the whistle fall back to your chest. Oh for god's sake, you tell yourself, laughing. But you sweet-talk her as she bustles merrily by.

Mearns' quail live in these mountains between four and six thousand feet. There are isolated populations in south-central New Mexico, the Texas Hill Country, and the Davis Mountains in southwest Texas, but these southern Arizona mountain ranges—also called the Sky Island Mountains—are the birds' stronghold. Like the mountains they live in, these quail have several names: Mearns' quail after naturalist Edgar Mearns; Montezuma quail because Mexico holds most of their habitat;

fool quail because the small coveys, family units actually, once held so tightly they could be clubbed to death; crazy quail because of their showy plumage and explosive flush.

Unlike the other quails, which feed primarily on seeds, Mearns' quail dig for sedge and oxalis tubers in the soft, moist humus beneath the oak overstory. Grass is the other critical component: side oats grama, hairy grama, and sprangle top among other familiar short- and midgrasses. Mearns' quail are late risers; hunting them before ten in the morning is generally fruitless. I like that. I spend more than enough time staggering about bleary eyed after waterfowl and today's lumpen bob-whites. Mearns' quail roost in relatively flat grassy areas on hilltops and valley floors. Sitting in their tight roosting circle, they put out virtually no scent. Around mid-morning they begin foraging, moving up or down the ridges or along the canyon floors, depending on food availability.

Mearns' quail hunting means hard walking in steep, rough terrain. I had spent the previous day hunting with new friends Web Parton, the Arizona guide, dog trainer, and writer, and Jim and Brenda Jordan of Tucson. Following excellent dogs—Web's big-running setters Emma and Musette and the Jordan's German shorthairs Bo and Chris—we moved one covey in five hours of hunting. I got a shot at a single, but in the failing light, lost the bird against the dark oaken background. Somehow Web knew exactly where the rest of the covey would be. He walked directly to a nondescript draw and walked up the singles, but none offered a decent shot.

Earlier that day we met a party of two hunters eating a tailgate lunch. They had moved one covey and had taken a Mearns' cock. One of the men took it from the cooler and laid it in my hand, and I wondered how such a gorgeous bird— breast, white polka-dots on jet black; powder blue legs and beak; russet crown; brilliant white nape and throat cut cleanly by the black ear patch—could be invisible on the open duff beneath the oaks.

I finished my coffee, swapped my parka for my vest, and picked up my shotgun. Right on cue, Molly, who had been watching me closely, jumped up and whined and wiggled about expectantly. I loaded my gun and cast her westward down the hill.

Within five minutes I was glad I had resisted the temptation to wear a sweater over my chamois shirt. I had been chilly sipping coffee, but now the steep terrain had me sweating. I let Molly follow her nose; she looped into the wind on the ridges to either side of me while I picked my way over the boulders on the canyon floor.

Relative to the surrounding desert, water is plentiful most years in these mountains. I walked along a narrow rill, crossing back and forth often as the terrain dictated. Molly stopped often to drink and wade. There were pools, some three feet deep, where catch basins had formed in the rock floor; the surrounding muck was covered with deer tracks. As Molly worked the slopes I occasionally caught distant movement and looked up to see Coues deer in twos and threes bobbing up the ridges, disappearing and reappearing amid the low oaks.

Mearns' quail are doing poorly these days. After several good years in the mid-1980s, populations plummeted due to drought and cattle grazing in the Coronado National Forest. I found many of the gentler hills essentially razed, and the dried cow turds along the rill made me wonder how far I would have to hike into these mountains to escape the cattlemen's blight. Maybe I'll try someday with backpack, shotgun, and Molly. There are designated wildernesses in these mountains, roadless tracts that are probably free of cattle and quail hunters alike. The idea gained appeal as we pushed further west exploring interesting draws and ridges. Cattle notwithstanding, we were hunting gorgeous, remote country. I periodically oriented myself with Mangus Peak and Apache Butte.[1]

photo by Web Parton

---

1   These rocky prominences actually exist. However I have
    selfishly renamed them in the interest of obfuscation. I'm sure
    you understand.

After two hours of hunting we had moved no birds. I was glad I had worn my hiking boots instead of my lightweight hunting boots. It was still and cool down in the canyons, but gray clouds scudded overhead, occasionally darkening the slopes, making the aloneness seem more acute. On the ridges above me, the wind whispered in the oaks. There was no hurry; I eased comfortably along.

A covey got up wild a couple hundred feet above me. Most of them—eight birds perhaps—flew up and over the ridge, but at least one bird peeled off, and Molly found and pointed it before I could climb fifty feet. I unloaded my shotgun and climbed toward her. The birds' wedge-shaped scratchings were everywhere. Molly had her bird under a chest-high canopy of oak, and just as I closed my gun after dropping in two shells, the bird flushed and bored away low. I crouched, looking frantically for a shot but lost the bird before it had flown twenty feet.

All right then. I had come to hunt Mearns' quail, not to collect what Web calls a "destination bird." Molly and I had stumbled over a covey on our own, and she pointed and held a single. The pressure was off now. We continued up the ridge after the rest of the covey.

I clamored over the top and found Molly on point. I walked past her, and she rolled her eyes at me and softened. I sent her on, and after sixty yards of animated snuffling she pointed again. Still nothing. Web had warned me about this. Hunting literature is full of descriptions of tight holding Mearns', but hunting pressure has done to the Mearns' quail what it did to the once genteel bobwhite. According to Web, most singles now run like jackrabbits.

Molly was blowing hard, so I made her stop and drink. The sharp wind quickly dried my sweat. We hunted hard but never found those birds. We hunted toward the truck through the labyrinth of draws and canyons, and whenever I had a high vantage point, I couldn't help but look toward the roadless areas to the north and west.

***

Arizona. I've been obsessed with the state since Jay Chesley, who is from Safford in the southeastern part of the state, first told me of the sixty bird coveys of Gambel's quail he walked up as a boy along the Gila River. And about the time Heidi joined the family, the magazines all reported a Mearns' quail boom. Unfortunately, I was gainfully employed at the time and couldn't bring myself to use four days of vacation to drive out there and back when I had good bobwhite hunting three hours away.

But I thought about it. Three quail species. Mourning doves. Whitewings. Tens of millions of acres of public land. Jay made it back to Safford once a year to visit his family and sometimes shot Gambel's quail within sight of his parents' house. Naturally he always took lots of pictures, which he was more than happy to show me.

Then, a couple of years ago, publisher Chuck Johnson suggested I give Web a call and get out to Arizona. Web felt we could take care of our "dove research" in a day or two; desert and Mearns' quail might take another two or three days. Anything for the job, that's my motto. I read Web's book *Wingshooter's Guide to Arizona*, ordered a few maps, and on New Year's Eve 1997, I loaded Molly and took off for the Sonoran Desert.

***

Web said that if I got lost between Tucson and his home in Oracle, I should roll down my window and listen for barking dogs. I found his house easily, but when I pulled into my drive I saw (or rather heard) exactly what he meant. He was busy cleaning his kennel, and his dozen or so dogs—several setters, shorthairs, and a Lab—greeted me loudly until he suggested rather strongly that they hush. Inside, while Web gathered his gear, I met and chatted with his wife, Nicole, and their ancient Chesapeake Bay retriever Sadie.

The hot weather worried me. Then Web appeared wearing snake chaps and a pistol. He offered me the use of his extra pair of chaps and explained the handgun: Years ago in California, a nasty run-in with a wild boar cured him of any desire to be in the boondocks without real stopping power. I considered the heat then decided against the chaps. I realize it's probably just a matter of time.

We loaded Molly and Web's big black Lab, Tucker, and headed for the Santa Cruz River for some dove shooting.

Arizona's white-wing dove hunting is all but finished due to the destruction of riparian nurseries and the conversion of grain crops to cotton. A few birds still fly north out of Mexico every year to feed on the fruit of saguaro and organ pipe cactus, but the shooting is spotty at best, and most of the birds leave for Mexico before the season opens on September 1. But millions of home-grown mourning doves swarm the grain fields and water holes in September, and millions of migrants from northern states fill in as resident birds fly south. Most years Arizona's mourning dove shooting remains good throughout the season.

Riding along the back roads, I got my first good look at the country. Dark granite mountains in the background, stately saguaro cactus, huge cholla, mesquite, creosote, and virtually no grass. Web explained that most of the land we were passing as well as the land we'd be hunting is state trust land, land held in trust by the state of Arizona and leased to ranchers and farmers, ostensibly to raise money for schools. State trust lands are open to licensed hunters, but unlike the Bureau of Land Management and the U.S. Forest Service, the State Trust Land Department has no wildlife management mandate. In practice, the lands are for cattlemen. Yet the hunting can be very good, which leaves Web shaking his head and wondering aloud how good it could it could be if wildlife were given as much priority as cows.

We met the Jordans at a designated spot along the road then drove on to the river. We went through an open gate with NO TRESPASSING signs on the fence to either side. I cringed. Texans take those signs very seriously. But Web pointed out that if you read the fine print, you'll see that persons with special permits can enter and that a hunting license serves as a permit. The problem is that lessees are tiring of trash and vandalism to windmill tanks, fencing, and equipment and are simply locking the gates.

We drove into a huge mosaic of milo fields bounded on the west by the Santa Cruz and cut by two-track roads and concrete agricultural canals. The area was new to Web too; he was acting on a tip from a friend. We stopped and got out to look things over. The river, which once floated paddle boats from Nogales, was a broken string of muddy pools I could've jumped across. Several doves flushed from the mesquite that lined the river channel.

Meanwhile the Jordans had arrived and were busy gathering gear and putting together shotguns. Their German shorthair, Chris, romped out to greet us. It was only 3:30, but already flocks of doves—twenty and thirty birds at a time— were whistling by, and hundreds of others were swarming in the milo.

Jim, who's vice president of sales and marketing for Precision Shooting Equipment Inc., the big archery equipment manufacturer, had a pair of prototype warm weather hunting vests for Web and me to try out. Jim has hunted big game all over North America, and he and Brenda have recently become engrossed in upland bird hunting. And like all southwestern bird hunters they noticed an absence of vests designed to carry water bottles, plenty of shells, and the accouterments that go with hunting in hot prickly country. These vests were second generation prototypes that Jim pronounced "close but not quite there." Web and I loaded up with shells and water bottles then stood there until all straps and buckles were adjusted to Brenda's satisfaction. I was actually relieved since the cheap camo game belt I normally use for dove and squirrel hunting pulls my pants down. And Web had his camera with him.

Molly jumped out of her box and lit out for the river, assuming, I'm sure, that we were after quail. She retrieves reliably and sits and stays on command, but I had never used her as a non-slip retriever. Nor had she ever picked up a dove. Unconcerned, I called her, and she barreled in wild-eyed and slavering and drank all of Chris's water.

Web uncased his Parker double, unloaded Tucker, and we all hurried off to take cover—Web and me in the mesquite above the river and the Jordans in a huge, ugly erosion cut.

Molly had no clue. She sat at heel, cocked and ready for launch. A pair of doves came whistling by, a perfect high-house four, and I dropped the leader into an erosion cut thirty yards away. Molly jumped straight ahead ten feet then whirled around to face me, ears perked, eyes bulging, and brow furrowed as if to say, "What the hell?" I said, "Dead bird!" and she spun and tore off into the cut and came back a half minute later with my bird. The downy feathers stuck to her gums and tongue, yet I couldn't interest her in a drink of water. I shot three more doves; she became more wild-eyed with each retrieve. Then she started breaking at every shot, and I wondered if perhaps one should take a big-running pointing dog out for a few low-key dove hunts before subjecting her to hundreds of birds and a shell expenditure of a dozen per minute.

Web dropped a dove, and Molly left in a cloud of dust to get to it before Tucker. Thunderous whistle blasts and various insults to her parentage brought her back before a fight ensued. I took out a leash and tied her to a small tree. With each of Web's shots her whines became more piteous, her drool more

photo by Web Parton

profuse, and her entanglement in the surrounding brush more ridiculous.

A dove flew along the river channel behind me. I spun and shot it. Amazingly, Molly marked it. I let her off the hopelessly entangled leash, and she dove off the bank and pounced on the stone-dead bird as if to give it a thorough stomping for good measure. Just as I took the bird from her, another one flew over my head and I dropped it too. (Yes, I was on that day.) I sent Molly to fetch, but there was no Molly. I blew the whistle until I was dizzy then walked over and picked up my dove. As I climbed out of the channel, I saw a flash of white in the milo a half mile away. It seems that after a quick visit with Chris and the Jordans, Molly set off to do what Molly does best; she went looking for birds. Why wait for them to come to you? I went to fetch her while doves poured over my spot on the river.

I dragged her back and tied her up, and things went to hell from there. She barked hysterically at Tucker and Chris and incoming doves, flushing meadowlarks and distant birds of prey. After another half-mile detour, I dragged her wheezing and foaming back to the truck and locked her in the Porta-Kennel.

By that time it was nearly dark and the doves had stopped flying.

But I had half a limit and some new friends. And there was the desert sunset that left me dazed.

Back at the little motel, the owner asked if I had any dogs with me. One, I told her. She said that was fine; she had a couple of rooms set aside for hunters with dogs. Looking at the spots on the carpet, I suspected she also occasionally boarded livestock. Molly sniffed about warily. I decided the owner wouldn't mind me cleaning my birds in the bathroom sink.

***

The blue or scaled quail is a grassland bird. Therein lies a problem for southwestern quail hunters. Grass is a valuable commodity in the desert southwest. Extended drought and heavy grazing are making both grass and blues scarce. Of course the desert grasses are quite capable of surviving drought; they simply bide their time underground, storing energy in their complex root systems, waiting for hospitable conditions above. Constant heavy grazing by cattle is another matter.

The Gambel's quail, on the other hand, is a true desert bird, inhabiting the sandy washes and arroyos from low desert to upper bajada. Find drainages lined with tamarisk, catclaw, or tarbush anywhere from the Chihuahuan Desert in south-central New Mexico westward through the Sonoran Desert and you'll find Gambel's quail. All things considered, Gambel's are doing okay. Given winter precipitation to bring on late winter and early spring forbs to trigger reproduction and summer monsoons for warm season brood rearing vegetation, Gambel's bounce back quickly from drought-induced busts.

In Arizona, blue quail are restricted to the desert grasslands in the southeastern corner of the state, the transition area between the yucca and agave flats of the Chihuahuan Desert to the east and the Sonoran Desert to the west. And on public grassland you typically find cattle, or the symptoms of their presence.

Unfortunately, environmental politics hardens dogma as much as it solves problems. Tenuous and unlikely alliances, formal and otherwise, form among groups on the political left and among groups on the political right. Environmentalists, vegetarian activists, and animal rights activists on the left. Hunters, ranchers, and business concerns on the right. Inviolate rules form to the detriment of the wildlife and people the groups want to help: Cows and logging are invariably bad; trees and grass are invariably good; hunters and ranchers are dinosaurs whose time has long since passed. From the other side: Environmentalists are all left-wing radical reformists, enemies of bedrock America who want to put hard-working Americans out of business and out of work.

There are many clear-cut (sorry) cases, of course. Grazing along sensitive riparian corridors and large-scale clear cutting are just plain wrong. On the other side of the coin, many so-called environmentalists would sell their souls to end hunting, ranching, and traditional wildlife management.

Too often we're forced to prioritize then compromise in the interest of some larger goal. The mature, thoughtful environmentalist who might privately concede that ranchers have contributed much and that grazing and logging, even very small scale clear-cutting, are appropriate in certain situations, finds herself in camp with noisy post-adolescent rebels with ludicrously simple answers. But then a vote is a vote; money is money. Politics is a nasty business.

Likewise, the environmentally conscious hunter senses animal rights, anti-hunting, anti-meat, anti-everything undercurrents in the environmental agenda—well out of the mainstream, but there—and finds himself in uncomfortable agreement on certain issues with interest groups he otherwise distrusts.

Economics and the politics of meat aside, most of our grasslands *need* to be moderately grazed to remain healthy. The Great Plains evolved under grazing by large ungulates, primarily bison. Given the absence of bison, we're left with cattle to fill that niche. A section of mixed prairie left ungrazed and unburned for several years, especially several wet years, becomes a rank, woolly mess no more natural or healthy than a feed lot.

So...

I'm a hunter and environmentalist—or conservationist; I'm never sure which. I love a nice greasy cheeseburger, and I believe responsible cattle ranching has a place in the ecology of certain grasslands, particularly the grasslands of the Great

Plains. And I tend to like and admire ranchers. Yet I believe most of our desert grassland should never have been grazed by cattle.

Bison never were plentiful in the desert southwest; the arid grasslands simply aren't adapted to grazing pressure from large herbivores. Tobosa, the dominant desert shortgrass is poor forage, but cattle will eat it roots and all in the absence of the more desirable gramas. A razed desert grassland is highly susceptible to invasion by brush, particularly mesquite. Once established in large stands, mesquite perpetuates a vicious cycle. Mesquite transpires huge amounts of water, and a lowered water table in turn gives the mesquite, with its deep running roots, a competitive advantage over the grasses. Today on the desert grasslands, mesquite, once limited to lower lying areas, is ubiquitous in the uplands and grotesque erosion cuts are nearly as common as cactus. And the grazing continues.

But the Southwest is changing. The cattlemen's time is running out and they know it. The economic potential for recreational use of public land far exceeds the paltry earnings from grazing leases. Fewer and fewer people are willing to support rapacious land use to preserve a myth.

But from a human standpoint, what are the ranchers to do after being propped up for three generations by ludicrously low grazing fees? Get a job in town? Over the long haul it probably will come to that.

In his book *The Rediscovery of North America*, Barry Lopez wrote that he is not deeply sympathetic to the frustrations of his neighbors in the Northwest who have logged themselves out of a job. They've known for years that this was coming, he wrote, and their employers have behaved like wastrels. All true.

Yet most of us find ourselves victims of momentum. By the time we're mature enough for real introspection, we're staggering under layers of adult obligation. Certain moral issues lose their clarity when the immediate quality of our children's lives are at stake. None of the ranches I've seen in Arizona would pass for South Fork. I wonder. What am *I*, thirty-seven-year-old extractive industries junkie, with my house in the suburbs, willing to give up? What adjustments am I willing to ask my family to make? These questions haunt my thoughts.

***

Grass or no grass, Web thought he could get us into a few blue quail. And he knew he could get us into plenty of Gambel's. Fortunately for the Jordans and me, Web had postponed a snake-breaking session with a customer's pointer; his three rattlesnakes were all too sluggish due to the cool nights. Hunting, writing, guiding, dog training, sculpting, taxidermy, photography, and grass roots activism; somehow he works them all in. I learned more about the desert in three days of hunting with Web than I could learn in ten years of reading and hunting on my own.

We began the morning in the Sonoran scrub near Oracle with Bo, Chris, Molly, and Emma, who lost a hind leg as a pup climbing out of her kennel. Emma is nonetheless a blur, tearing up the countryside with that smooth, lovely setter gait. I can't imagine the strength that must be in those three legs.

We started hunting three abreast through the prickly pear, mesquite, and chest-high cholla and barrel cactus, with Molly and Emma in the distance and Chris and Bo quartering sixty yards in front of us. The ground was naked save for occasional clumps of snakeweed, that noxious indicator of exhausted range. Fortunately quail will eat snakeweed seeds when nothing better is available. I wondered where on the bare dirt a covey of blues could hide. In the distance the bare, dark mountains, the Santa Catalinas and the Tortolitas, were at times difficult to distinguish from the low stratus clouds. Even razed, this is rough, wild country, sparsely beautiful, and I'm endlessly fascinated by it. A few days prior, a local quail hunter was badly shaken when he walked up to his rigid pudelpointer, and instead of quail, found a cougar crouching in the brush.

We topped a nondescript rise among scores of other nondescript rises, and Web announced that a covey of blues would be nearby. Within five minutes, all four dogs were birdy, trailing, cat-walking, dashing about, tails whipping furiously. After a half-dozen unproductive points by all of the dogs, Bo pointed and Molly backed him while Chris and Emma worked ahead in the scrub. Jim and I walked in, and a single quail flushed to my side. I shot it, and Molly brought it in—sure enough, a blue.

The rest of the covey did what blues do; they melted into the desert, leaving only faint tendrils of scent to frustrate the dogs.

We spent the rest of the morning hunting the arroyos for Gambel's quail. We had good hunting behind Musette and Web's efficient little solid liver shorthair Sage. Typically, Musette found the coveys; Web somehow knew which draws the singles would fly into; then Sage would snuffle in to work scattered pairs and singles while Musette ranged wide for another covey. Web carries a whistle but usually handles his dogs with a low, barely audible whistle between his teeth and a calm, soft voice that Emma and Musette hear from two hundred yards away.

At times we heard birds calling in the distance: *chi-ca-ca-go.* I had never taken quail calls seriously; then Web took out his call and conversed with a covey until we were able to locate it well enough to walk more or less straight to it.

(Web tells me that blue quail, though much less vocal than Gambel's, sometimes call *chuck-chuck-ping*, the *ping* being almost identical to the sound of a concierge's bell.)

I started the morning red hot then missed eight straight. The sky cleared around mid-morning, and the temperature climbed into the low seventies. I began to covet Jim and Brenda's knee-high snake boots. By early afternoon we were out of water and I was trying to decide if I had four or five blisters on each foot. Musette coasted to a stop and dug a nice cool hole in the shade beneath a catclaw thicket. Web checked the sun and said that if we hurried, we could make it to the Santa Cruz in time for the afternoon dove shooting.

Back at the milo fields, Molly stressed out the second she realized we were dove hunting. I had probably been too rough on her the day before. Web sweetened her up with a dove he had in his bag, and I put her back in her crate happy. Good dog trainers can make something positive out of nearly any mess.

Naturally I carried my new shooting slump with me to the dove fields. I had a perfect spot in a concrete canal and proceeded to shoot my way to a migraine. Web went through two rolls of Kodachrome 64 recording my misses.

I limped back to my motel room that night actually grateful I didn't have many birds to clean.

***

After a murderous day of Mearns' quail hunting in the mountains near Nogales, Jim and Brenda graciously invited me to stay with them at their home in Tucson. I hunted Mearns' quail alone the following day and moved one covey.

Jim sent me home with a hand-drawn map complete with cryptic symbology (it *could* fall into the wrong hands) of a canyon on the Arizona-New Mexico border. He assured me I would find Gambel's quail there, and it wasn't far out of my way.

I found the place, a series of remote bajadas cut with numerous drainages. Molly found plenty of Gambel's quail, and I shot my way out of the slump. But we found no blue quail in what is supposed to be Chihuahuan Desert grassland. There was not a single blade of grass as far as I could see, only cow flops and clumps of snakeweed on the bare ground amid the desert scrub.

I had planned to camp there and hunt the next morning, but standing on the rim of a stock tank at sunset, watching dust devils form on the lower bajada, I decided to leave.

I drove out in the dark. Tumbleweeds half the size of my truck rolled across the road in front of me. I thought of a conversation Web and I had two days prior. We were driving through the low desert toward our dove hunting spot on the Santa Cruz River, discussing "The Green Lagoons," Aldo Leopold's essay about the long canoe trip he and his brother made into the Delta of the Colorado; how they supped on Gambel's quail roasted in their Dutch oven; the geese they stalked. As we talked, I pointed toward the surrounding country—the huge saguaro cactus and the distant mountains—and wondered aloud what southern Arizona was like 120 years ago. "Oh it was a paradise!" he said. *"A paradise!"*

Rebuilding

*Beyond doubt, Bobwhite is the outstand-
ing optimist in our midst. Following
each bitter winter and chill spring, he
comes perennially to whistle his cheer
and to proclaim that more quail are on
the way. In troubled times, he never
grumbles for us to hear. Even at the
instant of violent death, his outcry is short and seldom
heard.*

H. D. Dogden in the foreword to Daniel Lay's Quail
Management Handbook for East Texas

The West Texas plains can be the best or worst place in the
world to hunt bobwhite quail. In good years, when rain comes at
the right times in the right amounts, November limits come
easy to the most rank beginners. Other years rain hardly comes
at all, and only the most ardent follow frustrated dogs across a
tortured landscape covered with dry stock tanks, rattlesnakes,
cactus, and bare mesquite.

I hunt during the bad years because I must. I am a hunter.
And my dogs' lives are too short to be squandered in a kennel.
Of course I hunt during the boom years, but frankly, I'm glad
they come only once or twice per decade. I don't like the effect
they have on me.

Yet I do love the boom years. Raucous diners at 5 A.M.; motel parking lots full of dog trailers; strings of pointers staked out at highway rest stops; the first wild weeks, coveys running in plain sight across ranch roads; dogs on overload running through coveys that shouldn't be where they are; looking for the singles and bumping other coveys, and me shooting at a dozen birds at once.

Things settle down by mid-December. The surplus has been taken. The birds are where they should be—in brushy draws, cedar breaks, and ragweed flats. The dogs, lean, calm, and workmanlike, hunt objectives as opposed to just running flat out. Best of all, after a month and a half of carnage, the fair weather hunters, happy with their full freezers, stay at home, leaving the remaining birds, skittish survivors, to us hard cases.

In January of our last big season, Brad and I cast our dogs up a mesquite-choked Panhandle draw. The morning was warm, overcast, and humid, but a norther was coming, and the birds were frantically filling their crops. We moved nine coveys in two hours. Our shooting was on, and the dog work was superb. We ended with quite a pile of birds, and the images stand clear: my graying shorthair, Heidi, running easily, swinging back and forth across the juniper-studded hilltops and down into the draws, her bell going silent, me fighting panic, sliding down steep banks into dry creek beds and pushing and pawing through the mesquite to reach her; the covey rises, some straight up through the mesquite, others low and fast just above the low scrub and then into the hills; Brad's Brittany, Dee, gaunt and gimpy after two days of hunting, completing a retrieve on three legs and then riding back to the truck on his master's shoulders. Boom year memories.

But I don't remember the deaths. The broken but immaculate bobwhite cocks with a single drop of blood on their beaks; the cripple running for its life and then the erect head and blinking eye protruding from my dog's mouth as she sat before me;

the feel of fragile bone breaking and sinew tearing and the death shudder in my hand. Excitement from copious gunfire obscured the most real part of the hunt. Those birds, like all others I have killed, saw dawn, sensed the impending weather, felt hunger and fear. I feel no remorse for their deaths, only regret and a touch of shame because I don't remember. Responsibility and respect are impossible without remembrance. Dog work and shooting are important, but not so much so that the end result—the death of a living creature for the sake of food, sport, tradition, or something more primordial—should be made trivial.

The big years, as welcome and celebrated as they are, can ruin perspective. February comes and I kick up dust and notice a lack of green matter in the birds' crops, and I know the crash is coming. Instead of thankfulness for what has been, I feel melancholy about what is to come.

photo by Henry Chappell

photo by Henry Chappell

And the crash does come. Spring and summer drought. The weed crop fails. Few birds nest with so little moisture, and then the chicks can't peck through the brittle, drought-hardened egg shells. The few that do hatch come into a blast furnace world devoid of brood rearing cover and protein rich insects.

But a few survive—genetically superior birds that prefer running to flying, that refuse to expose themselves to a hawk or bobcat or a bird dog; birds that flush wild and fly a half mile only to alight and then run or flush again; birds fit to start the comeback.

I curse and sweat my way through the drought seasons, driving four hours for one or two coveys per day, lugging quarts of water for my dogs, and hunting around windmill tanks. I tape boots on the dogs against cactus and sand burrs and camp in hot wind that mangles tent poles and blows sand into our pancake batter. I take a couple of birds per day if I'm lucky, and when I feel the warmth and perhaps the death shudder in my hand and open the nearly empty crop, I know full well that I am holding root stock, and I remember.

Best of all are the rebuilding years. Gentle regular rain comes in April and May and again in November. The ragweed, croton, bundle flower, partridge pea, and other warm season forbs spring up on ground left vacant by drought burned perennial vegetation. The few surviving bobwhite cocks, urged on by moisture and earth's fecundity, strut and whistle. Nests are built and chicks are hatched and raised in a lush, herbaceous, bug filled world.

The November hunting is much improved despite the small carryover. We find birds where we should; their numbers have yet to exceed the capacity of the available habitat. The autumn rains make perfect scenting conditions and bring on the cool season greenery that sustains the birds after the summer seed crop has been used up. Stock tanks are full. Creeks and rivers are strings of clear pools, perfect for cooling dogs and comforting quail hunters. Eight or ten coveys per day keep dogs interested and hunters' perspectives in order.

The season progresses. The hunting slows. By February hours pass between covey rises, but there is no late season melancholy. Next season's seed is in place, and history says that spring rain will come. I take a bird from my dog, stroke the brilliant white face, feel the warmth, and rejoice. The boom is coming and I'm ready. I've been rebuilt.

Other books from

After the Alamo

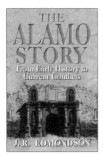

Alamo Story: From Early History to Current Conflicts

Antiquing in North Texas

Barbecuing Around Texas

Battlefields of Texas

Best Tales of Texas Ghosts

Born Again Texan!

Browser's Book of Texas History

Bubba Speak: Texas Folk Sayings

Cartoon History of Texas

Comanche Peace Pipe

Counter Culture Texas

Cowboy of the Pecos

Dallas Uncovered (2nd Ed.)

Daughter of Fortune: The Bettie Brown Story

Death of a Legend: The Myth and Mystery Surrounding the Death of Davy Crockett

Dirty Dining

Exploring Dallas with Children (2nd Edition)

Exploring Fort Worth with Children

Exploring New Orleans: A Family Guide

Exploring San Antonio with Children

Exploring Texas with Children

Exploring the Alamo Legends

Eyewitness to the Alamo

Famous Texas Folklorists and Their Stories

Fire on the Hillside

First in the Lone Star State

Fixin' to be Texan

Fixin' to Party: Texas Style

Funny Side of Texas

Ghosts Along the Texas Coast

Good Times in Texas: A Pretty Complete Guide to Where the Fun Is

Great Firehouse Cooks of Texas

Hesitant Martyr in the Texas Revolution: James Walker Fannin

Hidden Treasure of the Chisos

History and Mystery of the Menger Hotel

Horses and Horse Sense

Illustrated History of Texas Forts

King Ranch Story: Truth and Myth

Last of the Old-Time Cowboys

Last of the Old-Time Texans

Lawmen of the Old West: The Bad Guys

Lawmen of the Old West: The Good Guys

Lone Star Menagerie: Adventures with Texas Wildlife

Lone Stars and Legends: The History of Texas Music

Looking for Texas: Essays from the Coffee Ring Journal

Making it Easy: Cajun Cooking

Messenger on the Battlefield

Republic of Texas Press

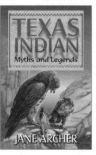